Rethinking

PSYCHOLOGICAL ANTHROPOLOGY

Second Edition

Rethinking PSYCHOLOGICAL ANTHROPOLOGY

Continuity and Change in the Study of Human Action

Second Edition

Philip K. Bock

WAVELAND
PRESS, INC.
Long Grove, Illinois

For information about this book, contact:
  Waveland Press, Inc.
  4180 IL Route 83, Suite 101
  Long Grove, IL 60047-9580
  (847) 634-0081
  info@waveland.com
  www.waveland.com

Cover: All drawings by David Levine. Reprinted with permission from *The New York Review of Books*.

10-digit ISBN 1-57766-055-2
13-digit ISBN 978-1-57766-055-2

Printed in the United States of America

12   11   10   9   8   7

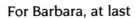

For Barbara, at last

Contents

Preface to the Second Edition

In the more than twenty years since this book was first conceived, psychological anthropology has undergone some major changes in concepts, methods, and goals. This seems to me to be a sign of a healthy discipline. The original book, *Continuities in Psychological Anthropology* (San Francisco: W. H. Freeman, 1980) was organized historically, and relatively few changes were necessary to bring its successor, *Rethinking Psychological Anthropology* (New York: W. H. Freeman, 1988) up to date. Specifically, the later chapters were revised to reflect increased interest in shamanism and mental illness, and a new chapter was added on "Emotions and Selfhood" to indicate the central place these topics had gained in the discipline. (This is the version that was reissued by Waveland Press in 1995.)

The present revision attempts to take account of continuing research interests while documenting new directions in cognitive and psychiatric anthropology as well as emerging work on evolutionary psychology and "embodiment." A good deal has been published lately on the history of anthropology, including its relationship with psychology and psychoanalysis; some of this material has been added to appropriate chapters, together with updates on the status of certain concepts and methods.

The theses of the original book, i.e., that all anthropology is psychological and that we should be aware of continuities between contemporary work and that of past scholars, are unchanged. Thus, rather than trying to integrate newer material into the text of 1988, I have chosen to add one new chapter and to place a supplement at the end of each older chapter presenting recent developments. New references have, however, been integrated into the bibliography.

I am grateful to Tom Curtin of Waveland Press for the opportunity to bring this work up to date, and to members of the Society for Psychological Anthropology for selecting me as their President (1998/99). In its meetings and publications, the S.P.A. carries on a lively debate about the relationship of individuals to their societies, keeping alive issues of great importance to the future of anthropology and of humanity.

It may be appropriate here to explain, to people who do not know us, the 1980 dedication of this book: "For Barbara, at last." My wife and I met in college, in 1954, but it was another 22 years before we were reunited. We have now been married for more than 22 wonderful years, during which her constant love and support have continued to light up my life, and for which I give daily thanks.

Phil Bock
Albuquerque, New Mexico
December, 1998

Preface

Over the past decade anthropology has become increasingly preoccupied with its own history. The writings of scholars such as George W. Stocking, Jr., Dell Hymes, and Regina Darnell have contributed to the reevaluation of the discipline while giving us a new appreciation for the works of its founders. Although some anthropologists are impatient with this trend, I embrace it, because I believe that the willingness to examine our roots critically without indulging in either hero worship or wholesale rejection of our ancestors signals a new maturity in the field.

I believe that psychological anthropology can be understood best from a historical perspective. As an interdisciplinary field, its development has been influenced by the interplay between anthropological problems and the psychological theories that were current when these problems were being formulated. Contemporary psychological anthropology is the product of a century of research, during which, all too often, investigators failed to learn from the errors of their predecessors. I hope that this critical survey of major schools and approaches will help to prepare the way for a much needed new synthesis.

This book is intended for use in courses on psychological anthropology, cross-cultural psychology, and the history of anthropology. It should be read together with some of the classics that are discussed in it (from Freud to Scheper-Hughes) or with one of the comprehensive anthologies now available (for example, LeVine 1974). In advanced classes or seminars, George D. Spindler's collection, *The Making of Psychological Anthropology* (1978), would be an excellent supplement, as would the historical essays edited by G. W. Stocking, Jr. *Malinowski, Rivers, Benedict and Others* (1986).

Because students in anthropology courses often vary in their preparation, I have tried to explain important psychological concepts when they first appear in the text so that readers can better understand their applications to anthropological data. For example, I introduce the key notions of perception, motivation, and cognition in the first chapter and include extra material on the "defense mechanisms" in the second chapter so the reader will be ready for the discussion of projective tests later on. In the sixth chapter I attempt to lead the reader to an intuitive understanding of correlational methods. Occasionally, I include long quotations to convey to the reader a sense of the *style* of certain leading figures. In most cases, I present each approach in its own terms before offering any critical remarks; nervertheless, I am certain that my own preferences and prejudices are quite clear.

Many teachers of anthropology will recognize that this book is in part an updated version of my text, *Continuities in Psychological Anthropology* (1980). I am indebted to Richard Shweder's three-part article, "Rethinking Culture and Personality" (1979–1980) for stimulating the revision and for suggesting a new title. Although his terminology differs from mine, our views on the "crisis in culture and personality" are remarkably similar; we agree that present methods of cross-cultural analysis are not the remedy for this crisis. Our shared goal of a productive synthesis continues to be pursued at the University of Chicago, the University of California at San Diego, and now at Emory University and Case Western Reserve. (See Shweder and LeVine 1984).

I am grateful to the following colleagues for commenting on part or all of the manuscript: Theodora Abel, Myrdene Anderson, Harry W. Basehart, Bruno Bettelheim, James Chisholm, James A. Clifton, Patricia Draper, Derek Freeman, William McGrew, Steven Piker, and David H. Spain. Thanks go to my editors at W. H. Freeman—Jerry Lyons, who encouraged me to undertake this "rethinking"; Philip McCaffrey, who guided the manuscript through press; and James Waller, whose careful copyediting improved many sections of the book. Thanks also go to my students at the University of New Mexico and Stanford University, who listened patiently and responded vigorously to the lectures on which this book is based.

Phil Bock

Prelude

All Anthropology Is Psychological

Psychological anthropology comprises all anthropological investigations that make systematic use of psychological concepts and methods. The goal of such studies is to understand the relationship between individual and sociocultural phenomena. This book traces the history of anthropological studies that have made explicit use of psychological ideas. Beginning with early speculation about the psychology of "primitive peoples," I shall examine the development of the discipline, including the impact of Freud's psychoanalytic theories and the rise of several approaches (configurationalist, basic and modal personality, national character, cross-cultural, and neo-Freudian). After surveying the school of social structure and personality and describing recent work in human ethology, I shall conclude by reviewing some recent studies of "the savage mind," shamanism, and the self.

The statement "All anthropology is psychological" is a deliberately provocative one. Depending on one's conception of the two disciplines, it might be taken as plausible, debatable, erroneous, or simply absurd. I propose to take it seriously and to offer four kinds of arguments in its support. The first is an argument of logical inclusion. If we briefly define anthropology as "the science of humanity" and psychology as "the science of behavior," it would appear that psychology, which deals with the behavior of all organisms, from protozoa to humans, includes anthropology as a special case. Certainly, if humans did not "behave," there would be no point to anthropology. Even those anthropologists concerned with fossil humans attempt to reconstruct the behavior of our extinct ancestors, and contemporary archaeologists use the material remains of past societies to understand such behaviors as subsistence practices, settlement patterns, and political relationships.

Many anthropologists who adhere to the goal of understanding behavioral systems show little interest in current psychological theories.

1

They prefer to operate with a "common-sense psychology" of human motivation and learning, using these ideas to account for changes or continuities in cultural systems. This preference is surprising, for they would certainly despise anyone who used a "common-sense chemistry" or "common-sense geology" in scientific research.

The most radical attempt to eliminate psychological considerations from anthropology is found in the work of Leslie A. White. White argued that the entire discipline should be redefined as *culturology,* that is, the study of culture independent of the individuals and societies with which it is associated. He viewed culture as a material system of objects and symbols that determines human behavior so completely that differences among individuals can safely be ignored (White 1949:121–145). The idea that individual differences are irrelevant to cultural processes is actually a most radical psychological assumption, which rules out, by definition, any study of the relationship between social and individual phenomena. However, as Anthony F. C. Wallace wisely pointed out,

> if people are going to essay explanations of institutionalized human behavior without reference to individual psychological processes, the psychology had better be pruned away by a sharper knife than simple denial or neologism; and if, as is more likely, explanation does have recourse to psychology, more use should be made of the resources psychology has to offer. (Wallace 1966a: 1255)

Wallace's statement leads to my second argument for the proposition that all anthropology is psychological. If we ask what a nonpsychological anthropology would be like, a *reductio ad absurdum* follows, for anthropologists within such a field would have to avoid any reference to perception, motivation, cognition, learning, or related topics. No consideration could be given to individual differences in performance or to the ways in which children (or adults) learn the culture of their society. The individual would be a mere "black box" exposed to certain inputs (culture) and responding with determinate outputs (behavior). But this is an image of humanity that satisfies only the narrowest behaviorists, and then only when they are writing about other people.

Another argument for the psychological nature of all anthropology is methodological: we cannot actually separate cultural from psychological phenomena because ethnologists and psychologists make use of identical kinds of data. Both sciences start from the observable behavior of individuals. but each analyzes these data with different *operations* and for different *purposes.* For example, a "life-history interview" might produce the same information whether conducted by an anthropologist or by a clinical psychologist. The anthropologist, however, would use the data to gain an understanding of the typical life cycle in a given society, or of the social factors affecting marital or occupational choice. The psychologist, on the other hand, might use the same data to make inferences about the personality of the subject: how he or she handles anxiety or relationships with authority figures, his or her need for achievement, and so forth. If a linguist now arrived on the scene, she might use the same material to make inferences about rules of syntax in the subject's language.

At least where human organisms are involved, the operations performed, not the data employed, make the difference between a psychological and an anthropological study. A given "slice" of behavior is subject to multiple interpretations. When Jack asks his mother for food by saying "I'm hungry," he may be expressing dependency *as well as* conforming to the norms governing mother-son interactions in his society. (Our linguist would point out that he is simultaneously following the phonological and grammatical rules of his language.) Every bit of human behavior is influenced by a host of cultural and noncultural factors, from climate to hormone levels. All these "influences" join together to produce the *unified experience* of the individual and the *intentional behavior* that flows from that experience.

A final argument for my position is obvious but nevertheless important: Anthropology is psychological because anthropology is a social enterprise carried out by all-too-human individuals who possess varying degrees of self awareness and quite diverse personalities. Clyde Kluckhohn believed that every ethnologist should be psychoanalyzed before beginning fieldwork. We do not have to go this far to recognize the part played by individual differences in the observation and inter- pretation of ethnographic data. Included here are differences in motivation, sensitivity, intelligence, and sheer energy level. On the practical side, qualities of personality may affect any anthropologist's ability to get along with people under study. This point is important because people are quite capable of refusing assistance or accurate information to investigators who personally offend them. As Bertrand Russell once observed, "All the data upon which our inferences should be based are psychological in character; that is to say, they are experi- ences of single individuals." (See Devereux 1967.)

If I have not yet convinced you that all anthropology is psychological, no matter. The following chapters will illustrate the range of psychological concepts and methods that have been used in anthropological studies. By the end of the book, we shall be ready to consider the converse proposition, "All psychology is cultural."

Chapter 1

The Psychology of Primitive Peoples

William James

Anthropology is the product of three great historical movements: the Age of Exploration, the Enlightenment, and evolutionism. The first of these brought European civilization into contact with alien cultures of both great complexity and great simplicity. Exploration of Asia, Africa, and the New World revealed peoples of diverse physical types living in a bewildering variety of ways. During the centuries that followed, many European nations carved out colonial empires around the world, subjugating and often enslaving the native peoples while expropriating their land and exploiting their labor and resources (Bodley 1982).

The European nations often found theological rationalizations for imperialism: the *souls* of the natives had to be saved, even if their bodies and their societies were destroyed in the process. Europeans even questioned whether "savages" were capable of understanding the revealed truth of Christianity. Missionaries usually took little interest in the superstitions they attempted to suppress, though some religious orders (especially the Jesuits) wrote extensive reports on the customs and beliefs of the peoples they ministered to.

Accounts written by early explorers, traders, and missionaries provide essential data on conditions of primitive peoples in earlier times, but they must be read and interpreted with care. These accounts often include statements and speculations about the psychological abilities and needs of native peoples: anecdotes report the bizarre, childlike, or uncomprehending behavior of non-Europeans. In most cases, cultural differences were assumed to indicate mental inferiority. Stereotyped images of "the savage" emerged, most of which were highly negative, as reflected in Shakespeare's phrase "dull and speechless tribes" (Sonnet 107), or Kipling's description of the native as "half devil and half child" (in "The White Man's Burden").

As Eliot Aronson has observed, stereotypes (past or present) are usually "ways of justifying our own prejudices and cruelty." Thus,

> it is helpful to think of blacks or Chicanos as stupid, if it justifies our
> depriving them of an education, and it is helpful to think of women
> as being biologically predisposed toward domestic drudgery, if we
> want to keep them tied to the vacuum cleaner. (Aronson 1980:175–
> 176)

The stereotypes that Europeans held during the Age of Exploration concerning "primitive peoples" were used to justify exploitation and indifference. They also contained many contradictory elements. Thus, the savage was considered to be "dull" but "crafty," "lazy" but "impul-

6

sive," and "superstitious" but "lacking in true religious feeling." Obviously, such contradictory notions made it possible for European observers to explain any kind of primitive behavior after it had occurred, and to rationalize any oppressive action on their own parts. During the Enlightenment, philosophers such as Hobbes and Rousseau drew selectively on the early accounts to document their opposing views of human nature. The classical (or Hobbesian) view was that human nature is fundamentally evil and violent and thus in need of constraint by the state. The Romantics maintained that humans (in a state of nature) are basically good but that they have been corrupted by artificial institutions. However, attempts to imagine a universal human nature independent of culture are based on a fallacy, for a human being is "not only a social animal, but an animal which can develop into an individual only in society" (Marx 1904:265).

In modern anthropology, the concept *human nature* refers to the entire range of human adaptations in all cultures that ever have existed and that ever will exist. Human organisms achieve articulate speech, satisfying interaction, and a secure sense of identity only when they encounter, at each stage of development, a cultural tradition transmitted with enough consistency to permit the unfolding of their potentials. Since we cannot know the form future cultures will take, we do not know what *Homo sapiens* may become. (See Geertz 1973:33–54.)

The rise of evolutionary thought in the mid-nineteenth century brought with it a new view of human development. Charles Darwin wrote of natural selection as "the preservation of favoured races in the struggle for life." Social Darwinism applied this idea to human affairs and interpreted the contemporary dominance of Europeans in evolutionary terms. The "inferior" races were destined to be thrust aside by the more highly evolved (white) race. Racial groups were ranked according to their resemblance to white Europeans, and their physical differences were related to levels of cultural development. Evolutionists such as Herbert Spencer developed a deep faith in the inevitability of progress, and they saw human society as evolving to higher and higher levels through conflict and survival of the fittest.

The field of anthropology was born in this milieu. Some early anthropologists rejected the racist explanations of cultural differences, but most retained the concept of levels or stages of culture and tried to understand the historical processes of development from lower to higher levels. Often, they assumed that peoples at any given level shared common psychological characteristics, including ways of experiencing the world, distinctive needs, and modes of thinking. Even today, students (and anthropologists) come to the study of primitive peoples with many irrational prejudices and contradictory stereotypes. It is important that we become aware of our own unconscious assumptions and critical of our common-sense knowledge. In the remainder of this chapter, I shall consider some early anthropological studies of primitive psychology while simultaneously introducing basic concepts of perception, motivation, and cognition that will be important throughout the book.

Perception, or "Do You See What I See?"

The term *perception* refers to all the processes by which an organism acquires information about its environment and its own internal states. We cannot directly experience the perceptions of another organism, but we can *infer* its perceptual abilities by finding whether changes in some stimulus can be linked to consistent differences in overt behavior. For example, if you can always push a button or say a word when a light goes on or a soft tone is heard, I infer that you can perceive these stimuli. Experiments of this type have shown that dogs can perceive high-frequency sounds that are inaudible to most humans, and that bees perceive ultraviolet light that the human eye cannot see. Still other animals (fish and insects) are sensitive to certain chemical compounds dissolved in water or diffused in the air.

The members of each species live in a perceptual world different from that of all other species. They receive different kinds of information because of differences in their size and sense organs, and their respective nervous systems interpret the information in different ways. An odor that is sexually stimulating to male muskrats may be repellant to members of another species (or quite imperceptible to them), while a sign of food to one animal is a danger signal to another. Even within a species, considerable individual variation in perceptual ability may exist, e.g., in sensitivity to cold or to odors.

As a result of our evolutionary history, human beings live in a rich world of colors and shapes, a somewhat narrower (though still diverse) world of sounds and tastes, and a rather impoverished world of smells. Each human nervous system performs the remarkable job of *integrating* these sensory inputs so that each of us experiences a colorful, three-dimensional world of familiar objects, meaningful sounds, and coherent events rather than a "buzzing, blooming confusion" of color patches and strange noises. Our reliable perceptual world is all the more remarkable, considering that it is in fact a *reconstruction* from information that has been coded into electrical impulses. As these impulses travel along our nerves to the brain, they differ only in their relative frequency and in the paths they take.

But do all humans live in the same perceptual world? How can we tell whether they do or not? And if differences exist, where are they located? In the sense organs? In the nervous system, which interprets sensory input? In both? Or are still other factors at work? And how are these differences distributed among human populations—where are they found and in what frequencies? Finally, are perceptual differences genetically determined, or are they due to differences in group experiences (such as learning and culture)? We are just beginning to answer these important questions.

For example, some people are unable to distinguish colors that others can easily discriminate. There are several kinds of color blindness. Some types involve only a weakness of vision in limited areas of the spectrum; others involve the total inability to see certain colors (red and green or yellow and blue). And in a rare condition called *monochromatism* all color vision is eliminated. We now know that these perceptual differences are primarily produced by inherited defects in the cone-shaped receptors of the retina, though blue-yellow blindness can also be caused by eye disease. Because of the way in which they are inherited, all types of color blindness are more common in males than in females. Rates also differ among racial and national groups, but this does not indicate any general group inferiority. Disturbances of color vision can also be produced by mental illness and hypnotic suggestion, indicating that the central nervous system may sometimes be involved as well as the retina.

Do people in primitive cultures have better or worse vision than "civilized" persons? Color blindness does not appear to be any more frequent in simple than in complex societies. Nevertheless, early investigators believed that primitives *must* have poor color vision because their languages have relatively few color terms; for example, many groups have a single word for the colors we call "blue" and "green." But recent studies indicate that the number of basic color terms in a person's vocabulary bears no relationship to his or her ability to perceive the full spectrum, although it affects classification and recall. (This issue will be discussed further in chapter 10.)

Another kind of stereotype involved the "sharp-eyed savage," who could supposedly detect objects (or hear sounds) that escape the civilized eye (or ear). People in every society develop culture-specific perceptual skills that enable them to detect subtle cues that outsiders are unlikely to notice. Beyond this, there is some evidence that hunters have better distance vision (on the average) than do settled agricultural peoples. Natural selection against poor visual acuity is probably relaxed for agriculturalists, since they perform fewer tasks requiring good sight: near-sighted people probably succeed better with a plow than with bows and arrows! Industrial civilization creates new hazards for the nearsighted (for instance, speeding automobiles), but it also provides corrective lenses that compensate for poor vision, thus relaxing selection still further. *Overlapping distributions* between populations occur for all such perceptual differences, however, so that some agriculturalists see as well as (or better than) some individual hunters.

Since we cannot directly experience other persons' perceptions, we must find ways of inducing subjects to respond to differences in stimuli, thus providing us with data that can be compared with those from other cultures. However, evoking such responses can present many difficulties in a strange society. Visual acuity, for example, is a fairly simple characteristic to measure, but this does not mean that one can simply grab an eye-chart and dash off to New Guinea or Alaska to test people's vision: "Okay, fellas, just line up over there and let's have you read off the third line from the top . . . the big guy first." Such an approach will not produce reliable data even in our own society, where people are used to being "processed." Some reasons for difficulties in cross-cultural testing of perception are these:

Unfamiliarity with the test situation The novelty of the situation may produce fear and confusion rather than cooperation. It is essential that an investigator establish rapport with test subjects first, if the responses are to have any consistent relationship to the subjects' perceptions. (See Triandis et al. 1971.)

Unfamiliarity with the test materials Even with good rapport, subjects may respond erratically if they have never before encountered materials such as those used in the test. As an extreme example, they may be illiterate, or literate in an alphabet different from that used in the test materials. (How would you respond to a chart printed in Hebrew or Arabic?) Subjects may be unable to understand or to follow the instructions.

Insufficient motivation Subjects may not see any reason to cooperate or to do their best. They may be too amused by the investigator to take the test situation seriously. Rewards for participation can help, but they can also cause problems: a strong desire for the reward may divert attention from the task or encourage fake responses.

Differing values In many societies it is considered poor manners to stand out in any kind of performance, so subjects may hold back in order to stay within group norms. Extreme cooperation or competition may lead some subjects to cheat on a perceptual test, either to do better than others or to help those who would otherwise fail. (See Price-Williams 1975:95–108.)

Additional problems arise due to conditions of investigation in the field. An eye-chart, for example, is only a rough screening device, but it does require standardized conditions and constant illumination. Elaborate testing devices that might be more accurate require electricity, which is not always available. For these and many other reasons, data on even basic perceptual abilities are hard to come by.

As early as 1900, the British psychologist and ethnologist W. H. R. Rivers compared Europeans with various "native" groups to determine what proportion of each group experienced various optical illusions, and how strongly individuals were affected. For example, in the familiar Müller-Lyer illusion (see figure 1-1), most Europeans see line A as longer than line B, though the two horizontal lines are in fact of equal length. Rivers used a device that allowed him to adjust the length of one of the lines until the subject reported the two as equal; this yielded an objective measure of the strength of the illusion. When he tested Melanesian natives with this device, Rivers found that (1) most of them were not affected by the illusion at all, and (2) those few who were affected made smaller adjustments than did the Europeans (in other words, the illusion was weaker for the Melanesians).

Such findings mean very little by themselves, although people who are already convinced that "primitives" have better (or worse) visual perception than "civilized" persons may use these facts to support their prejudices. Simple notions of "how savages perceive" will not do, for Rivers also discovered that populations that are barely susceptible to the Müller-Lyer illusion may be highly susceptible to certain forms of the horizontal-vertical illusion (see figure 1-2). It appears that different *classes of illusions* exist, and a person (or group) strongly affected by one will not necessarily be affected by another.

One plausible explanation for differential susceptibility to illusions is the "carpentered-world hypothesis." This hypothesis states that if one lives in a highly carpentered environment (in which buildings have rectangular floorplans, many straight lines, and right angles between floors,

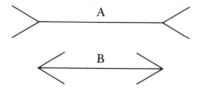

Figure 1-1 The Müller-Lyer illusion, in which most Western subjects judge line A to be longer than line B, although the lines are of equal length.

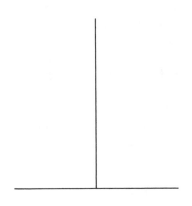

Figure 1-2 The horizontal-vertical illusion, in which most subjects judge the vertical line to be longer than the horizontal one, though the lines are actually of equal length.

walls, and parts of windows), one unconsciously *learns* to use angles as cues for distance. When these perceptual habits are applied to certain two-dimensional figures (illusions), they produce systematic under- and overestimates of length. People who have grown up in environments lacking these features (say, in houses with round or oval floorplans), or who have had no experience with two-dimensional representations of reality, have not acquired these perceptual habits, and their estimates of length will therefore be different.

Recent research has demonstrated that differences in illusion susceptibility exist between rural African natives who live in round houses and their urban relatives who have lived—if only for a few years—in a more carpentered world. Segall, Campbell, and Herskovits (1966) did tests in several related societies, showing a standardized series of visual illusions to people of various ages, both sexes, and different degrees of modernization. Like Rivers, they found that Western samples were more susceptible than non-Western peoples to the Müller-Lyer illusion, and that Western samples were less susceptible to the horizontal-vertical illusion than some non-Western peoples. They conclude that

> these and other differences are not "racial" or "primitive." They are differences produced by the same kinds of factors that are responsible for individual differences in illusion susceptibility, namely, differences in experiences. . . . For all mankind, the basic process of perception is the same; only the contents differ, and these differ only because they reflect different perceptual inference habits. (Segall et al. 1966:214)

Finally, what about the "special senses" that have often been attributed to primitive peoples? The anecdotal nature of most of the evidence should make us suspicious, yet many explorers have reported that "the natives have some kind of sixth sense" that allows them, for instance, to track game over barren ground, to find their way home "instinctively," or to navigate out of sight of land without a compass or other instruments.

Careful study of these alleged special senses has usually shown them to be romantic or racist nonsense. This is not to deny that peoples who have lived for generations in a given environment often develop abilities that puzzle outsiders. They do. Polynesian sailors routinely cross hundreds of miles of open water, and Algonquin trappers do find their way home in areas that strike non-Indians as featureless. But anthropologists such as Thomas Gladwin and A. I. Hallowell have shown that no "homing instinct" or other sixth sense is involved. Rather, these peoples possess large amounts of practical knowledge (of astronomy, topography, and ecology), and they give careful attention to detail (for instance, noticing changes in the direction of the wind or the displacement of a few pebbles). As Hallowell states, "It is not only the direct experience of the terrain which assists the individual in building up his spatial world; language crystallizes this knowledge through the customary use of place names" (Hallowell 1955:193; Bock 1974:174–178). The relation of perception to motivation and cognition will be dealt with later in this chapter.

Motivation, or "The Natives Are Restless Tonight"

The study of motivation is concerned with the biological needs and psychological drives that influence the behavior of organisms. Human motivation is a complex topic that generates many points of view and little agreement. Some psychologists write of hierarchies of needs, while others deal with biological tensions or unconscious complexes. Still others feel that "motivation" is a useless concept because it lumps together several different types of phenomena, each of which requires a different approach (Wolman 1973:673–733). Here I shall consider motives simply as those *needs* that have been claimed to influence human behavior, with special attention to alleged differences between those of primitive and civilized peoples.

The writings of early explorers and anthropologists often attribute brutish motives to native peoples. Comparisons with civilized men are usually uncomplimentary, and the contradictions and ambiguities often found in stereotypes are included in the picture. In 1771, John Millar wrote of "the savage" that "his wants are few, and in proportion to the narrowness of his circumstances. His great object is to be able to satisfy his hunger; and, after the utmost exertion of labour and activity, to enjoy the agreeable relief of idleness and repose" (quoted in Harris 1968:48). More than a hundred years later, L. H. Morgan wrote of the "inferiority of savage man in the mental and moral scale, undeveloped, inexperienced, and held down by his low animal appetites and passions" (1877:41). Morgan also felt that primitives lacked a strong *desire for property,* a "passion" whose dominance over all other motives "marks the commencement of civilization" (1877:6).

The notion of "savage passions" implies strong, uncontrolled urges that may at any moment erupt into violent action. It is understandable that such ideas might develop in the minds of European settlers and colonial officials who had good reason to fear the outbursts of the peoples they had displaced and exploited. The natives had to be controlled— prevented from "gorging" themselves in pagan feasts, from "slaughtering" one another in combat, or from "foolishly" giving away all their possessions. Their sexual desires had to be curbed—though the exaggerated tales of orgies and wife-sharing make one suspect the presence of wishful thinking on the part of missionaries and other reporters. As Frantz Fanon has shown, the increasing anxiety of settlers is expressed in repressive measures, which in turn provoke hostile outbursts among the natives that lead in a vicious circle to further anxiety (Fanon 1965).

The same natives whose violent passions had to be restrained and whose "undue generosity" had to be curbed were, under other circumstances, said to be incurably lazy and uncooperative. Their "laziness" had to be overcome, by force if necessary, but preferably by schooling and the development of new needs—for instance, for cash and consumer goods. Peoples who had lived close to a subsistence level for generations, working only long enough to provide themselves with food and the instruments of survival, quickly acquired a taste for canned fruits, brightly printed cloths, bicycles, metal tools, and rifles. If these desires did not sufficiently "motivate" them, a tax payable only in cash effectively forced them into wage labor (see Bodley 1982:128–132).

How can we measure motivation? Like perception, motivation can only be inferred from observable behavior. In animal experiments, we make such inferences indirectly, for example, by noting the number of hours since the animal last ate, or the level of electric shock it will endure to reach a goal (food, water, or a receptive mate). One infers positive and negative motives (desires and avoidances) by observing the overt responses of individuals to opportunities for gratification. However, making such observations is much more difficult when one is working with humans in a natural setting, though intensive observational studies do provide data relevant to assessing motives (see chapter 9).

One way that motives influence behavior is by lowering *thresholds*, that is, by making us more sensitive to certain kinds of stimuli, even to the point of distorting them. When we are very hungry, we notice smells, sights, and sounds (such as the opening of a refrigerator door) that might go unnoticed at other times. We may, if hungry enough, fantasize or "perceive" things that are not actually present. For example, one evening as I was driving along with my young daughter, who had not eaten for many hours, I pointed out the beautiful sunset; she replied, "Yes, it looks just like a big red enchilada on a blue plate." The degree to which individual needs distort perception provides a measure of the strength of motives; this process is basic to the so-called "projective tests," discussed in chapter 4.

Lists of human motives go back at least to Aristotle. Thomas Aquinas systematically analyzed the human "passions" of the body and soul in his *Summa Theologica*. These philosophers were more concerned with universals than with group differences. The plays of Shakespeare are filled with keen analyses of individual motivation, although his statements about groups—Jews, Moors, and Frenchmen—embody the stereotypes of his age (Bock 1984). The Swedish naturalist Carl Linnaeus divided *Homo sapiens* into four "major races," each characterized by physical and motivational features: Americans were copper-colored, erect, and "choleric"; Europeans were fair, brawny, and "sanguine"; Asiatics sooty, rigid, and "melancholic"; and Africans black, relaxed, and "phlegmatic." Unfortunately, racist theories that attribute motivational differences to group inheritance are still with us today.

Another venerable theory of differential motivation attributes social differences in activity to the direct influence of climate. Constant rainfall, for instance, is claimed to make people melancholy, whereas intense heat makes them lazy, and temperate climates stimulate creativity. (It is easy to guess what climactic zone the author of such a theory comes from.) While climate certainly does influence our moods and behavior, theories that try to explain cultural achievements or national character on such grounds invariably oversimplify the issue. They certainly cannot account for individual differences or for changes through time in a given climatic zone. Environmental factors can go a long way toward explaining cultural variability, though not by way of their direct effects on individual motivation.

Still another type of motivational theory attributes differences in present motivational states to differences in childhood experiences. Thus, if the members of a society seem preoccupied with food and eating, it is because early experience produced in most of them strong oral anxieties about getting enough to eat. If they frequently behave in what an observer interprets as a highly "aggressive" manner, this too is attributed to early training (socialization) that either encouraged or failed to control aggressive impulses (Dollard et al. 1939; Gladwin and Sarason 1953).

Most such theories are able to explain behavior fairly well *after the fact.* Given an individual or group preoccupied with food or with head-hunting, a creative observer can discover (or postulate) past events that plausibly account for present actions. (The Freudian theory to be examined in the next chapter is a good example of their kind of reasoning.) Inherent in such theories, however, is the danger of a logical fallacy of the following type: Johnny is aggressive; therefore, he *must have had* early experiences (teasing, frustration, and the like) that instilled the motives that produce this behavior. All too often, the early experiences are assumed rather than demonstrated to have occurred, and no proof is given of the *continuity* between those early experiences and present motives or behavior. This chain of reasoning contains too many debatable links to be accepted without additional independent evidence. Furthermore, behavior that one observer calls aggressive might be considered normal assertiveness by another, and attributed to quite different circumstances.

We shall return to the relationship between child training and motivation in several later chapters, but even in this introduction it is important to note the contradictory nature of many common ideas about primitive child training. Great variability exists in socialization customs. For example, early European explorers in North America were surprised that native Americans seldom used physical force to discipline children. Their reactions ranged from approval of the Indians' great love of children to horror at the "spoiling" that took place. For their part, most American Indians were shocked to see adult Europeans "beating" defenseless youngsters.

Human societies hold widely differing conceptions of what infants and children need. The child-training practices of primitive peoples range from little to much discipline, early to late weaning, ice-cold to scalding hot baths, much verbal instruction to almost none, and constant supervision to great freedom (Bock 1974, chap. 3). Some societies consider babies almost sacred, while others practice infanticide (child killing) during the early days of life with little apparent remorse. Childhood may be a time of freedom and independence or of important and increasing responsibilities. (See Lee 1959:59–77.) Societies (and subgroups within societies) affect the motivation of their members in three general ways:

Recognition   By giving public recognition to a motive, culture "codifies" it, making it available to people who can then attribute their experience to it (Schacter and Singer 1962; Aronson 1976:176–181). Every human society recognizes "hunger" as a motive; that is, all people have hunger available as an explanation for their own or another's behavior. But certain motives are limited to specific cultures. The need to "defend my sister's honor" or to "save face" or the desire for "union with the Eternal" or for "self- actualization" are quite unknown as motives in many societies. Other "needs" (such as those for whiter teeth and fresher breath) are even more obviously created by social recognition, while some motives that we might presume to be universal have been reported as absent among certain peoples. (For example, sexual jealousy is reportedly quite unknown among the Toda of central India.)

Emphasis   Both simple needs and complex social motives receive different emphasis in various societies. The very fact that a culture defines something as "worth doing" or "worth having" demonstrates that certain desires (for wealth, wisdom, or many wives) are valued more highly than others. The need to excel as an individual, usually referred to as "need for achievement," is by no means universal; it is probably emphasized less strongly in American culture today than it was even one or two generations ago. Some cultures place so much emphasis on people's "spiritual needs" that large proportions of their populations regularly withdraw from secular society into lives of devotion and contemplation (Spiro 1965). Other cultures place the communal needs of the group above those of the individual, requiring people to subordinate their personal desires to the good of the family, the fatherland, or the revolution. Culture, in a sense, creates motives, but as Abram Kardiner has noted, "no culture can interdict an emotion; it can only create conditions which render the emotion unnecessary; it can make the suppression of the emotion acceptable; or it may interdict its manifestation. The rest is a problem for the individual" (1939:87).

Canalization   Even where societies recognize similar needs and give them equal emphasis, the needs may be directed toward quite different *goals*. For example, two societies may recognize sexual satisfaction as important, but one may channel this motive into monogamous marriage while the other encourages its members to seek many partners of both sexes. The term *canalization* refers to the learning of specific types of satisfactions for a general drive (Murphy 1947:161–191), as when one is "thirsty for a cold beer" or "hungry for spaghetti." The staple foods that members of one society consider necessary to complete a meal (for example, rice, bread, manioc, tortillas) may be unknown or treated as occasional side dishes in another society. The canalization process applies to all types of motives.

We still have a great deal to learn about why human societies recognize and emphasize different needs and how these needs are directed, or canalized, toward diverse goals. In later chapters, we shall consider some theories that have been advanced to account for differential motivation. Let us now turn to a third area of primitive psychology: the comparative study of thought processes.

Cognition, or "Thinking Can Make It So"

Whatever their views on primitive perception or "savage passions," many people assume that primitives must think differently from "civilized" people. Up to a point, this is true. Modern science has left its mark on all of us who live in complex societies. We may speak of the sun "rising and setting," but we know better. For us, the stars are other suns vast distances away from our planet, though we may reserve judgment about their effects on human affairs. We determine matters of fact by empirical test, even if we choose to keep certain topics open to speculation or private faith.

The qualifications noted with respect to these characteristics are essential to my argument, for while one may distinguish civilized from primitive mentality by determining whether members of a society hold views anchored in scientific thought, one cannot thereby assume that all members of a complex society are equally rational in all areas of their thinking. The scientific part of modern culture is carried by a relatively small corps of highly trained thinkers, many of whom still exhibit large areas of irrationality in their own thought (for example, in believing in astrology or unsupported notions concerning reincarnation).

Probably more has been written about primitive thought than about perception and motivation combined. Cognitive differences have been inferred from language, ritual, mythology, and a large variety of psychological tests. Remember, though, that differences in thought processes—among individuals or groups—can only be inferred from observable behavior or its products, and all behavior is affected by many kinds of factors, including those discussed above in relation to cross-cultural tests of perception.

The characteristics of primitive thought were of great concern to early anthropologists and "folk psychologists." Many of these scholars attempted to trace the development of ways of thinking by the same historical and comparative methods that others were using to study the development of technology and social organization. For example, L. H. Morgan postulated a series of evolutionary stages from savagery through barbarism to civilization. These stages were based primarily on technological features (subsistence, metallurgy, housing), but Morgan also associated specific mental developments with each stage. He wished to demonstrate "the growth of the ideas of government, of the family, and of property," for he believed that modern institutions "have been developed from a few primary germs of thought" (Morgan 1877:6, 18).

The concepts *animism* (belief in spirits) and *animistic thinking* were the contribution of E. B. Tylor. Tylor was less of a stage-builder than Morgan, but he too tried to show that culture evolved from simple to complex forms, and to demonstrate the steps by which humans slowly arrive at better understandings of the universe. Tylor considered animistic thinking—the attribution of spirits or souls to animals, objects, and natural phenomena—to be the earliest type of religious thought. He argued that early people reasoned their way to a belief in spirits on the basis of their dream experience, and then generalized this belief to any other phenomena that were difficult to understand (Tylor 1958, chaps. 11–17).

The eminent German psychologist Wilhelm Wundt had as one of his many interests the study of *Völkerpsychologie* (folk psychology). Wundt defined its goal as "the psychological explanation of the thought, belief, and action of primitive man on the basis of the facts supplied by ethnology" (1916:7). Like Tylor, he attempted to link particular thought processes, whose existence he inferred from ethnographic reports, with specific stages of cultural evolution. Wundt contrasted the early "totemic stage" with an "age of heroes and gods," leading to the enlightened "age of humanity," and he associated each of these ages with a characteristic type of thinking. However, Wundt held that "the intellectual endowment of primitive man is in itself approximately equal to that of civilized man. Primitive man merely exercises his ability in a more restricted field; his horizon is essentially narrower because of his contentment under these limitations" (Wundt 1916:113). (Among Wundt's students were Émile Durkheim, Franz Boas, and Bronislaw Malinowski. His indirect influence on anthropology may have been far greater than is generally recognized.)

Many writers have considered primitives to be incapable of abstract thought. In his *Principles of Psychology* (1880), William James wrote that

> men, taken historically, reason by analogy long before they have
> learned to reason by abstract characters. . . . In all primitive litera-

ture, in all savage oratory, we find persuasion carried on exclusively by parables and similes (i.e., concrete rather than abstract thinking).

With his usual good sense, though, James recognized that "over immense departments of our thought we are still, all of us, in the savage state. Similarity operates in us, but abstraction has not taken place" (James 1981:988).

James Frazer researched extensively into mythological themes throughout the world; he combined ethnological sources with his great knowledge of Greek and Roman mythology in his classic fourteen-volume work, *The Golden Bough.* Frazer also wrote four huge volumes called *Totemism and Exogamy,* in which he sought to explain the origins and meanings of various primitive belief systems. Though Frazer constantly revised his conclusions, making a brief summary difficult, his basic approach was to infer the processes of primitive peoples' thought from a study of their myths and customs.

Frazer believed that primitive people can reason as well as civilized people, but that since primitives invariably start from *false premises,* their conclusions are necessarily in error. For example, if one starts from the premise that a person's discarded clothing, hair, or nail-clippings retain some spiritual connection with him, it is quite rational to conclude that one can affect the person by doing something to these objects. Frazer called the procedures related to this belief "contagious magic" and documented their occurrence all over the world.

Frazer is often called a "rationalist" because he insisted that differences exist not in the reasoning abilities of different peoples, but only in the assumptions that underlie reasoning. If this position is taken as one end of a continuum, the other extreme is best represented by the French philosopher Lucien Lévy-Bruhl, who in his early works argued for a distinctive primitive mentality. Lévy-Bruhl called this mentality "prelogical," by which he meant that primitives are usually indifferent to logical contradictions. Their thought, he said, is organized in terms of "collective representations" (socially derived complexes of thought and emotion), and anything unusual calls forth in them an attitude of "mystical participation" rather than rational analysis. In a recent study, Jean Cazenueve summarizes Lévy-Bruhl's position as follows:

> Certainly the "savage" has concepts, but they are less systematized than ours. The knowledge of primitive people is not classified rationally—it is "unpackaged." Since items of knowledge remain thus simply juxtaposed, the field stays open to mystical preconnections, and contradictions have little hope of being disclosed or rejected. Finally, it is the emotional element which compensates for logical generality. (Cazenueve 1972:12–13)

Lévy-Bruhl's position has often been ridiculed, and it does have racist overtones, but he was an original and careful scholar whose ideas deserve serious attention. (For an appreciation, see Needham 1965; for an early critique, see Bartlett 1923:282–286.)

In American anthropology, the question of cognitive differences between primitives and civilized peoples was considered settled—or at least irrelevant to the proper goals of the discipline—for nearly forty years. The man most responsible for this attitude was the influential Franz Boas. Boas was not opposed to psychology; indeed, having studied with Wundt, he knew more about the psychology of his time than did most anthropologists. But he fought against facile interpretations of culture that reduced complex historical phenomena to a few "elementary ideas" or common-sense "laws of association." Above all, he opposed all forms of racism, insisting that "there is no fundamental difference in the ways of thinking of primitive and civilized man" (1939:v). This position is called the *psychic unity* theory. Boas stated his program as follows:

> If [anthropologists] can show that the mental processes among prim-
> itive and civilized are essentially the same, the view cannot be main-
> tained that the present races of man stand on different stages of the
> evolutionary series and that civilized man has attained a higher place
> in mental organization than primitive man. (1939: 130)

Boas pointed out the extraordinary self-control required by many taboos and the persistence shown by natives when engaged in work that *they* consider important. Claims that "savages lack strong powers of attention" were shown to derive from situations in which the native people could hardly be expected to take much interest. Boas worked long hours with native informants, and he confessed that when the topic was one that interested them, *he* was usually the first to tire. His conclusions on this point are worth quoting for, as we shall see, they sound very modern:

> Perseverance and control of impulses are demanded of primitive man
> as well as of civilized man, but on different occasions. If they are not
> demanded as often, the cause must be looked for, not in the inherent
> ability to produce them, but in the social structure which does not
> demand them to the same extent. (p. 133)

Boas also criticized the ideas and methods of Lévy-Bruhl; for example, concerning mystical participation, he wrote:

> This conclusion is reached not from a study of individual behavior,
> but from the traditional beliefs and customs of primitive people. . . .
> However, if we disregard the thinking of the individual in our society
> and pay attention only to current beliefs [we shall] reach the conclu-

sion that the same attitudes prevail among ourselves that are characteristic of primitive man. (p. 135)

Actually, Boas and Lévy-Bruhl agreed more closely in their later work than either realized. In his posthumous publications, Lévy-Bruhl abandoned the notion of prelogical thought and came to agree with Boas that "the functions of the human mind are common to the whole of humanity" (Boas 1939:143). Boas in turn drew close to the Frenchman's concept of the "affective category of the supernatural," which is "rationalized" by civilization, when he wrote of "the emotional, socially determined associations of sense-impressions and of activities, for which intellectual associations are gradually substituted" (p. 226).

Primitive mentality was never a "taboo topic" in the United States (see M. Mead 1932; Radin 1957), but little original research was done on the subject until the late 1950s. At about that time, a rebirth of interest in comparative thought processes gave rise to the subfield of *cognitive anthropology*. Discussion of these developments will have to wait until chapter 10. My goal in the present chapter has been to indicate the kinds of psychological assumptions made by early anthropologists as a background for later developments. We turn now to the school of *psychoanalytic anthropology* and the work of its founder, Sigmund Freud.

Supplement, 1999

Approaching the main topics of this chapter in order, it must be said that most anthropologists have abandoned the study of *perception* to neurologists who now construct elegant models of how the brain and nervous system filter, integrate, and associate stimuli to construct our perceptual world. This study has become highly complex, depending on technological innovations that allow scientists to study changes in the brain and on computer programs that attempt to mimic brain functions such as visual and speech recognition.

While such work is certainly important, I believe that anthropologists would insist that the ability of a program to imitate the *results* of human thought does not prove that the same *processes* are involved. Anthropological linguists who are aware of the importance of cultural context and presuppositions in the interpretation of speech would insist that these human abilities cannot be simulated mechanically.

If perception has been neglected, the analysis of *motivation* has taken a central place, often fused with concepts of *emotion*. Traditional approaches to motives conceived as a set of universal needs, drives, or instincts has given way to a more culturally sensitive view, in which cultural models are said to possess "motivational force" that may "elicit desires" (Strauss 1992). Others write more generally of the "attribution of inner states" (Rosen 1995), raising broad philosophical questions about intentionality and possible knowledge of "other minds." Some of these newer trends seem to be related to Murphy's concept of canalization. (On Garner Murphy's relationship to anthropology see Bennett 1998:241.)

Cognition and "cognitive models" have thus been linked to motivation. The rise of evolutionary psychology has contributed to this linkage as scholars try to understand how our species has developed specific cognitive abilities in response to past adaptive problems, arguing against their derivation from a few basic needs such as hunger and sex. Other psychologists, from diverse traditions, try to demonstrate the existence of a "hierarchy of motives" with basic needs or drives at the bottom and more specific motives emerging as ways of satisfying them (Pyszczynski et al. 1997).

The most comprehensive discussion of the psychic unity issue, as well as an encyclopedic treatment of various types of "cultural models," is found in Bradd Shore's *Culture in Mind* (1966). Using case studies from the American Northwest Coast, aboriginal Australia and his own research on Samoa, Shore points out the existence of multiple and sometimes conflicting models in so-called "simple societies," and he proposes some far-reaching conclusions about the "problem of meaning." However, when he writes about four types of *motivation* (1996:330–332), readers should be aware that he is concerned with the ways in which "signs" are linked with meanings rather than motivation in the usual sense.

Anthropologists continue to be wary of the cross-cultural use of Western-inspired intelligence tests. Recent writing on comparative cognition emphasizes the *practical and emotional dimensions of intelligence*. For example, Richard Shweder (1984) insists that "there's more to thinking than reason and evidence," while, in a different vein, Daniel Goleman (1995) has written about "emotional intelligence," a topic that has also interested feminist scholars. The dangerous division between thought and feeling is discussed in many recent works, including one by Vice President Al Gore (1992)!

It would be wonderful to report that racism and other forms of prejudice have diminished as a result of anthropological research and publication, but no figures of the stature of Ruth Benedict or Margaret Mead have arisen thus far to carry the message of cultural diversity and tolerance to the public. Indeed, even works that seem to cry out for popular attention, such as Nancy Sheper-Hughes' study of child neglect in Brazilian slums or Tanya Luhrmann's analysis of the "serious play" of witches in modern England, often seem to convey public messages that are quite different from the author's intentions.

Many anthropologists continue to ignore the relevance of psychology to their work, so it would not hurt to remind them that, in 1904, Franz Boas regarded the two main branches of our discipline as "psychological anthropology" and "biological anthropology" (Stocking 1992:312). As we turn to early attempts to understand the relationship of culture to individual psyches, we will confront many ideas that may seem simplistic or perhaps offensive to some readers. Let us remember that their proponents were doing their best with the materials at their disposal to wrestle with questions for which we still do not have adequate answers.

Chapter 2

Psychoanalytic Anthropology

Sigmund Freud

The importance of Sigmund Freud to twentieth-century psychology can hardly be overestimated. From his early work in neurology, hypnotism, and drug therapy to his founding and leadership of the psychoanalytic movement, Freud's genius illuminated virtually every aspect of human behavior. Whether they have accepted, modified, or rebelled against his ideas, most workers in psychological anthropology from 1920 to the present have been stimulated and influenced by Freud.

As we saw in the preceding chapter, the problems of "human nature" and of "primitive mentality" were central to early anthropology. But whether scholars used common-sense psychology (as did Frazer) or the latest academic theories (as did Wundt), their attempts to reduce the data of ethnology to general psychological principles were seldom illuminating. Rivers' studies of primitive perception and Lévy-Bruhl's speculations on prelogical thought identified important problems and developed some useful methods, but until about 1910, when Freud began work on "the culture question," no one had formulated a general theory that brought these ideas together in a coherent way and pointed the direction for further research.

In his clinical practice, Freud had already created his unique *dynamic theory of mental processes*. By means of this theory, the thoughts and behavior of children and adults, normal and insane, and primitive and civilized could be brought together and explained by general principles as far removed from common-sense psychology as is molecular biology from folk notions of heredity. In Freud's dynamic theory, all behavior is viewed as the result of *conflict*. His work also included a scheme of individual development and a hypothetical "anatomy of the mind" consisting of "mental organs" (id, ego, and superego) that battle for control over behavior.

Elements of Psychoanalysis

Perhaps the most important element of psychoanalysis for a beginning student is Freud's insistence that we take seriously all kinds of mental phenomena: nothing is irrelevant to a psychoanalytic explanation. Seemingly trivial phenomena such as dreams, slips of the tongue, lapses of memory, or minor accidents are all clues to dynamic processes and hidden motives. Of course, this principle can be abused ("party psychologists" who eagerly interpret dreams or faux pas probably reveal more about themselves than about their unwilling clients), but in the hands of a skilled clinician, psychoanalytic theory provides a link between experience and imagination, motive and behavior, that has not been surpassed.

Let us begin with some generally accepted facts about memory, and then see what Freudian theory says about them. Human memory is highly variable and unpredictable. Most people retain few if any memories from the early years of their lives, and those few are often highly inaccurate. Still, we are occasionally favored with an exceptionally vivid memory, triggered by a smell, sound, or taste, and hypnotism or electrical stimulation of the brain can yield flashes of supposedly long-forgotten memories (Schachtel 1959; Penfield 1975). Furthermore, we do not walk about repeating important names, addresses, or phone numbers to ourselves, yet when we need them, they are usually available. Where have these memories been stored? How do we retrieve them when needed? And, more important, why do perfectly familiar facts sometimes elude our attempts to remember them, only to "pop into our minds" at another time, "for no good reason"?

Psychoanalysis assumes that a lapse of memory, whether momentary or extended (as in hysterical amnesia), always takes place for a good reason, though not one that is immediately obvious. Like others before him, Freud distinguished between conscious and unconscious mental processes (Whyte 1960). He maintained, however, that consciousness was only a tiny part of our mental life—like the tip of an iceberg—and that it developed out of the unconscious, both in the early life of each individual and in the evolution of our species. Forgetting must be understood as a dynamic process occurring within this context, not merely as the passive "decay of memory traces." One forgets, for example, because a memory is too damaging or too painful to enter consciousness, or because it is associated in some way with other unpleasant experiences. But a "forgotten" memory remains in the unconscious.

In Freud's view, every person strives constantly for pleasure—the immediate satisfaction of physical and psychic needs. We are born with a number of such needs, and these become more and more differentiated with experience. Freud referred to the inborn strivings for pleasure as *instincts;* in his later writings he grouped these into two categories: *eros* (life or sexual instincts) and *thanatos* (death or destructive instincts).

Some discussion of *eros* is necessary to prevent misunderstanding, for Freud used the terms "sex" and "sexual" in a much broader sense than most people realize. Sexual pleasure in psychoanalytic theory includes all the gratifications that an individual derives from his or her own body, through many different organs. Freud shocked many of his contemporaries (including his medical colleagues) with his insistence that despite their obvious dependency and presumed "innocence," babies are capable of experiencing a variety of sexual pleasures.

In psychoanalytic theory, each child is said to mature through a series of psychosexual stages. These stages are universal and rooted in human biology. The pleasures of the newborn child center on its *oral zone* (the lips and mouth), and are related to the nursing situation. Then for a time the *anal zone* becomes the center of pleasure; it also becomes a center of conflict during toilet training, when cultural constraints are imposed on the natural rhythm of the child's bowels. Still later, pleasure becomes centered in (and largely narrowed to) the *genital zone*. This stage occurs at about age five—long before sexual maturity for reproductive purposes is achieved in our species. In most cases (for reasons to be discussed), this genital stage is followed by a period of "latency," during which little overt sexual expression takes place. Genital sex has not vanished: it has only been repressed until it again erupts with the onset of adolescence.

The concept of *repression* is central to psychoanalytic theory. It refers to the dynamic process whereby an impulse, thought, or experience is kept from becoming conscious. In this process, a constant expenditure of energy is required to keep contents out of awareness. "Since the repressed continues to exist in the unconscious and develops derivatives, repression is never performed once and for all. . . . [t]he repressed constantly tries to find an outlet" (Fenichel 1945:150).

Why do we bother to repress thoughts and feelings, especially since to do so is costly in terms of mental energy? Repression is one way in which individuals "defend themselves" (their conscious egos) against unpleasant experiences, as when we "forget" a painful memory or a dentist appointment. The notion of *defense mechanisms* that protect the ego from pain or anxiety is central to psychoanalytic theory. It received its most influential formulation in a book by Anna Freud, the daughter of the founder. She distinguished a number of different mechanisms of defense (A. Freud 1946). The following are the most important for our purposes:

> **Repression** The mechanism by which, as we have seen, painful experiences are kept out of consciousness by unconscious forces. Repression may be accompanied by *denial* of a thought or feeling.

> **Projection** A process by which unacceptable impulses are attributed to external persons or objects, as when the unconscious hostility felt toward a parent or teacher is converted into the conviction that "he hates me." Freud recognized the positive functions of projection in each individual's construction of the external world (S. Freud 1950:64).

Introjection Through this process, external objects or persons are "incorporated" into the ego. A common form is *identification,* in which the individual introjects and adopts the characteristics of a loved or hated person, especially a parent.

Displacement By this mechanism, impulses and feelings are transferred from their actual (unconscious) objects onto other, less threatening objects, as when a man who has been frustrated by his boss yells at his wife or child. In dreams, displacement is one way in which a latent wish may be disguised.

Regression This mechanism is the tendency to return to earlier types of satisfaction when one meets with frustration; for example, a child may regress to thumbsucking (oral) during toilet training (anal) or as a substitute for masturbation (genital). "Any disappointment in or threat to adult sexuality may influence a person to revert to those levels of his infantile sexuality to which he is unconsciously fixated; in other words, to levels that have been repressed and remained unchanged in the unconscious" (Fenichel 1945:160).

Sublimation By definition, sublimation is a "successful" defense in which an unacceptable impulse is transformed and directed toward an acceptable substitute goal, often bringing the individual social rewards and recognition. This generally involves a "desexualization" of the impulse, as when an individual with a strong need for oral gratification becomes a radio announcer or a food-taster. Sublimation can involve a variety of mechanisms, including displacement and *reaction formation,* "a change from passivity to activity [or] a reversal of an aim into its opposite" (Fenichel 1945:141). For example, excessive cleanliness may mask an anal desire to play with dirt or feces.

Although Freud believed that society rightfully required people to find substitute gratifications for most of their erotic impulses, he also recognized the great pleasure to be found in direct satisfaction of needs. Best of all, thought Freud, would be a world in which individuals could become aware of all their impulses and then consciously decide which to gratify and which to sublimate, rather than being at the mercy of unconscious conflicts. (Under present forms of society, this goal can be achieved only through long-term psychotherapy; see Marcuse 1955.)

In work with his own patients, Freud developed ways of understanding and treating the symptoms of *neurosis.* Neurotic patients suffer as much as patients with physical diseases—perhaps more, since they are told that "it's all in your mind." Fears and headaches, the inability to eat or sleep, morbid fantasies, paralysis or impotence, the compulsion to repeat a word or gesture—such typical neurotic symptoms do not yield to drugs or to pep talks. Neurotics can become increasingly withdrawn from a normal social life; often they are fired from jobs, abandoned by friends, in conflict with family members, and too "nervous" (anxious) to engage in ordinary relationships.

Freud's approach to such symptoms (as to all mental phenomena) was to take them seriously and to interpret them symbolically in terms of his dynamic theory. He understood a given neurotic symptom to be the result of conflict between opposing impulses—an effort made by the patient's ego to defend itself against threats from within and without. Freud's "talking cure" was an attempt to trace the roots of the conflict and to make patients aware of the defenses they had erected against their problems. By encouraging them to "free associate" to words and dream events, he could discover the unconscious significance of symptoms. Freud saw that merely treating symptoms was ineffective, since the underlying conflict would only be expressed in a different form.

Before we turn to Freud's influence on anthropology, we should look briefly at his contribution to the study of dreams. When Freud published his first great book, *The Interpretation of Dreams,* in 1900, he was challenging a prejudice in Euro-American society which held that dreams were trivial and any interest in them frivolous. For Freud, dreams were the "royal road to the unconscious." In dreams, the repressions and constraints of adult life are relaxed, not destroyed. Here our minds are flooded with scenes and figures of strange and fantastic kinds: monsters mingle with old friends in wondrous landscapes, and events we fear are mixed with those we most desire. Psychoanalysis takes the *manifest content* of a dream (the images and words reported by the dreamer) and uses free association to arrive at the *latent content* (the symbolic meaning and unconscious conflicts concealed within the dream). The formula "every dream represents a wish fulfillment" underlies the Freudian strategy of dream interpretation.

Freud believed that "repressed infantile sexual wishes provide the most frequent and strongest motive forces for the construction of dreams" (S. Freud 1952:107). These wishes must be disguised in symbolic forms, for even in sleep we do not allow ourselves to become aware of socially unacceptable desires for incestuous objects or pregenital satisfactions. Dream messages are condensed and distorted: hostile or erotic impulses toward a parent or child are displaced onto other persons, animals, or inanimate objects; one part of the body may be symbolized by another part.

Not only dreams and neurotic symptoms but also myths, legends, fairy tales, jokes, and much of our daily behavior are symbolic substitutes for what we unconsciously desire (S. Freud 1952:107–111). These data must be interpreted to reveal their true meaning. A basic principle of such interpretation is that things are seldom what they seem to be.

The Origins of Psychoanalytic Anthropology

Throughout his life, Freud was fascinated by art, literature, history, and anthropology. He was well acquainted with the archeological and ethnological theories of his time. Around 1910, stimulated by the work of Wundt and of Carl Jung, Freud turned his mind to "the cultural question." In a series of books and papers, he attempted to show how psychoanalysis could help to explain the origins and functioning of cultural institutions. The problem occupied him for the next thirty years. His five major works dealing with social and cultural issues are *Totem and Taboo* (1913), *Group Psychology and the Analysis of the Ego* (1921), *The Future of an Illusion* (1927), *Civilization and Its Discontents* (1930), and *Moses and Monotheism* (1939).

In the Freudian view, *culture is to society as neurosis is to the individual.* If we accept this proposition, it follows that institutions may be analyzed to reveal their latent content and the conflicts that they at once mask and are meant to resolve. Freud used his understanding of neurotic symptoms to interpret cultural institutions.

I use the term *psychoanalytic anthropology* to designate attempts by Freud and his followers to apply psychoanalysis to a wide range of societies and cultural phenomena. Some of these followers, such as Ernest Jones, Erich Fromm, and J. C. Flügel, were practicing psychoanalysts who took an interest in cultural matters. Others, such as Géza Róheim, George Devereux, and Erik Erikson, were trained as psychoanalysts and also carried out ethnographic fieldwork. Still others were primarily anthropologists who were later analyzed and trained in psychoanalysis, for example, Geoffrey Gorer, Clyde Kluckhohn, William Caudill, and Robert LeVine.

Most accounts of Freud's pioneering effort, *Totem and Taboo,* emphasize (and criticize) his treatment of totemism. However, in my opinion, his analysis of taboo carries much greater conviction and has greater anthropological value. (See Keesing 1985.)

The word *taboo* refers to a great variety of prohibitions against eating, touching, or otherwise contacting certain objects or persons. Something or someone—especially a high-ranking person—may be considered inherently taboo, or a person who has the necessary power may impose a temporary taboo by performing the required ritual. Individuals may also become temporarily taboo due to contact with a taboo or polluting object (such as a corpse). Such pollution is usually highly "conta-

Taboo	violation	Pollution	which	Purification
(prohibition)	results in	(contagion)	requires	(renunciation)

Figure 2-1 Taboo and some related concepts.

gious," being spread by contact to other persons or objects, and it can only be removed by rituals of purification (see figure 2-1).

In anthropological usage, the term *taboo* has been extended to cover all types of prohibitions, from the "incest taboo" to the Jewish rule against eating pork or shellfish. In his book, Freud makes reference principally to the Polynesian types of taboo, hoping to illuminate them by showing "Some Points of Agreement between the Mental Lives of Savages and Neurotics" (the subtitle of *Totem and Taboo*). He begins with the observation that every psychotherapist "has come across people who have created for themselves individual taboo prohibitions of this very kind and who obey them just as strictly as savages obey the communal taboos of their tribe or society" (S. Freud 1950:26). After warning that the similarities *may* be only external, Freud proceeds to offer a dynamic hypothesis to account for both kinds of prohibitions.

Since a neurotic's self-imposed obsessional prohibitions are just as extensive and restrictive as social prohibitions, Freud suggests that both are produced by deep *emotional ambivalence*. For example, a typical "touching phobia"—whereby an individual fearfully avoids touching some common object or substance—is claimed to have originated when the patient's childhood desire to touch his or her own genitals was met by a parental prohibition. The prohibition was accepted—in part because of the child's love for the parents; however,

> the prohibition does not succeed in *abolishing* the instinct. Its only result is to *repress* the instinct (the desire to touch) and banish it into the unconscious. Both the prohibition and the instinct persist . . . and everything else follows from the continuing conflict between the prohibition and the instinct.
>
> The principal characteristic of the psychological constellation which becomes fixed in this way is . . . the subject's *ambivalent* attitude towards a single object, or rather towards one act in connection with that object. He is constantly wishing to perform this act (the touching) . . . and detests it as well. . . .(p. 29)

Using obsessional neuroses as a "model" (his term), Freud infers that taboos prohibit desires that are still strong. Just as the person who has given up masturbation may still unconsciously desire it, primitive peoples have highly ambivalent feelings toward their taboos:

> The desire to violate it persists in their unconscious; those who obey the taboo have an ambivalent attitude to what the taboo prohibits. The magical power that is attributed to taboo is based on the capacity for arousing temptation; and it acts like a contagion because examples are contagious and because the prohibited desire in the unconscious shifts from one thing to another. The fact that the violation of a taboo can be atoned for by a renunciation [ritual of purification] shows that renunciation lies at the basis of obedience to taboo. (p. 35)

Thus far, Freud has only offered an *analogy* between (1) a dynamically motivated type of neurotic behavior and (2) a class of social customs with a possible basis in ambivalence. He recognized that the value of this hypothesis depended on whether it resulted in "a clearer understanding of taboo than we could otherwise reach" (p. 35). He therefore proceeds to examine evidence from many cultures, dealing with three particular types of taboos. In each case, the hypothesis of ambivalence contributes to an explanation of the customs. Let us look briefly at each of these.

The treatment of enemies Ample evidence exists to show that tribal peoples throughout the world observe similar customs with regard to a slain enemy. The dead person is "appeased" with gifts and prayers, whereas the victorious slayer is placed under restrictions, notably isolation from social contact, food taboos, and rules against touching or being touched. These prohibitions persist for a certain period of time, or until rites of purification have been performed. Freud relates all these customs to "emotional ambivalence towards the enemy" (p. 41). That is, in addition to hostility toward the dead person, unconscious feelings of remorse and admiration are also present, and these conflicting impulses account for both the fearful appeasement of the enemy ghost and the taboo restrictions on the killer.

Taboos surrounding rulers Following Frazer, Freud tells of the various customs by which people attribute to their rulers far-reaching powers over nature, even as they impose many unpleasant restrictions on the rulers' lives. To the psychoanalyst, the "excessive solicitude" represented by the taboo rituals indicates the existence of an unconscious current of hostility or ambivalence toward the rulers. Freud suggests that the importance of the rulers is greatly exaggerated precisely in order that rulers may be blamed for any disappointments: "The ceremony is *ostensibly* [consciously] the highest honor and protection for them, while *actually* [unconsciously] it is a punishment for their exaltation, a revenge taken on them by their subjects" (p. 51).

Taboos surrounding the dead Taboos on bodily contact with the dead are widespread, and purification ceremonies are required following such contact. Many of these restrictions also apply to those who have had such contact "only in a metaphorical sense: the dead person's mourning relations, widowers and widows" (p. 53). Freud relates both these customs and the prohibitions against using the dead person's name to *fear of the dead*, as did Wundt, but Freud goes further by asking the important question: Why should a "dearly loved relative" change upon death "into a demon, from whom his survivors can expect nothing but hostility and evil?" (p. 58). His answer is that this fear is a reaction to the mourners' projecting their own hostility onto the dead, for survivors often deny their ambivalent feelings toward the deceased, as reflected in our own admonition against "speaking ill of the dead." Here too we find that "the taboo has grown up on the basis of an ambivalent emotional attitude, . . . the contrast between conscious pain and unconscious satisfaction over the death that has occurred" (p. 61).

In each of these examples, we see Freud reaching beyond the superficial or piecemeal explanations offered by others toward a more dynamic and comprehensive understanding of social customs. Whether we accept his conclusions or not, we must acknowledge the validity of these goals. His method here and elsewhere is to "submit the [ethnographic] facts to analysis as though they formed part of the symptoms presented by a neurosis" (pp. 48–49). Just as individual neuroses result from compromises between unconscious erotic and hostile impulses, many taboo customs may be understood as expressions of ambivalent emotions. In a suggestive passage, Freud states that "the neuroses are social structures [that] endeavor to achieve by private means what is effected in society by collective effort" (p. 73). He never confounds neurosis with culture, but he remarks that neuroses are like "distortions" of the great social institutions:

> It might be maintained that a case of hysteria is a caricature of a work of art, that an obsessional neurosis is a caricature of a religion and that a paranoic delusion is a caricature of a philosophic system. (p. 73)

Totemism and Exogamy

As noted earlier, I consider Freud's analysis of taboo much more successful than his treatment of *totemism*—the use of an animal as an emblem of a kinship group; yet most anthropologists who have dealt with *Totem and Taboo* have focused on the part of the book that attempts to explain the origins of certain ill-defined totemic institutions. In this attempt, Freud was following the most eminent anthropologists of his day, all of whom tried to elucidate totemism and its relationship to marriage prohibitions. (See Lévi-Strauss 1963.)

A *totem* is an animal species after which a kinship group is named and from which the group claims descent. Members are normally forbidden to eat the totem animal, but in certain circumstances, the members of a totem group (clan) are required to kill and ritually consume their totem animal. Freud asked why it is that "poor, naked cannibals," whom one should hardly expect to find observing rules of morality, go to the greatest lengths to avoid "incest" and even prohibit marriage with any member of their totem clan. The combination of the characteristics of clan exogamy with animal name, belief in descent, and ritual consumption of the usually taboo species stimulated Freud to produce an account that has been called variously a "hypothesis," a "myth," and a "just-so story." (See Brown 1966, chap. 1.)

Freud first sought a type of neurosis to serve as a model for the customs to be explained. In this case, he chose children's "animal phobias," that is, the irrational fears and avoidances that are frequently "attached to animals in which the child has hitherto shown a specially lively interest" (S. Freud 1950:127). Analyzing several cases in which young boys were terrified of large (but quite harmless) animals, Freud concluded that "their fear related at bottom to their father and had merely been *displaced* on to the animal" (p. 128; italics added). To understand why this displacement occurs, we must first consider a central concept of psychoanalysis as yet unexplained in this account: the Oedipus complex.

Most people are familiar with the myth of King Oedipus, who unknowingly (that is, unconsciously) killed his father and later married his mother, thus bringing disaster to himself and his city. When he finally discovered the truth about his ancestry, Oedipus blinded himself and went into exile. Freud used the term *Oedipus complex* to denote the constellation of unconscious tendencies affecting children at about the age of five—intense love for the parent of the opposite sex coupled with hatred of and desire to replace the parent of the same sex. Young boys and girls frequently express their intention to marry "mommy" or "daddy" and show, in various ways, their wish that the other parent should "go away" (die). Their feelings toward the rival are necessarily *ambivalent:* the same-sex parent stands between the child and the love object but is also admired and feared. The child is frequently frightened by his or her own hostile fantasies, for these may provoke fear of retaliation. In Freud's day, threats of castration were common deterrents to masturbation, and the sight of female genitals might have convinced a boy that "it could happen to me, too!" (The blinding of Oedipus is interpreted by Freud as the symbolic equivalent of castration, a punishment Oedipus incurs for loving his mother too well. For another interpretation of the myth, see Bock 1979.)

In normal individuals, the Oedipus complex is "resolved" at about age six or seven by (1) *renunciation* of the mother (or father) as an erotic love object, and (2) *identification* with the same-sex parent, who is taken as an ego-ideal, partly out of guilt for the former feelings of hostility. This initiates the latency period discussed above, under "Elements of Psychoanalysis." Even in the best of families, renunciation is based on repression of unconscious desires. Thus, when overt sexuality again appears, the adolescent seeks out a partner who is, in some respects, like the beloved parent. (In pathological cases, an unresolved Oedipus complex may contribute to regression, hostility, homosexuality, and various character disorders. See Stephens 1962.)

Freud believed that the Oedipus complex was *universal,* and he made it a central part of psychoanalytic theory. The universality of Oedipal feelings has been argued back and forth for many years, but psychoanalysts seem always to have the last word, for anyone who rejects the concept is accused of *resistance*: "You only oppose the idea because you never resolved your own Oedipus complex." Though the alleged castration fears may be difficult to accept, many people find that the Freudian notions of emotional ambivalence and early object-choice do correspond with their own experiences. Few can reject the following, *minimal* formulation of the Oedipus complex: children's erotic and hostile impulses are frequently directed toward family members, and this fact can complicate their later relationships.

We have seen that some children displace their fear of the jealous parent onto animals. For example, Little Hans (in a famous case study) was terrified that a horse would come into the house and "bite" him; Freud concluded that he was symbolically expressing his castration anxiety. If Hans had lived in a totemic society rather than nineteenth-century Vienna, he might have identified himself with the animal-parent (totemism) and renounced his desire for his mother or sisters as sex objects (thus demonstrating the incest taboo and exogamy).

We come here to Freud's myth. He asks us to envision, at the dawn of human society, a "primal horde" (the idea is Darwin's) dominated by a "violent and jealous father who keeps all the females for himself and drives away his sons as they grow up" (S. Freud 1950:141). Freud immediately admits that such a society has never been observed among humans, but he invites us to take it as a hypothetical starting point. Guided by psychoanalysis, we are to derive from it the equalitarian band that practices totemism and exogamy, which he believed to be a primitive form of human society.

Recalling the ritual meal in which the totem is solemnly killed and eaten by the whole group, Freud suggests the following sequence of events:

> One day the brothers who had been driven out came together, killed and devoured their father and so made an end of the patriarchal horde. . . . The violent primal father had been the feared and envied model of each one of the company of brothers: and in the act of devouring him they accomplished their identification with him. . . . The totem meal . . . would thus be a repetition and a commemoration of this criminal deed, which was the beginning of . . . social organization, of moral restrictions and of religion. (pp. 141–142)

After the sons had eliminated their father and, through physical incorporation, satisfied their wish to identify with him, their suppressed affection reappeared in the form of remorse. Then, following the psychoanalytic principle of *deferred obedience* (conformity to the will of a deceased parent whom one had resisted during his or her lifetime), the brothers

> revoked the deed by forbidding the killing of the totem, the substitute for their father; and they renounced its fruits by resigning their claim to the women who had now been set free. They thus created out of their filial sense of guilt the two fundamental taboos of totemism, which for that very reason corresponded to the two repressed wishes of the Oedipus complex. (p. 143)

Freud then went on to explain human culture in terms of these mythical events:

> Society was now based on complicity in the common crime; religion was based on the sense of guilt and remorse attaching to it; while morality was based partly on the exigencies of this society [fraternal solidarity] and partly on the penance demanded by the sense of guilt [exogamy and attempts at atonement]. (p. 146)

This highly condensed account of Freud's theory of the origin of culture again illustrates the steps constituting the approach of psychoanalytic anthropology: the choice of a "model" from clinical practice (animal phobia and castration anxiety); the selection of ethnographic data (totem meals, actually very rare; the "primal horde," actually hypothetical); the analogy between individual dynamics (guilt leading to "deferred obedience") and group process (the brothers' guilt leading to exogamy). From these steps a conclusion is drawn, in this case that "psychoanalysis requires us to assume that totemism and exogamy were intimately connected and had a simultaneous origin" (p. 146). Many other ideas, including the suggestion that "God is nothing other than an exalted father" (p. 147), are expressed in this essay. Freud also provides a discussion of animal and human sacrifice (p. 151), and an analysis of Christian communion as a descendant of the totem meal (p. 154). As in the essay on taboo, Freud draws together in his hypothesis the most varied phenomena and provides a dynamic and comprehensive explanation.

Nevertheless, the explanation of a universal (the incest taboo) and a highly specialized social form (totemism) in terms of hypothetical historical events is far from convincing. It has been subjected to devastating anthropological criticism. How could such a historical event, even if it were repeated in several groups, have such far-reaching effects? Freud's ethnology was not bad for its day, but his generalizations about totemism are unacceptable. Still, despite its many factual errors and logical fallacies, *Totem and Taboo* remains an important and influential book. A. L. Kroeber (a great anthropologist who was analyzed and who briefly practiced psychoanalysis) suggests that we strip away the historical claims and examine Freud's theory as "a generic, timeless explanation of the psychology that underlies certain recurrent historical phenomena or institutions like totemism and taboo" (Kroeber 1952:306; cf. Fox 1967:60–61).

Freud's insight that collective guilt is intimately related to the origins of social organization was further developed in his long essay *Civilization and Its Discontents* (1930). This is probably his most pessimistic work, but every anthropologist should read at least the first chapter for the extended analogy between the stratification of Roman ruins and the structure of the mind, as well as the last two chapters for their description of the superego as the internal representative of external social authority.

In *Group Psychology and the Analysis of the Ego* (1921), Freud turns his model around, so to speak, and asks what we can learn about individual psychology from an examination of crowd behavior and of institutions such as the church and the army. He expands the concept of identification, showing its role in group formation and morale, and offers several observations on the state of "being in love."

As we shall see, the whole thrust of neo-Freudian psychology has been *away from* Freud's historical, biological, and often provincial sexual theories and *toward* more ego-oriented and culturally sensitive interpretations. Anthropologists of the *culture and personality* school (see chapter 3) have generally felt more comfortable with the neo-Freudian version than with the orthodox one; but some of Freud's most penetrating insights are to be found in his most outrageous statements.

These ideas have periodically been rediscovered by scholars approaching cultural phenomena from perspectives quite different from that of Freud (Brown 1959; Goffman 1963; Paul 1976).

Psychoanalysis and Clothing

Perhaps a less exotic example will help clarify the psychoanalytic approach to culture. Unlike other animals, humans wear clothing, following the "dress code" of their particular society (Lurie 1976). Anthropological studies of clothing have usually been concerned with its history, manufacture, or practical functions, though some have studied its social symbolism or investigated changes in fashion as an example of general cultural processes (Kroeber 1952:358–372). But such studies rarely explain *why* particular garments are worn in one society rather than another. We turn to psychoanalysis in the hope that it may disclose the hidden meanings of clothing and the motives for its use: of what human neurosis is clothing the symptom?

The best-known work on this subject is *The Psychology of Clothes,* by the psychoanalyst J. C. Flügel (1950). Although much of the book is devoted to typologies of clothing and to functional analysis, scattered through its pages are hints of what a thoroughly dynamic treatment of the subject would be like. Flügel points out that the motives of modesty and display are fundamentally opposed to one another, and that therefore our attitude toward clothing is necessarily ambivalent:

> Clothes . . . are essentially in the nature of a compromise; they are an ingenious device for the establishment of some degree of harmony between conflicting interests. In this respect [the use of clothes] resembles the process whereby a neurotic symptom is developed . . . due to the interplay of conflicting and largely unconscious impulses. (Flügel 1950:20–21)

Clothing that can conceal the body may also serve to enhance its beauty and call attention to it. Claims of greater "comfort" or "hygiene" may actually be rationalizations of an unconscious desire to display one's body, whereas an excessive interest in clothes may be interpreted as a displacement of exhibitionistic tendencies. Exaggerated fear of the cold and a tendency to "bundle up" may signify an unconscious fear of losing maternal love (pp. 82–83).

Particular items of clothing have regular symbolic meanings, both in dreams and in the behavior of fetishists (individuals who derive sexual satisfaction in connection with items of clothing or other objects). Shoes, ties, hats, and trousers are male, or "phallic," symbols, whereas handbags, jewels, girdles, and (sometimes) shoes are female symbols. According to Flügel, "we can easily establish the existence of a continuous transition, from blatant exhibition of the actual genitals to the totally unconscious symbolism of them by garments which resemble them but very little" (p. 27). The padded and brightly colored "codpiece" of the English Renaissance is an intermediate example; long, pointed shoes are another, less obvious one. Protective amulets may also have phallic connotations:

> The "evil eye" was supposed to harm its victims . . . by damaging their reproductive powers or reproductive organs [and it is] intimately connected with the castration complex . . . [m]ost of the amulets used to ward off the evil eye appear to be symbols of the reproductive organs. (p. 74)

Transvestism (the wearing of clothing of the opposite sex) is considered an individual perversion in some societies, but in others it is an expected behavior on ritual occasions. The orthodox Freudian approach assumes that it is possible to explain these social customs by analyzing the motives of deviant individuals. Flügel suggests that the mechanism of identification is at work in both cases: every lover identifies to some extent with the beloved, and in abnormal cases this may be achieved by dressing in clothing associated with the love object.

The concept of identification is useful in understanding some social customs requiring transvestism (see Bateson 1958), but even Flügel recognizes that many such practices may result from any of several quite different motives:

> The direct transfer to one sex of some experience or characteristic of the other may be the end in view, as when in the couvade the magical transference of labour pains from the mother to the father is helped by some exchange of garments or when young male initiates are dressed as girls, or captured soldiers dressed as women. . . . Finally, the exchange of dress may only be a particular example of the general exchange of roles . . . that characterises special holidays. (p. 121)

What would Freud, Flügel, or Fenichel say about contemporary unisex styles and the adoption by many young people of "funky" clothing of uncertain age and origin? For many radical students, certain garments (for example, overalls or caps) consciously symbolize their identification with the working class, with blacks, or with farm laborers. For others, nostalgia or durability (or both) may be primary motives. Clothes may express more than one's conscious identification. The message of student styles of the late 1960s was brilliantly deciphered by journalist Garry Wills. Writing of the student demonstrators at the 1968 Democratic Convention in Chicago, he says,

> The keynote of the kids' clothing is softness. No edges. Even last year's military jackets have the padding torn out—droopy epaulettes, wilted fronts, frayed bottoms, every sag and hang eloquent: "I ain't a-marchin' anymore." . . . Their clothes are all of the muffling sort—blankets, capes, serapes, sheperd's coats, hoods, wooly sweaters, thermal underwear like tailored mattresses. . . . Bell-bottom pants are mandatory for the girls, worn with light sweaters. No bras, of course. No edges. (Wills 1971:297–299)

These insights are highly compatible with psychoanalytic ideas, for Flügel was quite aware that certain kinds of restrictive clothing (for example, tight, stiff collars) may be "symbolic of duty or moral control" (1950:196). It is possible that loose clothes "of the muffling sort" symbolize both conscious rebellion against "the system" *and* an unconscious sense of loss of parental affection. (We shall return to this issue in connection with the "swaddling hypothesis" and Russian national character in chapter 5.)

Summary and Critique

We have seen in this chapter how Freud and his disciples attempted to apply psychoanalysis to cultural topics. The basic analogy between neurotic symptoms and customs or institutions was developed in a number of different ways, some more enlightening than others. In the course of examining Freudian explanations for taboos, totems, and transvestism, I introduced several concepts that will be important in later chapters. These include Freud's dynamic model of mental life, in which conflict and ambivalence are to be expected; the defense mechanisms and their operation in daily life (for example, in forgetting) as well as in dreams or neuroses; and the Oedipus complex as a crucial stage in human psychosexual development.

Although I have presented these ideas with a minimum of critical commentary, the reader must realize that they were at first highly controversial. Some of them have passed into public knowledges and their origins may not be remembered. For example, the analysis of "dirty jokes" that Freud proposed in his book *Wit and Its Relation to the Unconscious* (1916) is now so generally accepted that George Orwell could summarize it without even referring to Freud:

> The reason . . . so large a proportion of jokes center around obscenity is simply that all societies, as the price of survival, have to insist on

a fairly high standard of sexual morality. A dirty joke is not, of course,
a serious attack upon morality, but it is a sort of mental rebellion, a
momentary wish that things were otherwise. (Orwell 1954:121)

Other aspects of Freudian theory are still considered highly controversial or even disproved (Fisher and Greenberg 1977). Yet the things
that make psychoanalysis a very powerful theory also make it virtually
untestable. The postulation of instincts, which are by definition unconscious, and energy, which is by definition unmeasurable, presents great
challenges to objective investigation. Given the notion that anything
may appear as its opposite in dreams or neurotic symbolism, the psychoanalyst can get out of any difficult position by claiming just such a transformation. In addition, the concept of resistance can easily be turned
against a critic: if you do not accept the idea of the Oedipus complex, it
is because your own complex is as yet unresolved.

Freud and his early disciples assumed that "primitives" were a
pretty homogeneous bunch. These writers shared many nineteenth-century ideas about "savage passions" and the "childlike" native. Thus,
they never came to grips with the immense variability of human cultures or with the tremendous diversity of psychological types in all societies. As we shall see, later developments in psychological anthropology
did account for this variability. Partly in reaction against earlier
overgeneralizations, later anthropologists stressed cultural differences
to the point where comparison and generalization became almost impossible.

Though Freud may have underestimated the differences among
primitive societies, the main thrust of his work emphasized the "primitive urges" that survive in all of us. In his analyses of religious and political institutions, Freud showed the illusions and neurotic needs on
which "civilized" accomplishments rest. And he demonstrated that "the
kind of thinking which underlies mythology is still at work today in the
minds of children and neurotics, of dreamers and artists" (Costigan
1965:301). Although this knowledge may make us uncomfortable (self-
knowledge usually does), it is now an inescapable part of modern life,
and we must learn to live with it. (See Endleman 1981.)

Supplement, 1999

Despite many detractors and defectors, psychoanalysis remains a major
influence within psychological anthropology (e.g., Heald and Deluz
1994). Several contemporary psychoanalytic movements such as "object
relations theory" and Lacanian psychoanalysis have introduced ideas

that extend the Freudian paradigm (see Ewing 1998), while Jonathan Lear (1998) treats Freud's metapsychology as a philosophical system comparable with those of Aristotle and Plato! Some of these ideas will be discussed in chapter 7 and its supplement. Here, it seems more appropriate to add only information about Freud's own ideas and methods in the light of further research.

An important source that was overlooked in the previous editions of this text is the study by Dr. Edwin R. Wallace, IV, *Freud and Anthropology* (1983). The author presents what he calls "a history and reappraisal" of Freud's anthropological essays with special attention to *Totem and Taboo*. He critically examines Freud's sources on totemism (many of which now seem exaggerated or distorted) and he discusses recent anthropological writings on this and related topics. Wallace argues that, although various defense mechanisms may be operative in religious belief and behavior, religion is no more "pathological" than other forms of human adaptation. Like Melford Spiro who regards religion as a "culturally constituted defense mechanism" that helps many people deal with their problems in living, Wallace writes,

> Even if one considers totemic practices to be the forerunners of religion (itself a very controversial notion) and even if one accepts Freud's oedipal explanation of their origin, it does not follow that these same motivations and meanings continue to be the decisive ones for any or all of the participants. (p. 183)

For a more orthodox interpretation of religious origins, see LaBarre (1970).

Of course, the "religious" actions and fantasies of some individuals probably are symptoms of mental illness; but most believers *use* the traditions of their faith for their own purposes, like any other part of their culture. Wishful and magical thinking are not confined to religion but may be found in politics, sports, business, psychology, and even anthropology! The disputes over Freud's legacy are sure to continue, revived from time to time by recognition of the irrational nature of much human thought and behavior.

During the past decade, claims concerning "recovered memories" of child abuse and murder have led to debates about the validity of repression, displacement, and other Freudian mechanisms. Freud's character as well as his ideas have been attacked and defended. And the keystone of his dynamic theory—the interpretation of dreams as wish-fulfilling products of unconscious conflicts—has also been questioned.

For example, work in neurobiology has revealed some of the brain mechanisms involved in the stage of sleep when most dreaming takes place. The study of sleep and dreaming in medical laboratories has produced many new ideas, and this "revolution" is far from being over. For example,

> Many researchers now believe sleep's main functions are to rejuvenate the brain and consolidate memory in various ways, but no one has proven that. Likewise, many think dreams are incidental side-effects of this process that evolution causes us to forget because the forgetting does no harm, while remembering might confuse dreams with reality, threaten our mental balance, and adversely affect survival. (Leonard 1998:68)

Psychological anthropologists must take account of these hypotheses, but their main concern continues to be with the *uses* to which people in different societies put their dream experiences. Are dreams shared or kept secret? In what contexts are they shared, and how does this affect their interpretation? Do people act on good or bad omens? And how are the meanings of symbolic dreams negotiated? These and many other questions are worth pursuing whatever the neurological source of a dream may be. (See Tedlock 1987; 1994)

It has also been suggested that the ethnographer's *own* dreams "can provide the ethnographer with important insights into emotional and conflictual aspects of their fieldwork situation" (Edgar 1994:111). Indeed, one anthropologist (Waud Krake) has reported that he "redreamed" an informant's dreams! I believe that—from throwing the I Ching to channeling or psychotherapy—*any approach that allows people to focus on their situation using creative hints from the unconscious can be valuable.* And the study of believers in any of these systems can also teach us a great deal about the larger culture to which they are responding (Ots 1994; Brown 1997; Krake 1997).

Finally, what might we say about 1990s clothing styles from a psychoanalytic point of view? Andrea Gillespie's study (1995) of the "Santa Fe Style" in clothing, a "look" that has been taken up nationally, draws mainly on historical sources and on ideas from research on fashion; but she makes clear the desires of customers to acquire what they consider "authentic" Southwestern clothes and jewelry, suggesting that they *identify* with the casual "life style" of New Mexico and the native peoples of the region. What this signifies in dynamic terms, however, is a topic for research in the next century.

Chapter 3

Configurations of Culture and Personality

The field of psychological anthropology goes by other names in many colleges and universities. The most common of these is "culture and personality." In this book, however, *culture and personality* is used to designate a particular school of thought within psychological anthropology (Hsu 1961:12–13). One reason for restricting our use of the term is that the word *personality* does not appear at all in the early work on primitive psychology; it occurs only rarely in Freud's own writing, though he did use the similar concept of character type. As we shall see, investigators in many recent studies avoid the term personality, or at least take a highly critical view of the concept, emphasizing instead direct and detailed observations of behavior in its natural settings (see chapter 9).

The culture and personality school comprises four major *approaches,* each of which will be treated in a separate chapter (chapters 3 through 6). These approaches are known, respectively, as configurationalist, basic/modal personality, national character, and cross-cultural (see table 3-1). Each approach has its distinctive methods, concepts, and subject matter, but important continuities exist among them, both of ideas and of personnel. The last three approaches were also influenced in important ways by psychoanalytic anthropology. Let us begin our survey of the culture and personality school by discussing the concept of personality as it was understood by the school's founders.

Personality in this context refers to persistent characteristics of an individual inferred from a sample of his or her behavior. These characteristics may be thought of in three general ways: as *traits* (distinctive behavioral regularities), as *character* (interpersonal dispositions), or as *modes of organization* (ways in which an individual's experience and behavior are integrated). The trait approach tends to be used by those concerned with the measurement of differences among normal individuals, as in skill, intelligence, or aptitude testing. Assessments of character or of modes of organization are more in the province of clinical psychologists and other professionals who deal primarily with disturbed individuals. In either case, literally hundreds of testing instruments and interpretive methods are available for the characterization of individuals. (See Wolman 1973:775–857.)

Personality, like culture, is one of the concepts we use to understand human behavior. When someone behaves in what is (to us) an unusual or bizarre manner, we usually try to make it fit with whatever else we know about that person. If we attribute the behavior to a childhood trauma or to anxiety induced by stress, we are using a personality type of explanation. On the other hand, if we attribute the same behav-

Table 3-1   Major schools and approaches of psychological anthropology

School	Approach and dates	Leading figures
Psychoanalytic anthropology	Orthodox (1910–)	Freud, Róheim, Flügel, Ferenczi
	Later Freudian (1930–)	Fromm, Erikson, Bettelheim, LaBarre, Devereux
Culture and personality	Configurationalist (1920–1940)	Benedict, Sapir, M. Mead, Barnouw, Hallowell
	Basic and modal personality (1935–1955)	Kardiner, Linton, DuBois, Wallace, Gladwin
	National character (1940–)	Kluckhohn, Bateson, Gorer, Hsu, Caudill, Inkeles
	Cross-cultural (1950–)	Whiting, Spiro, LeVine, Spindler, Edgerton, Munroe, D'Andrade
Social structure and personality	Materialist (1848–)	Marx, Engels, Bukharin, Godelier
	Positionalist (1890–)	Veblen, Weber, Merton
	Interactionist (1930–)	G. H. Mead, Goffman, Garfinkle
Cognitive anthropology	Primitive mentality (1870–)	Tylor, Lévy-Bruhl, Boas, Lévi-Strauss
	Developmental (1920–)	Piaget, Cole, Price-Williams, Witkin
	Ethnosemantic (1960–)	Conklin, Frake, Kay, Berlin, Hunn

ior to familial values, for example, or to the way Italian women are expected to act when ill, we are using a cultural type of explanation. Both types of explanation may be partly valid, but our decision to *accept* one or the other (or both) is a function of our own past experience and present needs. As Edward Sapir wrote in 1934,

> Our natural interest in human behavior seems always to vacillate between what is imputed to the culture of the group as a whole and what is imputed to the psychic organization of the individual himself. . . . The study of culture as such . . . has a deep and unacknowledged root in the desire to lose oneself safely in the historically determined patterns of behavior. The motive for the study of personality . . . pro-

ceeds from the necessity which the ego feels to assert itself significantly. (Sapir 1949:194, 198; cf. Wagner 1975:81–82)

This quote is of special interest here because, although Sapir was an outstanding linguist and ethnologist, he had a deep distrust of cultural explanations. It has been suggested that he emphasized the role of the individual in cultural processes in order to "prove that culture doesn't matter" (M. Mead 1959:201, quoting a letter from Ruth Benedict). The school of culture and personality involves much more than the subjective attribution of behavior to social or individual sources. The key to its early development can be found in the same essay of Sapir's that was quoted above. In it Sapir states that

> *the more fully one tries to understand a culture, the more it seems to take on the characteristics of a personality organization.* Patterns first present themselves according to a purely formalized and logically developed scheme. More careful explorations invariably reveal the fact that *numerous threads of symbolism or implication connect parts of patterns with others of an entirely different formal aspect.* . . . There is no reason why the culturalist should be afraid of the concept of personality conceived of as *a distinctive configuration of experience which tends always to form a psychologically significant unit* and which . . . creates finally that cultural microcosm of which official "culture" is little more than a . . . mechanically expanded copy. (Sapir 1949:201–203; emphasis added)

The three italicized passages in this quotation summarize the early approach of the culture and personality school. Let us closely examine the ideas they express:

- A culture, fully understood, is like a personality. This is the basic simile on which the configurationalist approach is founded. The similarity of patterning is not revealed in the usual ethnographic description of beliefs and practices within a culture: one can find the connections only by exploring beyond the superficial patterns of the "official culture." It is in its subtle, complex organization, integrated on many different levels, that a culture is said to be like a personality.

- The patterns of a culture are connected by "symbolism and implication," that is, by both symbolic and logical linkages. One must be alert and sensitive to discover them; for example, "a word, a gesture, a genealogy, a type of religious belief may unexpectedly join hands in a common symbolism of status definition" (Sapir 1949:201). Again, one must get *behind* conventional ethnographic categories—the orderly but mechanical descriptions of "kinship," "technology," "religion," and so forth—to find these linkages.

• Anthropologists need not shy away from studying individuals, provided that they understand personality as a configuration of experiences that tend to form psychologically significant (that is, meaningful) units. We can understand the growth, functioning, and integration of cultures only by realizing that the *human personality is a system that seeks and creates meaning*. It is because individuals are the ultimate locus of culture (the "cultural microcosms") that cultural integration can take place.

Sapir rejects a "trait psychology" and insists on viewing personality as an organized system. His choice of words clearly allies him with the school of Gestalt psychology, which was well established by the 1920s. Terms such as "pattern," "organization," and, above all, "configuration" indicate his debt to this school, which consistently emphasized the importance of patterns and configurations as well as the organization of experience in a "field" of psychologically significant units. (See Bock 1985.)

The German word *Gestalt* means literally "form" or "pattern." It was adopted about the year 1912 by three young psychologists (Max Wertheimer, Kurt Koffka, and Wolfgang Köhler) to designate their departure from the academic psychology of their time (especially the experimental approach of Wundt). In their early work, they emphasized the perception of colors, forms, and movement, maintaining that perceptual processes could be understood only when the thing perceived was viewed as an organized pattern *(Gestalt)* rather than a collection of separate elements. For example, when we recognize a musical melody, we perceive a pattern of relationships rather than individual tones. This mode of perceiving can be demonstrated if we transpose the melody into a different key: All of the notes are changed, but the melody remains the same because the relationships among the notes are maintained. A melody is not present in its separate notes, for the same notes can be rearranged to produce a number of other melodies. Thus, an *atomistic* approach, which breaks a melody down into its separate elements, destroys the meaning of the experience. The meaning is in the pattern.

In his analyses of language, Sapir (1921) described the unconscious patterning of sound and grammatical categories and attempted to identify the dynamic processes of linguistic change. David Aberle has argued that early culture and personality studies were strongly influenced by these linguistic theories (Aberle 1960). It is thus important to grasp the Gestalt notion of configuration and to see how this concept was applied by Sapir's friend, Ruth Benedict, to the study of culture and personality.

Configurations of Culture

Gestalt psychologists emphasize the fact that our perceptions are self-organizing; that is, we experience patterns according to certain principles (similarity, proximity, closure, and the like) that are rooted in the structure and functioning of our brains. They object to the atomistic theories of "associationism" and "behaviorism" on the same grounds: "Behavior no less than sensory experience shows us wholes that are not merely the sums of parts but have their own properties as wholes, and obsession with elements is never going to reveal the essential properties of the wholes" (Woodworth 1948:135). *Configuration* is another term for such whole patterns.

The concern for configurations in culture has a history similar to that of Gestalt psychology. In the first decades of the twentieth century, American anthropology had become highly atomistic and trait-oriented. Partly in reaction against speculative evolutionary theories, Boas and his students attempted a massive documentation of the basic elements of Amerindian cultures and their exact geographic distribution. (This research strategy is today often called *historical particularism*, for example, in Harris 1968, chap. 9.) At its best, this approach produced much valuable data that made possible the delimitation of culture areas, historical reconstructions, and detailed studies of cultural transmission. At its worst, it yielded a mechanical listing of "culture traits" and an indication of their presence or absence in various social units. For example, a typical trait list would resemble table 3-2, with a list of items down one side, and a set of social units ("tribes") across the top. A plus indicates that a given trait was present in the society, whereas a minus shows its absence; a blank or question mark indicates uncertainty.

The trait list served as a check on historical speculation, and in the hands of a master it could be made to yield interesting results. (For examples, see Sapir's famous essay, "Time Perspectives," 1949:389–462, or any of Boas' essays on folklore or primitive art, e.g., 1966:397–490; 535–592.) For all its appearance of precision, however, the trait list was far from being a dynamic model of cultural processes. It did not satisfy those who wished to understand the *reasons* for a distribution, or who questioned the meaning of "present" when applied to a complex mode of behavior. Note that the traits ranged from items of material culture (kinds of tools, shelters, clothing), through details of behavior (types of arrow release, techniques of cooking), to quite abstract types of social organization or religious belief (exogamous clans, totemism, puberty rituals). Each trait would be marked as present or absent in an entire society, often on the testimony of one or two elderly informants! The trait list implicitly defined a culture as equivalent to the sum of its parts, and

Table 3-2   A hypothetical trait list showing presence (+) or absence (–) of material, behavioral, and ideological "traits" in four societies

		Tribes		
Trait	A	B	C	D
1 Ground-stone axes	+	+	–	+
2 Wood-plank houses	+	+	–	–
3 Woven-bark capes	–	+	–	+
18 Primary arrow release	–	+	–	–
19 Stone boiling	–	+	+	–
20 Fish drying	+	–	+	+
57 Exogamous matriclans	+	+	–	–
58 Totemic beliefs	+	+	+	+
59 Male puberty rites	–	+	–	+

it assumed a homogeneity of behavior that is contrary to common experience in any society.

Critiques of this approach have taken many directions, but we are concerned here with two main points:

• *The meaning of a given trait will vary according to what other traits are present.* For example, in table 3-2 we see that trait 58 is present in all four societies, but its significance will be modified by whether 57 or 59 is also present.

• It follows that *a culture is greater than the sum of its parts.* A culture is a configuration in which elements interact with one another, producing meaningful patterns. The acceptance, rejection, or reinterpretation of a new trait depends on the preexisting patterns. Two societies with similar trait lists may nevertheless have cultures that are *organized* in quite different ways.

Let us examine how these criticisms affected the work of Ruth Benedict. Benedict began to study anthropology at Columbia University in 1921. This was "a period when Boas was still interested in diffusion and in having his students laboriously trace a trait . . . from culture to culture, showing the changes [in] the trait" (M. Mead 1959:11). Boas soon recognized Benedict's talent, and after only three semesters of study she completed her Ph.D. Her dissertation on "The Concept of the Guardian Spirit in North America," written under Boas' close supervision, was published in 1923. (A guardian spirit is a supernatural protector acquired by an individual—frequently in a dream or vision—who takes special interest in the person's welfare, often endowing him or her with spiritual powers.)

Benedict's study is based on a careful analysis of the *distribution* of guardian-spirit beliefs and their *association* with other traits. In good Boasian style, she concludes with the statement that "man builds up his culture out of disparate elements, combining and recombining them" (Benedict 1923:84–85). But despite this particularistic conclusion, Benedict's concerns already went beyond historical reconstruction "toward a more just psychological understanding of the data" (p. 7). While the "intricate fortunes of diffusion" might associate guardian spirits with one trait here and another there, elaborating now on one feature and then upon another, Benedict's main point was that in each society we are dealing with a unique type of *social patterning*:

> In one region [the guardian spirit] has associated itself with puberty ceremonials, in another with totemism, in a third with secret societies, in a fourth with inherited rank, in a fifth with black magic. Among the Blackfoot, it is their economic system. . . . Among the Kwakiutl, their social life and organization, their caste system. . . . It is in every case a matter of the social patterning—of that which cultural recognition has singled out and standardized. (p. 84)

Any individual trait may have a fortuitous distribution across the continent, but within a given society traits enter a *pattern* that selects, emphasizes, and combines elements. The pattern integrates the diverse elements provided by history, giving each a new significance, just as each individual integrates diverse life experiences into a coherent personality.

Benedict developed this basic insight over the next decade, as she struggled with what she called "the configurations book." Sapir contributed greatly to her thought, as a fellow poet, colleague, and critic, though I believe David Aberle (1960) overestimates the influence of Sapir's linguistics per se on early culture and personality studies. The key ideas came from many sources, especially Gestalt psychology; and Margaret Mead also played an important role as student, colleague, and confidante. (See M. Mead 1972:138; also 1953a:136.)

During this incubation period, Benedict published two important papers: "Psychological Types in the Cultures of the Southwest" (1928), and "Configurations of Culture in North America" (1932). But her ideas reached their fullest development in *Patterns of Culture,* published in 1934 (1946a). The impact of this book on anthropology and the general public was very great. For many laymen and future anthropologists it was a first introduction to the facts of cultural diversity and to the relativistic theories that were then central to the discipline. The book soon became a best-seller due to its clear and elegant style, its somewhat sensational contents, and its genuine contribution to the characterization of cultural wholes (see Redfield 1955, especially chap. 5). Let us examine the structure of this landmark book in some detail.

Patterns of Culture begins with a chapter called "The Science of Custom," in which Benedict describes cultures as learned solutions to the problems confronting every society. Culture is contrasted with genetic inheritance to point out the inadequacy of racial theories of social differences and to argue that there is no scientific basis for *racism* (compare Boas 1939). Her emphasis is on our need to understand culture and the ways in which it affects our lives.

In the next chapter, "The Diversity of Cultures," Benedict discusses the unique pattern each society develops to cope with the human situation. In culture, as in language, *selection* is "the prime necessity." Each language makes use of only a few of the sounds our vocal cords can produce, and each culture elaborates certain aspects of human experience, ignoring others. Monetary values, technology, adolescence, and warfare are examples of phenomena on which some societies have erected "enormous cultural superstructures" but which have been virtually ignored in other societies. For example, puberty rites (for males, females, or both sexes) may be central to a society's ceremonial life, or the transition to adulthood may be casual and unmarked. Benedict then summarizes her own research on "guardian spirits," concluding that "the diversity of the possible combinations is endless, and adequate social orders can be built . . . upon a great variety of these foundations" (p. 40).

Cataloging the details of cultural diversity is not enough, since each living culture is more than "a list of unrelated facts." As Benedict writes,

> It tends also to be integrated. A culture, like an individual, is a more or less consistent pattern of thought and action. Within each culture there come into being characteristic purposes not necessarily shared by other types of societies. . . . Taken up by a well-integrated culture, the most ill-assorted acts become characteristic of its peculiar goals, often by the most unlikely metamorphoses. The form that these acts take we can understand only by understanding first *the emotional and intellectual mainsprings of that society.* (p. 42; emphasis added)

This patterning of behavior around a few central concerns is not, says Benedict, an "unimportant detail." Like chemical compounds (and Gestalt configurations), cultural wholes are greater than the sum of their parts. There is nothing mystical about this cultural integration: it is the result of the operation of "unconscious canons of choice," such as those that produce (over several centuries) great unified art styles. Only when we abandon the fixation on isolated traits in favor of whole cultures can we appreciate the importance of this patterning.

Explicitly citing Gestalt psychology, Benedict insists, "The whole determines its parts, not only their relations but their very nature" (p. 47). Cultural configurations do exist in complex civilizations but, she suggests, "the material is too intricate and too close to our eyes for us to cope with it successfully." We must begin elsewhere. "The whole problem of the formation of the individual's habit-patterns under the influence of traditional custom can be best understood at the present time through the study of simpler peoples" (p. 50; but see chapter 5, below).

In the next section of her book, Benedict considers at length four societies: the Pueblo Indians of New Mexico; the Plains Indians, whom she contrasts with the Pueblo; the Dobu Islanders of Melanesia; and the Kwakiutl Indians of America's Northwest Coast. The first description is a generalized portrait for, in addition to her own work at Zuni Pueblo, she draws on a number of other Pueblo studies; her "Plains Indian culture" is also a composite based on several tribes. The goal is to characterize the basic configuration of each culture—its "emotional and intellectual mainsprings"—exactly as a clinical psychologist might describe the personality structure of a patient. Benedict draws on all kinds of ethnographic materials to formulate and document her configurations: economic practices, family structure, political authority, religion, warfare, folklore—all are grist for her mill. What follows here is a summary of Benedict's configurational types for the four societies:

> *The "Apollonian" Pueblo Indians* The central pattern of Pueblo culture (according to Benedict) is avoidance of extremes, and this characteristic requires that individuals be totally subordinated to the traditions of the group. The Apollonian ideal (this term is taken from Nietzsche) is adherence to "the middle way" and avoidance of all strong emotion: evenness of behavior is prized; violence, anger, jealousy, and other forms of individual assertiveness are condemned as disruptive of good social relations. Cooperation and communal responsibility are taught from childhood. "Sanction for all acts comes from the formal structure, not from the individual" (p. 95). Communal forms are provided for all important activities: elaborate group ceremonies insure fertility, cure illness, and guide the individual through various life-crises. Ritual office confers only limited authority, and "a man must avoid the appearance of leadership" (p. 91). The accumulation of personal wealth is deemphasized, and resources are channeled into ceremonial responsibilities from which the entire community benefits.

The "Dionysian" Plains Indians The configuration of Plains Indian culture is exactly the opposite of the Pueblo's. It follows the "path of excess" and glorifies the individual who can escape from the ordinary boundaries of the senses. The cultures integrated by this Dionysian pattern (again, the term is from Nietzsche) greatly "valued all violent experience, all means by which human beings may break through the usual sensory routine" (p. 73). Dreams of power and guardian-spirit visions were actively sought by means that included fasting, drugs, and self-torture. Prestige accrued to those individuals who showed themselves fearless and violent, courting danger in warfare, glorying in their victories, and displaying wild abandon in their grief.

The "Paranoid" Dobuans The Dobu Islanders live in an atmosphere of conflict and suspicion. Their institutions magnify these tendencies, setting husband against wife, neighbor against neighbor, and village against village. Like the *paranoid* character type who projects his own unacceptable desires onto others, the Dobuan pattern insists that one person's gain is necessarily another's loss. This pattern permeates marriage, gardening, economic exchange, and all other significant activities. A good yam harvest implies that one has magically lured the tubers from surrounding gardens into his own plot, so harvest size and magical formulas are guarded in the utmost secrecy. The Dobuan is "dour, prudish, and passionate, consumed with jealousy and suspicion and resentment," and it is assumed that any prosperous man "has thieved, killed children and his close associates by sorcery, cheated whenever he dared" (p. 155). In every aspect of social life, despite shows of friendship and cooperation, "the Dobuan believes that he has only treachery to expect" (p. 158). Constant watchfulness, powerful magic, and potent poisons are essential to survival in this culture, which views all existence as a "cut-throat struggle."

The "Megalomaniac" Kwakiutl The Kwakiutl configuration centers on "their special ideas of property and of the manipulation of wealth" (p. 168) and incorporates many Dionysian religious practices that emphasize the "divine madness" of initiates. Family groups own hunting, gathering, and fishing territories, but individuals hold exclusive rights to certain material and nonmaterial items (totem poles, masks, songs, myths, names, and titles of nobility) that confer status and privileges on the owner. Prestigious items are usually inherited, but possession has to be "validated" by the distribution of wealth in the competitive feast known as the *potlatch*. The goal of these events is to shame one's rivals: "This will to superiority they exhibited in the most uninhibited fashion. It found expression in uncensored self-glorification and ridicule of all comers" (p. 175). Such a pattern would be called *megalomania* in an individual. Kwakiutl culture is integrated by this constant round of competitive gift-giving and/or destruction of property, for to avoid being shamed one has to repay (or destroy) a greater amount of wealth in a return *potlatch*. Triumph in such a contest increases a chief's claim to greatness—even if it means loss of all his possessions—and he arrogantly sings his own praises. This pattern permeates all Kwakiutl institutions: succession to office, marriage, religious ceremony, mourning, and warfare (pp. 186–205). (One could also acquire title to a prestigious ceremony by killing its owner!)

The lesson to be drawn from these case studies is that a dominant cultural configuration integrates many different activities: therefore, these activities can only be understood in relation to the total configuration. Not all societies have achieved neat configurations: "Like certain individuals, certain social orders do not subordinate activities to a ruling motivation [and] their tribal patterns of behaviour are uncoordinated and casual" (p. 206). Furthermore, Benedict insists, each configuration is an "empirical characterization" probably unique to a single culture. It would be a mistake to treat configurations as "types" and then attempt to fit other societies into the same categories. Even within the cases considered, "the aggressive, paranoid tendencies of Dobu and the Northwest Coast are associated with quite different traits in these two cultures" (p. 220). Our own culture centers on the desire "to amass private possessions and multiply occasions of display" (p. 226), but the American configuration is quite distinct from that of the Kwakiutl. (See the discussion of American national character in chapter 5.)

In her final chapter, Benedict deals with essentially the same problem she treated in her paper "Anthropology and the Abnormal" (1934): What is the relation of the individual to the cultural pattern? Most people, she says, manage to adapt and conform (at least outwardly) to the configuration that dominates their society, but for many, the psychic cost is great. People whose individual temperaments are suited to the culture pattern of their time and place will be "at home" in their own society, pursuing its goals with genuine satisfaction. However,

> just as those are favored whose congenital responses are closest to that behaviour which characterizes their society, so those are disoriented whose congenial responses fall in that arc of behaviour which is not capitalized by their culture. These abnormals are those who are not supported by the institutions of their civilization. They are the

exceptions who have not easily taken the traditional forms of their culture. (p. 238)

In other words, the individual who is frustrated and maladjusted in his or her own society—say, an aggressive, individualistic Pueblo Indian—might have been successful and content in another, for instance, on the Plains or in Dobu. "Normality" is relative to the dominant configuration of one's society; it is not an absolute quality of the personality, since "culture may value and make socially available even highly unstable human types" (p. 249). (See the excellent discussion of this point in Endleman 1967:580–598.)

This conclusion probably sprang in part from Benedict's own situation as a poet and "career woman," trapped in an unhappy marriage and finding little support for her ambitions in the institutions of her society. Her concern for the deviant, the person who in Sapir's phrase is "alienated from an impossible world," was shared by Margaret Mead. Benedict recognized that the "misfit" may develop a "greater objective interest" in his or her situation, for example, by becoming an anthropologist. She insisted in all her writings that an understanding of cultural patterning is liberating for the individual and essential in the modern world.

Benedict viewed *Patterns of Culture* as a "popular" book, one that was important because "people need to be told in words of two syllables what contrasting cultures mean" (letter to Reo Fortune, quoted in M. Mead 1959:321). There is no doubt that she selected and simplified her materials to suit this aim (some criticisms of this approach are cited in the Interlude, below). Underlying her popular message and personal motives is yet another level that, I believe, has been overlooked by most readers of the book: a Darwinian metaphor. Each cultural configuration functions as a kind of evolutionary *niche* within which well-adapted persons flourish, while the poorly adapted are constantly "selected against" by cultural pressures. Those whose characteristics are most opposed to the configuration (like the trusting and cooperative Dobuan who was considered a "simpleton" by his peers), and those who are unwilling or unable to conform, frequently become mentally ill and are isolated from their fellows.

Benedict comes very close to Freud's view of culture when she writes that "Tradition is as neurotic as any patient; its overgrown fear of deviation from its fortuitous standards conforms to all the usual definitions of the psychopathic" (p. 252). Our own culture, for example, with its great emphasis on material success, necessarily creates "failures." She pleads for greater tolerance of individual diversity and suggests that future cultures may develop in this direction. Freud himself was more pessimistic:

A good part of the struggles of mankind centre round the single task of finding an expedient accommodation—one, that is, that will bring happiness—between this claim of the individual [to liberty] and the cultural claims of the group; and one of the problems that touches the fate of humanity is whether such an accommodation can be reached by means of some particular form of civilization or whether this conflict is irreconcilable. (S. Freud 1961:43)

We shall deal with some of Benedict's later work in connection with studies of "national character." Let us now turn to the early writings of another founder of the culture and personality school, Benedict's friend and colleague, Margaret Mead.

To and from the South Seas

Margaret Mead must be considered *the* major figure in the culture and personality school. Her long and productive career spanned all four approaches of the school. With Benedict and Sapir she was a founder of "configurationalism"; she then moved beyond them into firsthand studies of growth and development, cross-cultural socialization, sex roles and temperament, national character, and investigations of the relationship between personality and culture change. Like Ruth Benedict, Mead was concerned with the application of anthropological findings to contemporary American life, and a continuing theme of her work was the relations between the generations. We shall examine only her early work in this section, reserving her later contributions for other chapters. Her first three major books—*Coming of Age in Samoa,* published in 1928 (1949), *Growing Up in New Guinea,* in 1930 (1953a), and *Sex and Temperament in Three Primitive Societies,* in 1935 (1963)—were all based on her fieldwork in the South Pacific. (Her more technical works on kinship and technology are not discussed here.)

Coming of Age in Samoa was the product of Mead's original research on a problem that was set for her by Boas: She was to investigate "the way in which the personality reacts to culture" (M. Mead 1949: foreword). Specifically, Mead was interested in sexual attitudes and the "crisis of adolescence" in a society with standards very different from our own. Samoa in the late 1920s had long been subject to Christian missionary activity, yet it had retained much of its traditional culture. Small villages subsisted on fishing and horticulture; there were titles of nobility and an elaborate ranking system; births and marriages were validated by property distributions similar to those of the Kwakiutl. The general *tone* of life and the expressive behavior of the Samoans was highly distinctive. Children were raised mainly by their older siblings, and adolescents had great personal freedom even though the culture permitted relatively few "choices" of occupations or goals.

In such a cultural setting, Mead asked, are the "conflicts and distress" characteristic of American adolescence inevitable? Or are these produced by aspects of our own culture that we take for granted, and that are thrown into relief by a comparison with the Samoan experience? To a large extent, she concluded, the crisis of adolescence is relative to the demands a culture places on young people during the transition to adulthood. The homogeneity of Samoan culture and its casual attitude toward early sexuality and responsibility make "growing up" relatively easy. As in the Pueblo culture, "excessive emotion, violent preferences, strong allegiances are disallowed. The Samoan preference is for a middle course, a moderate amount of feeling, a discreet expression of a reasonable and balanced attitude" (p. 89). Mead showed that the organization of families and villages encourages a greater *diffuseness* of relationships:

> Disagreements between parent and child are settled by the child's moving across the street, between a man and his village by the man's removal to the next village, between a husband and his wife's seducer by [the gift of] a few fine mats. . . . Love and hate, jealousy and revenge, sorrow and bereavement, are all matters of weeks. From the first months of life, when the child is handed carelessly from one woman's hands to another's, the lesson is learned of not caring for one person greatly, not setting high hopes on any one relationship. (p. 132)

Two important characteristics of Mead's work are evident in the above quotation: the fluency and persuasiveness of her style (based on her intimate knowledge of an exotic culture) and her emphasis on the early learning of cultural patterns through nonverbal communication. Mead does not attempt to sum up Samoan culture in a single configuration, but she does write of "the lack of deep feeling which the Samoans have conventionalized until it is the very framework of all their attitudes toward life" (p. 133).

This *shallowness,* she feels, largely accounts for the painless transition from childhood to adulthood. There are exceptions. In her treatment of "The Girl in Conflict" (chap. 11), we learn about the unhappy deviants who, through accidents of birth or temperament, are prone to special kinds of suffering: the shy and awkward girl whom the rank system has cast in the role of household "princess," expected to entertain and dance for her chiefly father's guests; or the beautiful but brash and assertive young woman whom no high-ranking man will marry. For all its charm and grace, Samoan society is not a paradise, and the range of individual temperaments is always wider than the types selected as ideal.

In *Growing Up in New Guinea* Mead describes her second trip to the South Pacific, in 1928, to study the Manus of the Admiralty Islands. (See M. Mead 1972:190–205.) The emphasis in this book is on the development of personality, "the manner in which human babies born into these water-dwelling communities gradually absorb the traditions, the prohibitions, the values of their elders and become in turn the active perpetuators of Manus culture" (1953a:13). The book offers a rich description of the traditional way of life, with its emphasis on the accumulation of wealth through trade and exchange. (Mead was to revisit this society twenty-five years later; she recounted the extensive changes that had taken place during her absence in *New Lives for Old*, 1956.)

Manus child-training patterns are highly distinctive. After the first year of life, the father plays a greater role in child-care than the mother, but both parents invariably "give in" to the child's demands for food or attention. There are a few basic taboos and skills, classified by the Manus as "understanding the house, the fire, the canoe, and the sea," but once the child has acquired these, he or she is left to play almost completely independently of adult control. A strong identification with the father is nevertheless established in the early years. Repetition and imitation play a large role in socialization, but the basic taboos—shame regarding the body and its functions, respect for the property of others, and fear of ghosts—are also communicated nonverbally.

Mead's treatment of the contrast between child and adult social life, and the ways in which this contrast affects personality development, is of great interest to psychological anthropologists. Manus children, says Mead, "live in a world of their own . . . based upon different premises from those of adult life" (p. 55). Exchange holds no interest for them:

> No attempt is made to give the children property and enlist their interest in the financial game. They are simply expected to respect the tabus and avoidances which flow from the economic arrangements, because failure to do so will anger the spirits and produce undesirable results. (p. 59)

All of this changes when marriage approaches. Gradually for girls, more suddenly for boys, the kinship and economic systems that have always surrounded them take on new meaning and begin to affect their behavior. Similarly, the spirits who guarded them (or perhaps made them ill) in childhood now become forces to be reckoned with. Manus children "reject the supernatural in favor of the natural" (p. 70), but Manus adults must engage in séances, divination, and magical rites of protection. Children's play is described as unorganized and unimaginative, and children's talk is practical and dull compared with adult conversations concerning "feasts and finances, spirits, magic, sin, and confessions" (p. 79). This situation has interesting implications for the issue of "primitive mentality," especially regarding "animistic" or "prelogical" thought. According to Mead,

> From this material it is possible to conclude that personalizing the universe is not inherent in child thought, but is a tendency bequeathed to him by his society. . . . Children are not naturally religious, given over to charms, fetishes, spells, and ritual. They are not natural story tellers, nor do they naturally build up imaginative edifices. . . . Their mental development in these respects is determined not by some internal necessity, but by the form of the culture in which they are brought up. (pp. 83–84; cf. pp. 170–172; also M. Mead 1932)

On her third trip to the Pacific (1931–1933), Mead investigated several contrasting New Guinea societies, giving special attention to the social roles of men and women. One product of this research was *Sex and Temperament in Three Primitive Societies,* published in 1935 (1963). The message of this book can be condensed as follows: if we designate biological gender by the terms "male" and "female," we can speak of the ideal *temperaments* attributed to each sex as "masculine" and "feminine," respectively. The American pattern assumes that males will be strong, aggressive, and concerned with commercial and worldly achievements; females, by contrast, should be dependent, maternal, and concerned with domestic matters. Despite recent changes, American culture takes this association between sex and temperament for granted and punishes those who display the "wrong" temperament with ridicule, ostracism, and names such as "tomboy" or "sissy."

Table 3-3   The relationship between sex (male, female) and temperment (masculine, feminine) in four societies (adapted from M. Mead 1935)

	Society			
Sex	*United States*	*Arapesh*	*Mundagumor*	*Tchambuli*
Male	Masculine	Feminine	Masculine	Feminine
Female	Feminine			Masculine

Mead discovered that each of the three New Guinea societies she studied had conceptions of appropriate temperament for each sex, but that these did not accord with the American pattern. The mountain-dwelling Arapesh saw little difference in the temperament of men and women; both were expected to behave in what we might consider a "feminine" manner—emotionally warm, nurturant, and peaceful. The Mundugumor of the Sepik River also saw little difference between male and female temperaments, but their ideal person (of either sex) was aloof and aggressive. Finally, the lake-living Tchambuli did recognize temperamental differences linked to gender, but these were quite the reverse of the American pattern: the ideal women were energetic, assertive traders, whereas Tchambuli men stayed home, occupying themselves with domestic tasks and engaging in gossip, personal decoration, and artistic endeavors! (The relations of temperament to sex in these societies are summarized in table 3-3.)

What conclusions can we draw from this comparison? In each case, the conventional assignment of a standardized temperament to a given sex is partly arbitrary, though fitting the general configuration of the culture. The insistence that all members of a gender (or a society) display a single temperament is destructive and wasteful, causing misery to those who cannot (or will not) conform. It is far better, says Mead, to recognize the diversity of temperamental endowments present in every group and to use it for positive social ends: "If we are to achieve a richer culture, rich in contrasting values, we must recognize the whole gamut of human potentialities, and so weave a less arbitrary social fabric, one in which each diverse human gift will find a fitting place" (1935:322). (For an appreciation of Mead's work, see the Summer 1975 issue of the journal *Ethos*.)

Summary

We have seen how discontent with the historical and atomistic character of American anthropology led Sapir and Benedict to use the concept of personality in analyzing the integration of culture. Douglass R. Price-Williams has commented on the connection between configurational studies and the contemporary development of *functionalism* in ethnology. Just as functionalists such as Bronislaw Malinowski and A. R. Radcliffe-Brown emphasized the interdependence of customs and institutions within a single society, the configurationalists tried to match cultural elements with aspects of personality: "One might say that the aim was to interpret personality as being identical with an institutional feature, so that it could be fitted into the interdependent framework of society like any other social trait" (Price-Williams 1975:71). Marvin Harris made a similar point in his lengthy critique of the culture and personality school (1968:393–421). But in addition to this implicit functionalism, I believe that Benedict and Mead used a Darwinian model in which each configuration was viewed as selecting for personality types most in accord with its ideals.

Introducing the culture and personality school through the pioneering works of Sapir, Benedict, and Mead has given a somewhat uneven view of the development of psychological anthropology. Many other anthropologists who were attracted to psychological problems began at the same time to investigate and publish on a variety of topics. In addition to appearing in the standard anthropological journals, articles by anthropologists were published in such diverse places as the *Journal of Abnormal and Social Psychology,* the *American Journal of Psychiatry,* and *Character and Personality.* In 1937, the journal *Psychiatry* was founded under the direction of Harry Stack Sullivan; for many years it served as a major forum for the discussion of culture and personality issues.

Another important leader in early culture and personality studies was the ethnographer, A. Irving Hallowell. While still a graduate student at the University of Pennsylvania, Hallowell began to study Freudian and Gestalt psychology, and he traveled regularly to New York to participate in seminars with Boas and Benedict. During the 1930s, he attempted to synthesize concepts from several psychologies with data from his work with Ojibwa Indians in order to demonstrate that the human environment is "culturally constituted." By this phrase he meant that human beings do not simply perceive what is "out there" in nature but, rather, that their perceptions are mediated by learned ways of perceiving and thinking, by "cognitive orientations that organize and confer meaning upon them [and that] are acquired in large measure . . . from cultural symbol systems" (Spiro 1976:608). This is a point that many psychologists have just begun to appreciate (see Tart 1978).

Hallowell's ideas were far ahead of his time, and he was an influential teacher. Although never a Freudian (or follower of any "ism"), he made creative use of psychoanalytic concepts and was one of the first anthropologists to employ the Rorschach test in non-Western societies (see chapter 4). (Mead had tried using it in Manus but with discouraging results; see Kaplan 1961:302–304.)

Hallowell's major writings have been collected in two anthologies (Hallowell 1955; Fogelson 1976). Together, these volumes cover an enormous variety of topics, from stress, anxiety, and aggression to psychological aspects of cultural change and human evolution. Although he does not "fit" into any of the schools or approaches defined in this book,

Hallowell contributed to most of them, and his works will be cited wherever appropriate. Like certain other scholars—A. Douglas Haring and Dorothy Lee among them—his major influence on the field will probably be effected through his students.

In the next chapter, we will examine the ways that psychoanalytic theory was blended with configurational interpretations to create new approaches to the study of culture and personality. These approaches, known as *basic* and *modal* personality, continued the configurationalists' concern with the integration of culture, adding to it a dynamic analysis of social institutions and a search for causal relationships between institutions and personality.

Supplement, 1999

Historical research on the configurationalist approach is represented in Stocking's volume (1987) and in the reflections of John W. Bennett on "classic anthropology" with special reference to Benedict and Mead (1998: Chapter 13). The loving attempt by Judith Irvine to reconstruct Sapir's fragmentary manuscript on the psychology of culture was largely unsuccessful. But the enduring message of the configurational approach—that any element of culture receives its meaning from its place in a larger pattern—remains important today. Indeed, this is part of what Boas and his students meant by "cultural relativism." Recent arguments, both for and against relativism, often seem to miss this point, though it was eloquently expressed in a distinguished lecture by Clifford Geertz (1984). (Derek Freeman's assaults on Mead's Samoan research and on relativism will be discussed later in this book.)

Even within our own society, the interpretation of supernatural beliefs is a difficult task. What, for example, are we to make of the widespread appearance of *angels* in U.S. culture? Why the sudden spate of "angelic" books, plays, television shows, clothing, and jewelry? How can the psychological meaning of this phenomenon be discovered?

In the absence of genuine research, many speculations have been offered, to which I shall add my own. I suspect that the angel fad is related to conscious and unconscious anxiety about the coming millennium. Thus, "angels" may correspond to something missing in our society. Perhaps we sense a *lack of protection and guidance* from parents, teachers, and other authority figures, and this interpersonal void is filled by fantasy figures supplied by our (commercial) culture. If so, it seems likely that as the year 2000 approaches, sightings of angels (and angelic merchandise) will increase.

Chapter 4

Basic and Modal Personality

Sigmund Freud

T hroughout the 1930s, Columbia University remained the American center of activity for culture and personality studies. At the University of Pennsylvania, Hallowell continued to develop his distinctive style of analysis, while at Yale, a number of social scientists under the leadership of Edward Sapir and John Dollard undertook studies that were to lead to the cross-cultural approach after World War II (see chapter 6). In this chapter, we shall be mainly concerned with developments at Columbia, where, by the end of the decade, the configurational approach to culture and personality had been replaced by an approach based on the concepts of *basic personality structure* and of *modal personality.*

The leading figures in developing this new approach were the psychoanalyst Abram Kardiner and the anthropologists Ralph Linton and Cora DuBois. Kardiner was the catalyst around which this approach took form, but we shall begin by considering the skills and knowledge that Linton brought to the enterprise.

Ralph Linton came from the University of Wisconsin in 1937 to replace Boas as chairman of the department of anthropology at Columbia. Linton had extensive field experience as an archaeologist and as an ethnographer in the Marquesas Islands (Polynesia), in Madagascar, and among the Comanche Indians. He had also been involved in studies of acculturation, but aside from one chapter in his influential textbook, *The Study of Man* (1930), there was little in his work to indicate an interest in psychology. The circumstances of his appointment caused extreme coolness in his relationship with Benedict (since she had hoped to succeed Boas as chairman), and the two never worked together closely.

Linton was soon deeply involved in a series of culture and personality seminars in which he and other anthropologists "presented" the cultures with which they were most familiar, after which Kardiner and other psychologists "interpreted" the data to reveal their dynamic significance (Linton and Wagley 1971). Kardiner's seminars had begun in 1935 at the New York Psychoanalytic Institute; after 1940 they were moved to Columbia and became part of the anthropology curriculum. By 1939, when he and Linton published *The Individual and His Society,* the basic methods and concepts of this approach had been worked out, especially the concept of *basic personality structure* (BPS). According to Linton, this concept

> suggests a type of integration, within a culture, based upon the common experiences of a society's members and the personality charac-

teristics which these experiences might be expected to engender. This sort of integration differs sharply from that which the functionalist anthropologists have made a focal point in their researches and from that posited by Benedict in her well known *Patterns of Culture.* (Kardiner and Linton 1939:viii)

Basic Personality Structure

Linton calls the functionalist approach to institutional integration "superficial" and describes it as yielding an image of culture as "a mass of gears all turning and grinding against each other," but lacking any focus. Benedict's configurational approach has greater potential, says Linton, but it runs into difficulties in cultures that "are not dominated by an *idée fixe.*" The concept of BPS, on the other hand, "places the focal point of culture integration in the *common denominator of the personalities* of the individuals who participate in the culture" (pp. viii–ix; emphasis added). He further suggests that BPS may help us understand phenomena of cultural change, such as acceptance or rejection of culture traits, or their "reinterpretation" (the imposition of new meanings by the borrowing society).

The BPS approach thus extends the configurationalist assumption that culture and personality are integrated in similar ways; Linton and Kardiner wish to understand the *causal* relationship between the two. Culture is integrated, they say, because all the members of a society share certain early experiences that produce a specifiable basic personality structure and because this BPS in turn creates and maintains other aspects of the culture. This assumption leads to a division of culture into two parts: *primary institutions*, which produce a "common denominator" of basic personality, and *secondary institutions*, which are produced by the BPS. This causal chain is diagramed in figure 4-1.

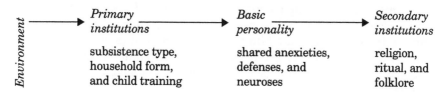

Figure 4-1 A causal chain linking primary institutions (viewed as adaptations to the environment) to basic personality structure (individual adaptations to the primary institutions), which in turn develops and maintains secondary institutions (because of the projection of shared conflicts). (Based on Kardiner 1939; 1945.)

The other key concepts used in this approach are *adaptation* and *projection*. Kardiner does not usually attempt to account for the origins of the primary institutions; he assumes that they are largely the result of a society's historical adaptation to its environment. That is, he regards subsistence technology, social organization (household and community), and child-training disciplines as "givens" for a particular society. Individuals born into a society with a certain set of primary institutions are thus "obliged to adapt to them one way or another." "The particular constellations caused by the necessity of the individual to adapt to these institutions become a part of his effective functional tools of adaptation, and eventually a part of his sense of reality" (Kardiner and Linton 1939:248–249).

Kardiner places great stress on the "ego functions" of reality testing and adaptation to objective frustrations; however, he insists that the "secondary institutions can . . . be understood only from the effects of the primary ones on the human mind" (p. 249). These effects include unconscious conflicts and anxieties produced by early experience. Secondary institutions such as "taboo systems, religion, ritual, folktales, and techniques of thinking" (p. 471) are to be analyzed (as in Freud's *Totem and Taboo)* as symptoms of intrapsychic conflict that are given form by projection and other defense mechanisms. In his later work, Kardiner referred to the secondary institutions as the "projective system." Let us examine some examples of this type of analysis.

In a series of brief "preliminary studies," Kardiner discussed data on the cultures of the Trobriand Islanders, the Zuni Pueblo, the Kwakiutl, the Chuckchee, and the Eskimo. Since he, like Linton, criticized Ruth Benedict's characterizations as vague and inaccurate (pp. 84–85), it is interesting to see how Kardiner approaches the Zuni and Kwakiutl materials: "The whole point of Zuni culture is . . . the formation of a powerful in-group with great increase in security for the individual" (p. 116). Kardiner emphasizes the cooperative and peaceful nature of Zuni social life, which rests on a strong sense of shame as well as "mutual advantages" of the complex social organization. He relates these to a strong dependency on, and fear of desertion by, the mother, and to the relative insignificance of sibling rivalry. Elaborate taboos affecting a Zuni who kills an enemy are interpreted as revealing strong ambivalence concerning aggression (see the discussion of taboos on the dead, in chapter 2).

Kwakiutl customs are said to "permit ample opportunity for expressing aggression in unsublimated or displaced forms," but "their religious practices show deeply repressed anxieties and methods of draining these [including] typical Oedipus myths and rituals" (p. 117). Intense rivalries and desires to humiliate others are common, and Kardiner attributes these factors to the frustrations imposed by the strict ranking system. He interprets the Kwakiutl Cannibal Society initiation as an acting-out of Oedipal fantasies and sibling rivalries. Kardiner relies on the principle that "certain basic disciplines . . . will create a definite type of personality which will lead to the formation of institutions according to the needs and perceptions of the personality" (p. 120). On this assertion rests the entire basic personality structure approach. (See Abel, Métraux, and Roll 1986; also Whiting and Child 1953:3–7.)

The remainder of *The Individual and His Society* deals with three cultures that Linton had studied at first hand. Although his field research had been directed to different ends, Linton's phenomenal memory provided rich data for Kardiner's dynamic analyses. For example, Linton presents (in forty pages) a description of the Tanala and Betsileo—two related societies of Madagascar—following which Kardiner analyzes (in sixty pages) the psychological "constellations" that connect primary with secondary institutions in those societies. According to Kardiner, the key to Tanala basic personality is the principle that obedience brings safety and security. Early child discipline and the structure of the family (powerful father, polygyny, and primogeniture) insure that "the pattern of love or security in return for obedience is the most prominent pattern of adaptation for the greatest number of people in the culture." A younger son in particular "must suppress hatred toward father and oldest brother, be diligent, ingratiate himself with his superiors real and supernatural, anticipate offence with prophylactic sacrifice, or atone afterward" (p. 361).

In a chart outlining the relation between primary and secondary institutions in Tanala culture, Kardiner indicates that the repressed hatred, submission, and ingratiation of (younger) sons are elements of the BPS that result in fear of ancestral ghosts, who are believed to cause illness when displeased by the sins of their descendants. Similarly, the severe and early toilet training of Tanala children is related to "obedience" in the BPS; this, in turn, results in a cultural emphasis on cleanliness and on "compulsive acts" as part of all cures for illness. Finally, the primary institution of *sibling inequality* (primogeniture) produces sibling hatred in the BPS. When repressed, this aggression results in the secondary institutions of blood brotherhood and male homosexuality; when expressed, the aggression takes the form of special social roles—the *ombiasy* (shaman) and the warrior who directs his hostility against the out-group (1939:326). Women are less subject to these dynamics, although conflict between a chief and his secondary wives in polygynous households does lead to the occasional practice of sorcery.

Even more interesting than Kardiner's characterization of Tanala BPS is the contrast with Betsileo culture and personality. Like the Tanala, the Betsileo were originally small-scale horticulturalists living in isolated, egalitarian, and highly endogamous communities. With the shift from dry to the more productive irrigated rice cultivation, however, Betsileo culture changed markedly in its "social organization, and hence created important changes in the basic adaptation of every individual" (p. 329). Changes in the primary institutions included use of new techniques of labor (especially related to water supply), diversification of village structure (including slaves), increases in exogamous marriages, an increase in the importance of personal property with a decrease in the significance of family ties, and the development of new levels of organization "from joint family to tribal organization to kingdom" (pp. 329–330).

Such changes are exactly what cultural-evolutionary theorists would expect under conditions of population growth and adoption of a more intensive form of food production. However, Kardiner is primarily interested in the consequences of these changes for *individual adaptation* and, ultimately, for the secondary institutions of the society. For example, under the irrigated rice system, the power of the father was diminished and the authority of the "king" became both great and arbitrary. New conflicts and new types of loyalties developed, while accumulation of property became "the most important element in the security system of the individual" (p. 331). The technique of ingratiation no longer worked:

> New needs as well as new anxieties were added to the individual's problem of adjustment. New needs were created in that the individual required different qualities to get along in this new society, and new anxieties in that he was susceptible to new dangers, dangers of poverty and degradation. (p. 331)

Obedience no longer insured security. There was also an increase in homosexuality, spirit possession, ritual, and sorcery. The king and the sorcerers replaced the father and ancestral ghosts as agents of social control.

These examples illustrate the explanatory model used in the basic personality structure approach. Changes in subsistence technology and social structure (primary institutions) produce changes in ritual and belief (secondary institutions), but the "functional integration" of these institutions is *mediated* by psychological processes. "The new [secondary] institutions can be derived from the anxiety defenses made necessary by the alteration in basic personality structure" (p. 346).

It is essential to note that the only *individuals* who appear in this analysis are several of Kardiner's American clinical patients. They are introduced (anonymously) to illustrate the "dynamics of projection" or the "psychology of ingratiation." There simply are *no data* on Tanala or

Betsileo individuals! What Kardiner has done (ingeniously) is to link one part of a cultural description with other parts by means of an invented BPS for which there is no independent evidence. Used in this way, the BPS has the logical status of a *hypothetical construct*—an entity or process having interpretive value even though it is not directly observed (see MacCorquodale and Meehl 1948). The reader must decide just how valid a given BPS is in relation to a body of data. However, when the data have been preselected by the analyst, the danger of confounding fact with interpretation is very great (see the Interlude, below).

Like Freud, Kardiner uses individual neuroses as models, but he emphasizes ego structure as well as instinctual processes, so the BPS is an adaptation both to reality and to intrapsychic conflicts. Kardiner is highly critical of those psychoanalytic anthropologists (Róheim, Reik, Fromm, Erikson) who rely heavily on Freud's instinct theory, but he also denounces "those without psychodynamic training who employ psychological concepts in cultural studies" for their errors concerning the nature of adaptation (Kardiner and Preble 1963:222). In one of his last statements on this topic, Kardiner insists that

> the functioning of a society depends on the social arrangement necessary to insure co-operation in dealing with the environment, on the impact of this arrangement on the integrative processes of the human unit, and on the institutions created by the members of society in response to the adaptive problems associated with a particular process of individual integration. The human unit is the variable that makes a functional analysis of cultural institutions possible. (Kardiner and Preble 1963:221)

Kardiner was fully aware of the need for independent evidence concerning the "human unit" to validate and to enrich his construct of basic personality. An opportunity for this kind of validation came in the person of Cora DuBois, a Berkeley-trained anthropologist who participated in Kardiner's seminars in 1936–1937. Working from descriptions of culture was, she felt, "a good exercise," but it provided no opportunity to *verify* one's inferences. The key question was this: "Were individuals predominantly what we might suppose them to be from the institutions under which they lived, the childhood conditioning they received, the values they shared, the goals for which they strove?" Her conclusion was that "only field work could test the procedure" (DuBois 1961:viii).

DuBois undertook fieldwork in the Dutch East Indies during 1938–1939. The book that resulted from this experiment, in 1944, is *The People of Alor* (1961; see also Kardiner et al. 1945:101–258). Although written in the days before confessional complaints came into style, her book makes it clear that this was a difficult field situation. DuBois had first to learn Dutch, then Malay, and finally an unwritten native language, which she named Abui. She lived for eighteen months in a small mountain village on the island of Alor among hostile people (formerly head-hunters) who found her strange, clumsy, and somewhat frightening. She worked hard and learned well.

The Modal Personality Approach

The People of Alor is a collaborative effort. As in the seminars, DuBois presents ethnographic data (stressing childhood experience) and life histories (autobiographies of eight Alorese, four men and four women); Kardiner provides chapter-by-chapter commentary on child development and an analysis of adult character. The final part of the book contains the results of psychological tests that DuBois administered in the field: the Porteus maze test, word associations, children's drawings, and the Rorschach test (discussed in the following section).

In *The People of Alor*, DuBois uses the logic developed in earlier basic personality studies. She links primary institutions such as gardening techniques and household structure to maternal neglect of young children; this neglect produces a typical personality structure that lacks the capacity to engage in sustained human relationships. In turn, the weak superego, instability, and distrust characteristic of Alorese personality find outlets in the secondary institutions: ritual competition for status and wealth, mythology, and (formerly) warfare.

Nevertheless, the Alor study differs from earlier BPS work in several important respects. First, the data were gathered by an experienced ethnographer who had also been trained in psychological methods and who knew what was important to the approach. Thus, DuBois's material on Alorese early childhood is much richer and more systematic than Linton's recollections about Marquesan childhood or the brief notes on this topic in many ethnographies.

Second, ample data are presented on selected individuals, in both autobiographical accounts (including dreams) and test *protocols* (response records). Thus, the inferred basic personality can be checked against concrete cases. The value of this evidence was enhanced by the independent analyses performed by Emil Oberholzer (a psychiatrist) of the thirty-eight Rorschach responses. DuBois compared these analyses with Kardiner's character analyses, which were based on cultural and biographical materials. In addition, Stanley Porteus analyzed the results of his maze test, making brief comments on the intelligence and personalities of the subjects. Alorese children's drawings are reproduced, and both word associations and Rorschach protocols are included so that the reader can compare them with the suggested interpretations.

These important improvements over earlier works have been incorporated into many subsequent culture and personality studies. The close accord between these relatively independent analyses led Kardiner to claim that the Alorese material had validated his basic personality approach. Nevertheless, in addition to receiving high praise, *The People of Alor* has been intensively criticized, partly *because* the inclusion of data on individuals permits alternative interpretations. For example, Rorschach tests can be scored and evaluated in many different ways (see Rickers-Ovsiankina 1977). The eight biographies displayed such diversity of character types that many readers questioned whether any significant "common denominator" existed. Others wondered how a handful of biographies (including some of admitted deviants) and several dozen test protocols could accurately represent the 70,000 culturally and linguistically diverse people of Alor.

Kardiner parried many of these criticisms by insisting that, though some details may be wrong, "there can be little doubt about the main trend." He argued that BPS is a result of primary institutions and that, in Alor, the "combination of influences acting from birth to adulthood *must* create a deeply insecure and isolated individual" (Kardiner et al. 1945:169; italics added). DuBois, perhaps because she knew these people first hand, was more reluctant to accept this global interpretation. Without explicitly rejecting the notion of BPS, she put forward an idea that many psychological anthropologists have found more acceptable than Kardiner's formulation—the concept of *modal personality* (MP). The term *mode* refers to a statistical concept that can be simply expressed as "most frequent." Therefore, when we speak of the modal personality of a group, we are referring to the most frequent type encountered in our sample. The modal type need not be the "average" person. Indeed, it may not even be in the majority; it is simply the most frequent. For example, for the ten scores 20, 30, 30, 50, 60, 80, 80, 80, 80, and 90, the average score would be 60 (the total of 600 divided by 10), but the mode would be 80 since it is the most frequent score even though it is not the majority.

For DuBois, modal personality is primarily a *descriptive* concept, "an abstraction and a generalization" comparable to a racial type (1961:4). MP also has a *dynamic* aspect: it helps us to understand processes of stability and change. Suddenly sounding a great deal like Sapir, DuBois states that "only when we have some comprehension of the link between institutions which the individuals bearing those institutions may make on an emotional level, shall we begin to grasp the repercussions involved in social alterations" (1961:5).

In her preface to the paperback edition of *The People of Alor*, DuBois considerably modified the claims made (mainly by Kardiner) in the original (1944) edition. She admits that their analysis "may have oversimplified the congruities and largely ignored incongruities and discrepancies" between institutions and personality (1961:viii). The use of projective tests, even in "homogeneous" groups, is now expected to give "high probability that only a small percentage of people in a society belong to these modal groups" (p. xx).

In my opinion, modal personality has two important advantages over basic personality as a way of conceptualizing relations between culture and personality.

- The MP approach does not assume that all or even most of the members of a society share the same personality structure. The degree of sharing becomes an empirical problem rather than an assertion based on purely cultural data.

- In MP studies, biographical and test data on individuals are invariably collected (and usually published). In theory, such data could be collected by researchers using the BPS approach. However, since test data always show a wide range of variation, they are much more compatible with an MP approach, which gives careful attention to techniques of sampling and of statistical analysis.

These advantages later attracted a number of young scholars to the MP approach, but before we can consider their contributions, we must examine the methods of testing and scoring in some detail.

Projective Tests:
Rorschach and Thematic Apperception

Since the remaining studies to be considered in this chapter make use of projective tests, this is a good point at which to pause and consider the nature of these tests. Projective methods for the study of personality include a great variety of "devices that enable the subject to project himself into a planned situation." When using such methods, we are primarily interested in what a person "indirectly tells us about himself through his manner of confronting the task" (Murphy 1947:669). For example, a *sentence-completion test* can be viewed as a projective method because it presents an open-ended situation in which a person may express his or her thoughts, needs, and anxieties. A sentence such as

When I have to take an examination, I feel _____

may tap both conscious and unconscious attitudes and feelings. In addition, the speed or hesitancy of response, or the refusal to respond at all, may be as significant as the word or phrase supplied. Using these factors, the analyst can supposedly get behind individual or cultural defenses to understand thoughts and motives of which the subject is not aware.

Projective methods are used both to *characterize* the personality structure of normal individuals and to *diagnose* psychological problems. Probably the best known of these methods is the Rorschach, or "inkblot," test, developed early in the century by the Swiss psychiatrist Herman Rorschach. The traditional test consists of ten white cards, each with an irregular but symmetrical inkblot. These cards are presented to subjects in a standard order, and the subjects are asked to report what they see in each card. Half the blots show differences in black-gray shading and half include color. Besides the total number of responses, three aspects of the responses are used in scoring the Rorschach test:

Locations Whether the response is to the whole blot (W), to large or to small details (D,d), or to the white spaces (S).

Determinants Use of form (F), color (C), and/or perception of movement (M), including various combinations of these.

Content Perception of animal, human, or botanical forms with or without movement, and whether these responses are common, original, or bizarre relative to the population on which the test has been standardized.

The test is scored and the ratios of certain types of responses are calculated. The scoring is then interpreted. Several alternative methods of interpretation exist, but Gardner Murphy gives a good summary of the traditional method:

> In general, the use of form represents objectivity, a disciplined recognition of fact. The affective (i.e., emotional) life of the individual is revealed primarily through color; the person with an outgoing emotional disposition piles up a considerable color score. To use both form and color indicates integration of objective and emotional tendencies. To give numerous form-color responses (form being the primary determinant, and color the secondary) indicates control, but control with some appreciation of affective realities; to give numerous color-form responses, color being dominant, is likely to mean loss of control through dominating affect. A person with a rich inner life typically has a high human movement score. A richly intuitive, subtle, responsive person, the very gifted or artistic, typically gives many responses of both color and human movement; the pedant gives neither. (Murphy 1947:674–675)

By scoring the test in other ways, and by looking for responses and ratios that are often indicative of psychological problems, it is possible for an investigator to obtain a quick estimate of a subject's overall adjustment level. Experienced diagnosticians can tell a good deal from this test, but they make use of the entire pattern of responses, and do not rely on any "single indicator" of pathology.

Great caution must be exercised in using the Rorschach cross-culturally. When Oberholzer analyzed the thirty-eight Alorese protocols, he warned that errors of interpretation were likely because of the small sample (less than a hundred) and the fact that the test had been standardized on a European population: what would be a bizarre detail for a Swiss adult might be fairly common in Alor. Nevertheless, he thought it significant, for example, that Alorese males produced many responses to small and unusual details (24.4 percent) and that they showed a high ratio of color to movement responses (27 percent as against less than 1 percent). "The more there exists a predominance of the C over the M, the less there exist self-control and balance of mind" (Oberholzer in DuBois 1961:590–591). However, in the absence of local norms, interpretation and (above all) comparisons between populations must be evaluated critically (Henry and Spiro 1953; Kaplan 1961; Spain 1972).

During the 1940s and early 1950s, the Rorschach test was a favorite tool of psychological anthropologists (Hallowell 1955:32–74). They hoped that it would be especially useful with nonliterate peoples. It is currently in disfavor, partly for the reasons just mentioned and partly because attempts to validate its findings on Euro-American clinical subjects have often been disappointing. New types of inkblots, techniques of scoring, and ways of integrating findings with other types of tests continue to be proposed by clinicians; some of these may turn out to have cross-cultural relevance (see Edgerton 1970; LeVine 1982: chap. 12).

The other projective method used most frequently in anthropological studies is the Thematic Apperception Test (TAT). Developed during the 1930s by Henry Murray at Harvard, this test consists of a set of cards each showing an ambiguous picture of one or more human figures. Ten of the cards are for men only, ten for women only, and ten for both sexes. The subject is asked to tell a story about each card as it is presented. There is no time limit and the stories are recorded verbatim. Subjects tend to identify with one of the figures (usually of their own age and sex) and tell their stories from the point of view of this character; in doing so, they reveal their own self-concepts. The number of responses and the subjects' general emotional tone during the test are also noted.

Protocols are usually scored in relation to Murray's theory of human needs (for example, the need for aggression, affiliation, dominance, nurturance, autonomy, and the famous "need for achievement").

Many subjects find the TAT less threatening than clinical interviews or the Rorschach: The pictures are familiar and "anyone can tell a story." With the TAT, a subject may "betray his deep wishes without consciously focusing on them" (Murphy 1947:672). When used cross-culturally, TATs have usually been modified to make the figures and situations more familiar to subjects, and alternative methods of scoring have been developed; however, these alterations affect the kinds of comparisons that can be made. TAT-like scoring procedures have also been used to interpret literature, drawings, folklore, and reports of dreams, often with interesting results (see Colby 1966).

Applications of Projective Tests

Throughout the 1940s, Hallowell had demonstrated the potential of the cross-cultural use of Rorschachs in a series of papers that dealt not only with pathology but also with intelligence, emotional structure, and the psychological consequence of acculturation (Hallowell 1955:125–150, 345–357). In the late 1940s, one of his doctoral students, Anthony F. C. Wallace, undertook an ambitious study of an Iroquoian Indian community near Buffalo, New York. The full title of Wallace's study, published in 1952, is *The Modal Personality Structure of the Tuscarora Indians as Revealed by the Rorschach Test*. Wallace went on to become one of the most significant figures in psychological anthropology. I shall give an extended account of the Tuscarora study, for I believe it represents an important advance in the MP approach.

Wallace states the problem to be investigated as follows: *"What is the type of psychological structure most characteristic of the adult Tuscarora Indians of this community, insofar as it can be inferred from the obtained Rorschach sample?"* (1952:1; emphasis in original). The sample consists of seventy adult Rorschach protocols, and to these data Wallace applies an intentionally mechanical type of analysis. He takes the statistical definition of "mode" seriously, and attempts to establish the modal class for Tuscarora personality through explicit and replicable operations.

The sample was similar in age and sex distribution to the adult population of the Tuscarora reservation. It consisted of thirty-six males and thirty-four females whose ages ranged from sixteen to more than seventy years. Wallace reports that looking at the inkblots became "a minor fad, in certain circles" (p. 41), and only two or three of the persons approached refused to take the test. A larger sample would have been desirable, but seventy out of 352 adults is certainly adequate. Though there might be some biases, Wallace felt that the sample was "a fair representation of Tuscarora society" (p. 42).

Wallace's goal was to describe the "distribution of individual personality traits or types which distinguishes a population" without making any prior assumptions about how these traits relate to culture (p. 50). Furthermore, he was not concerned with isolated traits as such, but with the pattern of association among them.

In their earlier Rorschach studies, Hallowell and Oberholzer had calculated *average* scores for each of the main factors of the test (locations, determinants, content, and ratios); they then interpreted the average profile of their entire sample as if it were the Rorschach of a single, typical individual. This approach assumes that a common denominator can be discovered by averaging all cases. Wallace, however, used the *mode* for each of twenty-one factors to establish a *modal class of individuals*. (This class included only these individuals whose scores were within one standard deviation of the modal score. See Hay 1976 for a discussion of these methods.)

Wallace found that twenty-six of the seventy individual records fell within his modal class; another sixteen records (called *submodal*) clustered around the modal class, differing in only a few factors or ratios. He then calculated an average profile for the twenty-six members of the modal class only. Working with Hallowell, he interpreted this profile as if it were the record of a single individual. What kind of person is this? According to Wallace,

> one might describe the Tuscarora modal personality type as displaying: (1) on a basic but presumably largely unconscious level, a strong urge to be allowed to become passive and dependent; (2) a fear of rejection and punishment by the environment and by the self for these demands; (3) a compensatory drive to be hyperindependent, aggressive, self-sufficient; (4) an ultimate incapacity to feel, to adapt, to evaluate the environment realistically, and a concomitant dependence upon categories, stereotypes, and deductive logic. (p. 75).

Although this characterization of Tuscarora MP structure is the core of his monograph, Wallace also presents a concise description of Tuscarora culture, past and present. He discusses sex differences in personality and the relationship of Tuscarora MP to culture. He then presents an intriguing comparison of his findings with a series of Ojibwa Indian Rorschach protocols, which had been gathered and scored by Hallowell. The comparison showed a core of personality traits common to both peoples, but the method also revealed several important differences in modal personality—differences that are "congruent with the obvious cultural differences between Tuscarora and Ojibwa" (p. 107).

One of the most interesting observations in this monograph is tucked away in a footnote. Describing a Tuscarora woman with a highly deviant Rorschach record, Wallace comments that although one might think Tuscarora culture would be "uncongenial" to her, this woman "functions well" as a widely respected and well-liked clan mother. He suggests that Ruth Benedict may have overemphasized the dependency of personality on culture: "It would seem that people with widely differing personalities can within certain limits use the same culture—for different purposes perhaps—and thereby play successful and rewarding roles" (p. 82n). This brief note anticipates Wallace's later concept of the "organization of diversity" (1970:23–24), which focuses attention on the way in which diverse personalities are organized into functioning, changing social groups. It will be discussed further in the Interlude and in chapter 8.

The other major work to be considered here is *Truk: Man in Paradise* by Thomas Gladwin, an ethnographer, and Seymour B. Sarason, a psychiatrist (1953). Truk is a cluster of small islands in that part of the South Pacific known as Micronesia. This area came under U.S. control following World War II and was the subject of intensive study by the federally funded Coordinated Investigation of Micronesian Anthropology (CIMA). Gladwin gathered ethnographic, life-history, and projective-test data during a seven-month period, supplementing his material with studies by other CIMA professionals; Sarason was in charge of test interpretation.

I shall try to give a brief account of the culture, the kinds of data collected, and the conclusions reached in this massive, 650-page book. The subtitle, "Man in Paradise," refers to the natural beauty and equable climate of the islands as well as the assured food supply and rather casual attitudes towards sexuality (especially for unmarried adolescents). As Gladwin writes,

> the natural environment of Truk is remarkable in the degree to which man can find in it fulfillment of his needs with a minimum outlay of effort and hazard. This [is] important . . . for here is a case in which it is clear that any anxieties which the Trukese may feel acutely are, in the last analysis, of their own making. (Gladwin and Sarason 1953:33–34)

The underlying question of this study is, Can human beings be happy, even in "paradise"? The first quarter of the book is devoted to the essentials of Trukese culture—the setting, the technological system, the social structure, and the life cycle from birth to death. The remainder deals with Trukese modal personality. For a sample of twelve men and eleven women of various ages and degrees of local "popularity," we are given detailed life histories, Rorschach protocols, and responses to a modified TAT, together with Sarason's interpretations of the test data. Working without knowledge of Gladwin's cultural description, Sarason interpreted the TATs in terms of *themes* characterizing men, women, and the group as a whole. These themes include the following:

- Conflict between men and women, particularly regarding sexuality and female "assertiveness"
- Inconsistency of parent-child relationships, with a lack of opportunity to identify with stable parent figures
- Anxieties concerning adequacy of food supply apparently deriving from early frustrations
- Separation anxiety involving fear of loss and isolation, present throughout life and related to food anxieties
- "Laziness," in the sense of a strong preference for an easy, passive life (Sarason comments on the great number of stories in which people are relaxing, playing, eating, strolling, or bathing)
- Suppression of hostile feelings such that "the Trukese have difficulty in giving overt and direct expression to their hostility" (p. 238)

Gladwin felt that the TAT analysis had validly portrayed many aspects of Trukese social life. Commenting on the last theme, he notes, "This of course coincides with our observation of the high incidence of gossip and fear of sorcery, the latter being a classic mechanism of anonymous aggression" (p. 241). It appears that "man in paradise" is *not* entirely happy. Inconsistency in child training tends to produce an individual who "has great difficulty in formulating a mode of behavior which . . . will be effective in dealing with his social environment," and who becomes a conformist intent on avoiding conflicts and difficult choices (p. 457). Paradoxically, in a society in which food supply and male dominance are assured, people show deep-seated food anxieties, and the men display a variety of anxieties in relation to women (p. 458; cf. Gregor 1985).

Gladwin and Sarason acknowledge their methodological debt to *The People of Alor* but state that they tried to improve on DuBois and Kardiner's approach by using more representative samples and by using projective tests "as a primary datum in the definition of personality rather than as a corroborative device" (p. 459). They also suggest that projective tests can be of value to anthropologists as a means of guiding their attention to areas or problems they may have overlooked or failed to emphasize sufficiently. The Rorschach and TAT yield different kinds of data, and the authors feel that, wherever possible, *both* tests should be utilized (p. 455; cf. Spain 1972; DeVos 1978).

Summary

We have seen in this chapter how the basic personality approach developed out of the configurationalist approach by the infusion of psychoanalytic concepts and the construction of a causal model of explanation. Further, the modal personality approach employed a systematic collection of individual data and was based on the assumption that the proper object of investigation was the most frequent personality type rather than a basic structure shared by all members of a society. We noted that the MP approach was refined further in the work of Wallace and of Gladwin and Sarason: the former using inductive statistical procedures to define the modal class, the others a combination of different tests integrated with observational data. In the next chapter, we turn to the approaches developed during the 1940s for the study of national character, after which, in the Interlude, I shall critique the entire range of studies so far considered.

Supplement, 1999

An excellent account of the ideas and career of Abram Kardiner is presented by William Manson (1987; 1988) in an article and later book that give readers a better appreciation of Kardiner's contribution and influence. Manson argues that Kardiner offered a "neo-Freudian alternative" to the intuitive configurational approach, and that his causal model was very important to later cross-cultural studies, discussed below in chapter 6.

The neo-Freudian movement in psychoanalysis tended to emphasize the functions of the ego in adapting individuals to interpersonal reality in their immediate social environments. It differed from orthodox Freudianism which was more concerned with the erotic and aggressive drives of the id and with processes that take place *within* the psyche. Although these two approaches should be complementary, during the 1930s they were very much opposed. Karen Horney, Erich Fromm, and Erik H. Erikson were leading neo-Freudians and, like Kardiner, they were concerned with how people adapted to the diverse cultures into which they were born (see Erikson 1963, discussed below in chapter 7).

Manson claims that the appearance of Kardiner's book, *The Individual and His Society* (1939) seemed to many anthropologists "'the crystallizing event' in the emergence of neo-Freudian culture-and-per-sonality research" (1987:72). He tells of Kardiner's anthropological training under Boas and Alexander Goldenweiser at Columbia and of his decision to return to medical school where he studied psychiatry. Later, he journeyed to Vienna where he was analyzed by Freud himself. However, his Boasian training made him skeptical of Freud's anthropological theories, and he determined to find another way to apply psychoanalysis of mythology, religion, and cultural differences.

Manson relates many details of Kardiner's seminars and his work with DuBois and Linton that led to the theory of "basic personality structure." Kardiner focused on "the adaptive modalities of the ego in relation to impulse regulation" and the development of a "security system" that resulted from childhood discipline (1987:82). Drawn into studies of national character during World War II, Kardiner was guilty of the same over-generalizations that characterized that approach (see Interlude). But Manson is correct in his statement that

> Despite the gradual demise of "national character" studies in the early 1950s, a young generation of psychologically informed anthropologists incorporated Kardiner's formulations of basic personality, projective systems, and personality mediation into the various syntheses of neo-Freudian theory, behaviorist learning models, and cross-cultural methodology which came to comprise the field of "psychological anthropology" (1987:90)

This is what I have called the "Yale Synthesis." (See chapter 6.)

If some of Kardiner's ideas seem over-simplified and dated today, let us recall that they were attempts to integrate new psychodynamic theories with anthropological data. Cora DuBois, one of my own teachers, introduced the idea of a statistical distribution of personality types within a society, breaking through the assumption of uniformity, while Anthony Wallace continued this important work, turning later in his career to biographical and historical studies.

When reviewing the basic and modal personality studies of the 1930s and 1940s, I was struck by their emphasis on *obedience to authority* (of a king, dictator, headman, or elder) as the defining pattern in other cultures. It occurred to me that this implicitly contrasted with the supposed *individualism and independence* of Americans. These works were characteristic of the Depression in the U.S. and the near triumph of fascism in Western Europe. Yet after the war, when investigations were made into American character, subjection to authority and to demands of the peer group emerged as central themes, e.g., in *The Lonely Crowd* (Reisman et al. 1950), and *The Organization Man* (Whyte 1956). Instead of seeing "ourselves" as different from the Zuni or the

Alorese, the Germans or the Japanese, we began to recognize similarities in adaptation and dynamics (Milgram 1974). Contemporary disputes over egocentric and sociocentric self concepts repeat many of these arguments, often without realizing their history.

Perhaps this is a good moment to recall a central tenet of Freud's teachings. As he viewed it, *all human beings sacrifice their individual happiness in exchange for the security that culture promises* (Freud 1961). That is, by accepting the constraints of social and ideological systems we gain certain forms of security; but the trade-off is that we cannot do exactly what we wish, or say what we truly mean. This is one reason that the late Kenneth Boulding once called civilization a "protection racket."

If Freud is correct (and I believe he is), *every culture* requires people to give up direct erotic and aggressive satisfactions in the interest of survival. Even the psychopath tries to appear normal and takes care not to be caught! It is the particular balance between restraint and release that gives to each society its dynamic quality. Psychoanalysis thus asks us to recognize the necessary compromises in our own lives as in those of others, while it warns that repressed desires often find indirect means of expression (e.g., in work, art, dreams, and bodily symptoms). Of course, in some cases the impulses are directly acted on despite danger to the life and reputation of the actor, whether she is a provincial doctor's wife (Flaubert 1957) or he is the President of the United States (Starr 1998). The implications of this insight will be further explored in chapter 7.

Chapter 5

National Character Studies

Adolph Hitler

I n the last two chapters, I outlined the development of several approaches to culture and personality. No doubt identifying differences among these approaches is easier than recognizing similarities. However, these viewpoints all share the assumption that a one-to-one correspondence exists between a type of personality structure (ideal, basic, or modal) and a culture (or society). Despite explicit disclaimers and occasional references to deviant individuals and groups, the entire culture and personality school assumes that each society can be characterized in terms of a typical personality and that these characterizations can be compared. The logical outcome of applying culture and personality methods to larger and larger social units is the study of *national character*.

"Everyone knows" that the English are "reserved," the French "excitable," the Spanish "proud," the Germans "industrious," and so forth. The tradition of nonscientific and literary characterizations of nations dates back at least to Theophrastus (372–287 B.C.) and continues with Tacitus, Thucydides, and de Tocqueville to recent best-selling authors (for example, Luigi Barzini, *The Italians,* or Hedrick Smith, *The Russians).* In short, there is a widespread popular assumption that citizens of a given nation have certain distinctive psychological characteristics in common. This opinion is held with varying degrees of certainty and explicitness. Like most stereotypes, popularly agreed-upon national characters are difficult to verify or refute, since such constructions usually contain contradictory elements (for example, the "reserved" English are also thought to be highly "eccentric"); thus, they can account (after the fact) for virtually any kind of behavior, and are therefore scientifically useless.

Still, stereotypes do perform important social functions: they are often used to justify modes of behavior (slavery, discrimination, exploitation) that are advantageous to those holding the stereotypes. It is not surprising that, in the United States, scientific studies of national character were first undertaken in connection with World War II. It was thought that understanding the psychology of our enemies and their leaders could be helpful in planning wartime operations and postwar policy. Similarly, it would be useful to know the psychological characteristics of our allies—especially if they might someday become our enemies! For that matter, knowledge of American national character could help the war effort by indicating ways to increase morale and effectiveness under stress.

As early as 1939, Margaret Mead, together with Gregory Bateson, Eliot Chapple, and Lawrence K. Frank, worked with the Committee for

National Morale "to consider ways in which the sciences of anthropology and psychology... could be applied to the problems of morale building in wartime." After America entered the war, Ruth Benedict, Clyde Kluckhohn, and other anthropologists moved to Washington to take part in research and planning: "By 1943 there were a large number of anthropologists in various government agencies in Washington... interested in the problems of studying national character and in developing techniques for research on cultures at a distance" (M. Mead 1974:57–58).

The notion of studying cultures *at a distance* was one of the more interesting developments of this period. Making a virtue of a necessity (since the enemy was naturally unwilling to be studied at first hand), Mead and others devised methods for analyzing literature, films, newspapers, travelers' accounts, and government propaganda. These studies combined the logic of configurationalist and BPS approaches. When possible, recent immigrants, refugees, and war prisoners were intensively interviewed and tested. They did not constitute a representative sample of their countrymen, but Mead argued (1953) that *any* member of a society could contribute to the study of national character provided that his or her position in the society was specified (see chapter 8).

The Yellow Peril

America's most "exotic" enemy in World War II was, of course, Japan. The behavior of Japan's government and its soldiers was puzzling to Americans in many ways. For example, even allowing for American racism and propaganda, the Japanese did seem "fanatical" in their devotion to the emperor and their willingness to endure hardships or undertake suicidal missions. Paradoxically, Japanese soldiers who were captured seemed to be willing immediately to "change sides" and work enthusiastically for their captors! It took some time for anthropologists to analyze this apparent shift in loyalty and then to convince the U. S. Army of its genuineness. As Clyde Kluckhohn explained, a Japanese war prisoner conceived of himself as *socially dead*. He regarded his relations with his family, his friends, and his country as finished. But since he was physically alive, he wished to affiliate himself with a new society:

> To the astonishment of their American captors, many Japanese prisoners wished to join the American Army.... They willingly wrote propaganda for us, spoke over loud speakers urging their own troops to surrender, gave detailed information.... To anthropologists who had steeped themselves in Japanese literature it was clear that Japanese morality was a situational one. As long as one was in situation

> A, one publicly observed the rules of the game with a fervor that impressed Americans as "fanaticism." Yet the minute one was in situation B, the rules for situation A no longer applied. (Kluckhohn 1957:137)

We are dealing here with an aspect of culture (situational versus absolute ethics). However, we may inquire about the kind of personality adapted to a situational ethic, with its reliance upon external authority and "shame," as opposed to a personality with internalized (absolute) standards and a strong, guilt-producing superego. (See Piers and Singer 1953.)

Japanese concepts of the self and of responsibility were one focus of Ruth Benedict's wartime studies. Although she continued to resist psychoanalytic formulations, Benedict increasingly made use of materials on child training. She "developed her own style of approach . . . in which published materials were integrated with interview data," and she devised methods for "extracting cultural regularities from a very miscellaneous assortment of literary sources—history, travel accounts, plays, and novels—and from a variety of sources on current wartime behavior" (M. Mead 1974:59).

Following the war, Benedict spent a year in California compiling research on Japan (much of which was still classified). *The Chrysanthemum and the Sword* (1946b), as its title indicates, focuses on the contradiction in Japanese character between restrained aestheticism (seen in art and ceremony) and fanatical militarism (typified by the ideal of the samurai warrior). Benedict felt that one key to this complex character lay in the distinctive Japanese notions of social responsibility and obligation. From their earliest experiences and well into adult life, Japanese are drawn into a web of social relations in which their personal desires must be subordinated to family and group demands. The childhood emphasis on "shame" develops into the pervasive adult concern for "face," and individuals must be constantly aware of their social positions to avoid disgracing themselves and their families. Serious disgrace can only be wiped away by an honorable death in battle or by suicide.

Benedict considered *The Chrysanthemum and the Sword* her most important book and, despite forty years of criticism from American and Japanese scholars alike, it stands as a landmark in national character studies (see Stoetzel 1955). The necessity for working at a distance led to some errors and overgeneralizations, but many of Benedict's conclusions have been validated by more objective methods. For example, she pointed out that Japanese moral categories cut across American concepts in ways that can be most confusing: *giri* is a term usually translated as "repay-

ment" for a social obligation, but it refers to both what we call "gratitude" and "revenge."

> A good man feels as strongly about insults as he does about the ben-
> efits he has received. Either way it is virtuous to repay. He does not
> separate the two, as we do, and call one aggression and one non-ag-
> gression because so long as one is maintaining giri and clearing one's
> name of slurs, one is not guilty of aggression. One is evening scores.
> (Benedict 1946b: 146)

Does this statement describe national culture or national character? For Benedict, the distinction was never that important: she wished
to demonstrate the *isomorphism* (formal identity) of cultural patterns
with personality structure. In this case, the cultural value on repayment
of obligations corresponds to the Japanese notion of a "good man," and
cuts across the Western distinction between gratitude and revenge.
Although she described patterns of child training, Benedict's main
interest was in the kind of adults that a cultural system produced. In the
case of Japan, she emphasized the centrality of *obligation* to adult
character, pointing out that middle-aged Japanese have less personal
freedom than either young children or elderly persons. This is exactly
the opposite of the American pattern, in which children and older persons have little freedom relative to persons in what we consider the
"prime of life." The real value of Benedict's work lies in her intuitive
grasp of such general patterns. (See Befu 1971, chapter 6.)

Benedict also detected an isomorphism between the structure of
the Japanese family and the political organization of the state. In both,
"the officials who head the hierarchy do not typically exercise the actual
authority" (1946b:301). However, as Alex Inkeles has noted, these generalizations assume a homogeneity within large populations that has yet
to be demonstrated:

> The basic difficulty with this approach, one pervasive in the culture
> and personality literature, is its failure to take adequate account of
> the differentiation within large national populations. It emphasizes
> the central tendency, the existence of which it presumes but does not
> prove, and neglects the range of variation within and around the typ-
> ical. (Inkeles 1961:173)

On the Western Front

This same criticism applies to such famous studies of German national
character as Erich Fromm's *Escape from Freedom* (1941). Fromm was
concerned with why the German people had submitted to Hitler's dic-

tatorial rule. He tried to explain the appeal of the Nazi movement in terms of the prevalence in Germany of the *authoritarian personality*. A person of this character type is exceptionally obedient and subservient to superiors but behaves in an overbearing and scornful manner toward social inferiors—especially those under the individual's control. Fromm felt that persons with this character react with anxiety to democratic institutions and thus show a strong tendency to "escape from freedom" into authoritarian systems in which they are more comfortable. These ideas helped many Americans to understand the European enemy, and "authoritarianism" became a key variable in social psychology for several decades (Adorno et al. 1950; cf. Bettelheim 1971:260–292).

Other approaches focused on Hitler himself. Walter C. Langer was called on by the OSS (an American intelligence agency) to produce a study of Hitler's personality. After thirty years, his secret report was published; it contains fascinating material on the Fuhrer's private life, neuroses, and style of leadership (Langer 1973). For example, although most Germans refer to their country as the "Fatherland," Hitler almost always called it the "Motherland." From this and other evidence about his early life, Langer concluded that Hitler transferred his Oedipal feelings for his mother onto the German nation while projecting his hostility toward his father onto the old and declining Austrian Empire. Thus, when Hitler writes of his longing to go to Germany, "where since my early youth I have been drawn by secret wishes and secret love," and when he contrasts his intense love for Germany with his "bitter hatred against the Austrian state," Langer infers that the alliance between Austria and Germany represented his parents' marriage:

> Unconsciously, he is not dealing with nations composed of millions of individuals but is trying to solve his personal conflicts and rectify the injustices of his childhood. [Thus, when World War I broke out, Austrian-born Hitler joined the German army.] To him it did not mean simply a war . . . but an opportunity of fighting for his symbolic mother, of proving his manhood and of being accepted by her. (Langer 1973:159–160)

Erik Erikson, whose work will be discussed at length in chapter 7, also analyzed German national character. He was interested in Hitler's appeal to German youth. In particular, Erikson looked at the *image* that Hitler tried to project through his autobiography and other propaganda, and at the kind of *identity* he offered to the angry, frustrated adolescents of prewar Germany. (On the background of this study, see Evans 1967:65.)

Erikson's analysis is highly suggestive. He points out the mythical elements in "The Legend of Hitler's childhood" (1963:326–358). These include the "striking use of parental and familial images" (for example, the father is shown as a harsh, autocratic man who has betrayed his own youthful idealism, and the son—Adolf—rebels against him in order to shape his own destiny). To German youth, Hitler's image became that of "a glorified older brother, who took over prerogatives of the fathers without over-identifying with them." His appeal was that of the "gang leader who kept the boys together by demanding their admiration, by creating terror, and by shrewdly involving them in crimes from which there was no way back" (p. 337; on the theme of "shared guilt," see S. Freud 1950:143–150).

Like Langer, Erikson notes the "abundance of superhuman mother figures" in Hitler's imagery (p. 339), but he also stresses the *new identity* that was offered to adolescents by fanatical German nationalism and racism. Hitler used anti-Semitic stereotypes as a projection of a *negative identity* against which the German "master race" could view itself as good, pure, and strong. Unfortunately for the rest of Europe, Hitler's personal pathology corresponded to the unconscious conflicts of an entire generation, giving him an uncanny power over them. Millions of Germans responded to Hitler's megalomaniac visions: "Let everything go to pieces, we shall march on. For today Germany is ours; tomorrow, the whole world" (p. 343).

The Slavic Soul

For reasons that are easy to divine, Russian national character became the focus of research in the immediate postwar years. In this connection, the British anthropologist Geoffrey Gorer developed the famous (or infamous) "swaddling hypothesis." Margaret Mead also had a role in the formulation and popularization of this hypothesis, while Erikson adapted it for his own purposes in the article "The Legend of Maxim Gorky's Youth" (1963:359–402), a parallel to his study of Hitler's childhood.

The swaddling hypothesis is a good deal more subtle than it appears at first. Gorer pointed out that Russian infants were traditionally tightly swaddled during the early months of life. The rationale for this practice was that swaddling enabled infants to grow straight and strong, and that, without swaddling, children might "hurt themselves." Children were released from the wrappings for short periods each day, during which time they were cleaned off and actively played with.

Gorer imaginatively related this alternation between long periods of externally imposed immobility and short periods of intense social interaction and muscular activity to certain aspects of Russian character and politics. Many Russians are said to experience intense mood swings between long periods of introspective depression and short bursts of frantic social activity; also, Russian political behavior seems to consist of long periods of willing submission to a strong external authority punctuated by brief periods of intense revolutionary activity.

It would be a mistake to view this hypothesis as a causal argument, for it is actually a configurationalist statement of isomorphisms. Gorer does *not* claim that the practice of swaddling children causes Russians to have autocratic political institutions (Tsarism, Stalinism), nor that it produces a manic-depressive basic personality in all Russian adults. Rather, he is content to note the formal similarity among various cultural patterns, and to suggest that prolonged, tight swaddling is *one of the means* by which Russians communicate to their children that a strong external authority is necessary.

What does it mean to say that "the Russians swaddle their children"? In this form, the statement is equivalent to a + on a culture trait list (see chapter 3): Russians "have" the trait of swaddling. Gorer, of course, is interested in this practice as part of a larger pattern, but the impression remains that swaddling is an objective "social fact" rather than an inference from highly variable human behavior. Several kinds of variability must be considered in dealing with such statements (see Bock 1974:54). These may be applied to swaddling as follows:

> **Spatial variability** How large a group is denoted by "the Russians"? After all, the Soviet Union was the largest nation in the world, its borders encompassing great industrial cities, peasant villages, numerous ethnic groups, and even some tribes of nomadic pastoralists. Gorer and his collaborator John Rickman entitled their book *The People of Great Russia* (1948). "Great Russia" refers to the geographic district within which only the Russian language is spoken. This territory too is enormous, and general statements about its population call for careful and extensive sampling.

> **Temporal variability** This term refers both to the *period* of time for which the statement is true and to the *duration* of the swaddling. Swaddling is probably a very ancient custom, but when was it first used? Is it still practiced in postrevolutionary Russia? If not, when was it abandoned, and why? The length of time during which babies were swaddled may also have varied considerably, from a few weeks to more than a year. Different durations might have very different effects on children, and might be consistently related to other types of variability (spatial or intracultural).

> **Intracultural variability** Within the specified area (Great Russia) and time period (say, 1850–1920) other types of variation may have existed. Rural-urban differences may be significant, since rural

peoples frequently cling to a custom long after it has been modified or abandoned in cities. Social classes also differ with regard to child training, and duration of swaddling may have varied considerably among individual families. Obviously, establishing the range of variation and the mode for this one practice would require considerable effort and expense. Even if swaddling were found to be rapidly disappearing in Russia, Gorer could maintain that the "message" concerning the need for strong authority is transmitted in many different ways. (See Gorer and Rickman 1962:198.)

It is also essential to state the kind of *sample* on which a given statement about child rearing is based. Fortunately, we have some fairly detailed data on this topic from the Russian Research Center at Harvard (Kluckhohn 1962:210–243). In a sample of 172 Russian defectors, the research staff found only three persons who denied any knowledge of swaddling. It was clear that swaddling was an emotional-laden topic, since the "majority of the subjects manifested some tension or uncomfortableness in this part of the interview" (p. 238). Several of the informants had heard of the Gorer hypothesis and rejected it with some force! Nevertheless, most of the subjects agreed that swaddling had been practiced in all sectors of Russian society before the revolution and that it had become less prevalent in the last few generations.

Swaddling is found more frequently in rural than urban areas. Except for a few who defended the practice, almost all of Kluckhohn's informants considered it "old-fashioned." Reasons given for swaddling included protecting the baby against self-injury and giving strength to the bones. It was also claimed that the swaddled child sleeps longer and more quietly, particularly in nurseries with several infants, and that swaddling makes children easier to handle. (People who rejected the practice spoke of it as unhealthy and a "torture.") The interviews revealed a wide range of reported durations: "The modal figure for the duration of swaddling was three to five months, but a number of informants extended the period to a year and one to a year and a half. . . . Some stated that hands and/or feet were left free 'after the child could sit up' or 'after eight months'" (p. 239).

There is, of course, much more to the study of Russian national character than the swaddling hypothesis. Clinical interviews and psychological testing of large samples showed the Great Russian modal personality to be "warmly human, tremendously dependent upon secure social affiliations, labile [emotionally unstable], nonrational, strong but undisciplined, and needing to submit to authority." However, the Communist Party sets forth a very different ideal, demanding "stern, ascetic, vigilant, incorruptible, and obedient personalities who will not be deflected from the alms of the Party and the State by family or personal ties and affections" (pp. 214–215). According to Kluckhohn, this conflict sets the stage for a "national character drama" in which a small ideological elite attempts to remake an entire people to suit an image that is quite contrary to its traditional personality type. The conflict is summarized in table 5-1.

Table 5-1 Themes in the Russian "national character drama." (Adapted from Kluckhohn 1962:241–242)

Traditional Russian personality	Ideal Soviet personality type
"Oral-expressive"	"Anal-expressive"
Warm, expansive	Formal, controlled, orderly
Trusting, responsive	Distrustful, "conspiratorial"
Identification with primary group— personal loyalty	Loyalty directed upward to superiors—impersonal
Emphasis on "dependant passivity"	Emphasis on "instrumental activity"

Inkeles has suggested that socialization is always future-oriented, that is, that parents raise their children in ways that anticipate the situations that the children will have to face. Though it is difficult to understand how this process operates, some evidence indicates that at least people at the "managerial" levels of Russian society are training their children in line with the new Soviet ideal (Inkeles 1967).

Deliberate attempts at socialist character building are also found in the Russian school system, which emphasizes collective responsibility over individualism. In his excellent book *Two Worlds of Childhood,* Urie Bronfenbrenner contrasts the Russian and American educational systems with special reference to their effects on values and personality structure. Although the Russian system emphasizes cooperation and conformity, Bronfenbrenner notes that in the late 1960s Soviet "upbringing" (*vospitanie*) was showing many signs of increasing flexibility: "In particular, both within and outside the family, there is a shift away from features which foster dependency and conformity, toward new configurations more conducive to the emergence of individuality and independence" (1973:94). Bronfenbrenner concludes that

> if the Russians have gone too far in subjecting the child and his peer group to conformity to a single set of values imposed by the adult society, perhaps we [Americans] have reached the point of diminishing returns in allowing excessive autonomy and in failing to utilize the constructive potential of the peer group in developing social responsibility and consideration for others. (p. 170)

The Lonely Crowd

Americans are inordinately fond of being told what a great (or miserable) people they are and have made best sellers out of many works on their national character, from Alexis de Tocqueville's *Democracy in America* (1830) to Philip Wylie's *Generation of Vipers* (1946). Here we shall examine a few examples that come out of the culture and personality tradition.

Aside from Margaret Mead's World War II morale-booster, *And Keep Your Powder Dry* (1942), the earliest study of American national character is Geoffrey Gorer's *The American People,* published in 1948 and revised in 1964. As a wartime liaison officer between American and British officials, Gorer became convinced that most misunderstandings between the two groups were due to the false assumption that they shared an identical culture, when England and America had in fact evolved "most strongly contrasting national characters" (Gorer 1964:12). He claims that a distinctive character is found in "a significant number" of Americans, and that these modal characteristics and patterns of behavior have been "influential in molding the institutions in which the whole society lives" (p. 17).

Gorer's book is filled with fascinating insights based on his travel, reading, and interviews with Americans from all walks of life. For example, he maintains that American society is based on a *rejection* of the European ancestry and traditions of its largely immigrant population:

> The individual rejection of the European father as a model and a moral authority, which every second-generation American had to perform, was given significance and emphasis by its similarity to the rejection of England by which America became an independent nation. (p. 27)

Gorer sees this rejection as analogous to Freud's myth of the primal parricide, "which establishes the legal equality of the brothers, based on common renunciation of the father's authority and privileges" (p. 29). The themes of *equality* and of *resistance to authority* in American life thus have a deep psychological basis. This insight explains why all persons in positions of power must present themselves as "conspicuously plain citizens, with the interests and mannerisms of their fellows" (p. 40; see also Wills 1971:140–145, on Richard Nixon).

Since respect and awe are highly painful emotions for most Americans, debunking leaders and institutions is a favorite pastime. These attitudes also permeate family life, where "the father is not a model on which the son is expected to mold himself," but rather someone to be surpassed (p. 46). American children, especially males, are "constantly urged toward independence and activity and initiative" (p. 86), while the admiration of other people "becomes essential to the American sense of self-esteem" (p. 108).

Gorer finds in the comic strips, especially *Blondie,* an exaggerated but accurate portrayal of American family life. Dagwood, the untidy, incompetent, greedy, lazy, and easygoing father, is "kind, dutiful, diligent, well-meaning within his limits; but he has so completely given up any claim to authority that the family would constantly risk disintegration and disaster, if it were not for Blondie" (p. 49). The American child, who during the 1930s and early 1940s was fed on a strict time schedule, often grows up with an irrational fear of hunger. This is the unconscious motive for the "great erotic fetishist value given to women's breasts." Gorer believes the addiction of American men to drinking milk probably has "symbolic significance" (pp. 77–78).

Gorer also comments on American attitudes toward love, friendship, youth, machinery, and material acquisitions, skillfully pointing out patterns of behavior that Americans take for granted but that are clearly related to the dominant values of "Americanism." Although his evidence is fragmentary and anecdotal, many statements ring true even forty years after the first publication of the book. He anticipates the "male liberation" movement in his remark that "the lives of most American men are bounded, and their interests drastically curtailed, by [the] constant necessity to prove to their fellows, and to themselves, that they are not sissies, not homosexuals" (p. 129).

One of the most influential books of the 1950s was *The Lonely Crowd* by David Riesman (written with Nathan Glazer and Reuel Denney and published in 1950). Subtitled "A Study of the Changing American Character," it documents a shift in the modal personality of Americans, using extensive interviews together with sociological surveys and analyses of books and films. Riesman uses three general "modes of conformity" to describe character types:

> *Tradition-directed* Most persons in premodern societies who look to cultural tradition when making decisions, on the premise that "one must do what the ancestors did."

> *Inner-directed* Persons, primarily in developing societies, who listen to their "inner voice" for guidance, and whose internalized "moral gyroscope" enables them to act effectively in times of rapid change.

> *Other-directed* A character type found increasingly in affluent societies, mainly among the "organization men in gray flannel suits," but also the consuming public whose tastes and decisions are determined by what they think others value.

Much of *The Lonely Crowd is* devoted to describing the other-directed personality and documenting its rise to dominance in the United States. Inner-directed people are shown to be out of place in modern bureaucratic-corporate society; their "moral gyroscopes" have given way to the "psychological radar" of the other-directed, who are constantly scanning their social environment for cues to the correct ("in") behavior, attitude, or purchase.

Riesman does not glorify either of these character types. Inner-directed individuals may have been necessary during the rapid industrial growth of the nineteenth and early twentieth century, but they were often unfeeling and unresponsive to the needs of others, driving themselves and their dependents ferociously to achieve distant goals. Other-directed people, however, seem to be without *any* guiding principles, easy prey to the advertisers and "image-makers" of contemporary America, substituting peer approval for substantive achievement. The inner-directed person conforms as readily as the other-directed person, although the voices he listens to are "more distant, of an older generation, their cues internalized in his childhood" (Riesman 1961:31). Furthermore, "each of us possesses the capacity for each of the three modes of conformity," and individuals may change from one mode to another during their lifetimes (p.30).

It must be noted that the three modes of conformity have no real cultural content. Since any mode may be found in any individual in any society, only the degree of dependence on a mode or the frequency of its occurrence vary among groups and over time. Riesman associates each mode of conformity with a particular phase of socioeconomic development; he states in reference to Benedict's *Patterns of Culture* that all of the tribes, "as long as they are in the phase of high population growth potential, would be more or less dependent on tradition-direction" (p. 231). The unique configurations that Benedict described vanish at this level of analysis.

Riesman asked students who had read Benedict's book which of the societies they felt was most similar to America. (Stop for a moment and formulate your own answer before reading further.) He was somewhat surprised to discover that

> the great majority see Americans as Kwakiutls. They emphasize American business rivalry, sex and status jealousy, and power drive. They see Americans as individualists, primarily interested in the display of wealth and station.
>
> A minority of students . . . say that America is more like Dobu. They emphasize the sharp practice of American business life, point to great jealousy and bitterness in family relations, and [in politics. However,

no students argue] that there are significant resemblances between the culture of the ... Pueblos and American culture—many wish that there were. (p. 227)

Riesman's own view is quite contrary to that of the students. He feels that the tone of Pueblo life, with its insistence on equality, coopera- tion, and emotional restraint, is most like "the American peer-group, with its insulting 'You think you're big.'" One of the striking patterns in the interviews with young Americans was that so many considered their *best* trait to be their ability to "get along well with everybody." The most frequently mentioned *worst* trait was "temper," though it usually turned out that the interviewee did not really have much of a temper! Riesman reports his impression that "temper is considered the worst trait in the society of the glad hand. It is felt as an internal menace to one's cooper- ative attitudes" (p. 232). (For a different view of the American configu- ration as compared to the societies studied by Benedict, see Kardiner 1939:115.)

Riesman is, at heart, an apologist for individualism. His solution to the negative aspects of other-directedness is the development of an *autonomous* character structure that would remain sensitive to others and capable of conformity, but that would also be "free to choose whether to conform or not" (p. 242). Is this really possible? On what basis would the autonomous individual make the choice? In what spheres of life? Do the many cultural "alternatives" that our complex culture offers really make "more room for autonomy" (p. 257), or are these alternatives simply the icing on the cake of conformity, like mass- produced consumer items personalized with "your very own initials"? In a later book, Riesman clearly sounds the individualist's creed: "no ideol- ogy, however noble, can justify the sacrifice of an individual to the needs of the group" (1954:27). But Philip Slater has pointed out that this creed is contrary to a basic principle:

> Riesman overlooks the fact that the individual is sacrificed either way. If he is never sacrificed to the group the group will collapse and the individual with it. Part of the individual is, after all, committed to the group. Part of him wants what "the group" wants, part does not. No matter what is done some aspect of the individual . . . will be sacrificed.

> An individual, like a group, is a motley collection of ambivalent feel- ings, contradictory needs and values, and antithetical ideas. He is not, and cannot be, a monolithic totality, and the modern effort to bring this myth to life is not only delusional and ridiculous, but also acutely destructive, both to the individual and to his society. (Slater 1970:27)

This quotation is from Slater's seminal book *The Pursuit of Loneliness*—in my opinion one of the most significant studies of American culture and character (see also Lifton 1970 and Wills 1971). Written at the height of the Viet Nam War, it is a passionate indictment of the old "scarcity-oriented technological culture," and a call for revolutionary change to a "true counterculture" based on social consciousness and recognition of our interdependence. Insightful, humorous, and more realistic than most books on the counterculture, it ranges critically over every aspect of American society, pointing out our enormous ambivalences (for instance, our desire for privacy versus the craving for community). Slater insists that "nothing will change until individualism is assigned a subordinate place in the American value system—for individualism lies at the core of the old culture, and a prepotent individualism is not a viable foundation for any society in a nuclear age" (p. 118).

A different approach to American national character can be found in the work of Francis L. K. Hsu. Born in China, educated there and in England, and for many years a professor in the United States, Hsu has a distinctive view of American culture. His analyses tend to be more critical than those of American-born scholars. He writes of the deep value conflicts in the United States, especially between the official ideology of equality and the actual practice of racial and ethnic discrimination. He also says that "our understanding of American values is today no better than it was several decades ago. Periodically we note the conflicts and inconsistencies among the different elements, but we leave them exactly where we started" (Hsu 1961:212).

Hsu argues that in examining the positive connections among these contradictory values we find that they are actually manifestations of one core value, "*self-reliance*, the most persistent psychological expression of which is the fear of dependence" (p. 217). Self-reliance is similar to individualism but it also implies "the individual's militant insistence on economic, social, and political equality" (p. 217). From this core value Hsu derives both the *resentment of status and authority* noted by Gorer and the *fear of dependence* discussed by Slater. Hsu does not maintain that all Americans are self-reliant, but he does argue that self-reliance is an ideal taught in the home and the school, and that "an individual who is not self-reliant is an object of hostility and called a misfit" (p. 219). In America it is an insult to call someone "dependent," even though each of us is necessarily dependent on others

> intellectually and technologically as well as socially and emotionally. Individuals may have differing degrees of needs for their fellow human beings, but no one can truly say that he needs no one. It seems that the basic American value orientation of self-reliance, by its de-

nial of the importance of other human beings in one's life, creates contradictions and therefore serious problems, the most ubiquitous of which is insecurity. (p. 219)

These inherent contradictions include the fact that successful competition in America today requires the "individualist" to conform to the norms of many organizations and peer groups. "In other words, in order to live up to their core value orientation of self-reliance, Americans as a whole have to do much of its opposite" (pp. 219–220). Unlike Riesman, Hsu sees contemporary Americans as highly individualistic, but forced to use "other-directed" means to achieve self-reliance. Hsu believes that several other contradictions are causally related rather than accidental. These include the connection of

a) Christian love with religious bigotry.

b) Emphasis on science, progress, and humanitarianism with parochialism, group-superiority themes and racism.

c) Puritan ethics with increasing laxity in sex mores.

d) Democratic ideals of equality and freedom with totalitarian tendencies and witch hunting. (p. 220)

Many anthropologists would agree with Hsu's statement that, in those societies where self-reliance is not a core value, and where obedience to authority and dependence relations are encouraged, individuals "tend to have much less need for competition, status seeking, conformity, and, hence, racial and religious prejudices" (p. 224; see Dumont 1970).

And Elsewhere

Among the other interesting studies of national character is *Themes in French Culture* by Rhonda Métraux and Margaret Mead (1954). The authors stress the role of *orality* in French behavior as well as the importance to the French of intellectual and emotional *control*. Métraux and Mead are also concerned with general patterns of the national culture. For example, they discuss at length the concept of *le foyer*—an "untranslatable" term that connotes the warmth, comfort, and family relationships of the idealized French bourgeois household.

Salvador de Madariaga, in his classic *Englishmen, Frenchmen and Spaniards* (1928), also analyzed "key terms" as a way of comprehending cultural differences. Madariaga contrasts the French emphasis on *thought* with the Spanish stress on *emotion* and the English emphasis on *action*. He suggests that "fair play" is a key term in English culture. An alternative view of English personality is found in Gorer's *Exploring English Character* (1955), which should be read in conjunction with Gorer's *The American People* (1964).

G. Morris Carstairs' *The Twice Born* (1957) is a study of high-caste Hindus in Rajasthan, India. The book is based primarily on psychiatric interviews. Carstairs emphasizes the passive-dependent element in many Hindu personalities, relating it to religious ideology and strong pressures for obedience both in early socialization and later family experience. Carstairs presents a good deal of life-history material, and cautions the reader that his conclusions should not be generalized beyond the caste or region for which they are valid. Others have suggested that strong tendencies toward dependency and conformity, and a lack of "initiative" (self-reliance?) are in fact common to much of India's population. Louis Dumont (1970) has even stated that hierarchy and inequality are so fundamental to the social structure of India that humans there should be designated as *Homo hierarchicus* in contrast to the individualistic, achievement-oriented *Homo aequalis* of Western civilization. Erik Erikson (1969) takes up this theme in his psychobiography of Mohandas Gandhi (to be discussed in chapter 7).

Gregory Bateson and Margaret Mead authored an innovative book, *Balinese Character* (1943), in which they used hundreds of still photographs to document Balinese behavior patterns and modes of interaction (including the extraordinary development of postural balance and of trance). They produced a series of films on Balinese childhood, as well as a film in which family life in Bali was compared with that in France, Japan, and Canada. As usual, Mead emphasized the nonverbal learning of values and interaction patterns in her commentary (*Four Families*, National Film Board of Canada).

In a seminal essay written in 1949, Bateson describes Balinese culture and character. He claims that, in Bali, rather than being directed to a goal, activity is "valued for itself" (1972:117). Balinese enjoy doing things in large crowds—fortunately so, since the island has the highest population density of any area on earth. Conformity to complex cultural ideals is "aesthetically valued," so that deviants are considered stupid or clumsy rather than immoral. In general, Balinese children learn to avoid any kind of "cumulative interaction" that might build to a climax, and daily life is structured in ways that prevent "competitive interaction." For these reasons, Bateson refers to the society as existing (ideally) in a "steady state" (p. 125).

Summary

We have surveyed the history of the national character approach. Although such studies were made less frequently in psychological anthropology during the 1960s, they have by no means come to an end; they are presently in vogue in sociology and political science. (See Bellah et al. 1985.) My emphasis in this chapter has been on the "findings" of the studies rather than their methods, because the method used was primarily the application of the basic and modal personality techniques to national states. In the Interlude, which follows, I assess the early culture and personality approaches, after which I will turn to the cross-cultural correlational approach, the final flowering of the school.

Supplement, 1999

Once again, criticism of this chapter focussed on the drawing of Hitler rather than the content of the text. Some readers felt that Levine's drawing was too humorous while others believed that attributing the war and the Holocaust to one person's pathology excused the actions of those who followed a "madman." These are interesting responses, but they suggest to me that this drawing functioned as a target for the projection of some viewers' anxieties. This is as it should be. Even laughter, as Freud has taught us, reveals the release of unconscious tensions.

Of course many factors—political and economic as well as psychological ones—contributed to German (and French and English and American) behavior during the war years. The best recent work on Germany is *Explaining Hitler* (Rosenbaum 1998), in which the author interviews historians and psychologists, eliciting their competing theories ranging from Allan Bullock's idea that Hitler was a rational schemer to Daniel Goldhagen's controversial notions about German character and national responsibility.

Although the national character approach was pretty well discredited by the 1960s, popular works continued to appear, explaining why "the French" or "the Chinese" behaved as they (supposedly) did. As new markets opened to U.S. products in Asia and the Middle East, writers in business schools and private consultants produced guides to "doing business with" this or that country. Most of these guides included rather superficial analyses of cultures, but also gave some good advice such as: learn the language, observe local rules of courtesy, and do not make a pass at your host's spouse. An early anthropological example is Edward Hall's book, *The Silent Language* (1959). Originally written for Foreign

Service personnel, it includes a useful discussion of cultural variation in the use of interpersonal space and of differing concepts of time.

National stereotypes are still fascinating topics, and some anthropologists have been tempted to do research that confirms or contradicts them, or that attempts to explain why people, including those stereotyped, continue to believe them. When parts of a stereotype are *positive*, they may be used in assertions of ethnic identity; e.g., Jews are "good family men," Japanese are "hard workers," or Italians, "great lovers." The problem is that, once one starts thinking in such terms, *negative* traits may also be attached to a social category with no attention to individual variation. Whether positive or negative, stereotyping is a form of prejudice that can have dangerous consequences.

One recent approach in personality psychology seems to me to be, if not dangerous, at least mistaken. It is called the "Five Factor" approach because it is based on personality tests that appear to show the same five "trait dimensions" in all subjects, including those in other societies. At present, these dimensions are labeled *neuroticism, extraversion, openness* (to experience), *agreeableness*, and *conscientiousness*, with several specific "facets" under each of these headings (Costa and McCrae 1992).

This is not the place for a critique of these particular instruments, but it may be well to warn against some implications when they are used cross-culturally. Despite extremely careful translation procedures, there is a tendency to impose the five factors with their English labels on responses that may have quite different meanings. The researchers are aware of this possibility. Nevertheless, it is alarming to read of supposed *national differences* in personality based on a few percentage points difference in responses to a dozen or so questions indicating levels of "neuroticism" or "extraversion." The averaging of scores from a sample (usually of college students) is made to represent an entire nation and then compared with other averages. This procedure really ignores what had been learned from several decades of anthropological research (see Bock 1999).

On the other hand, a remarkable series of books by folklorist Timothy Mitchell seems, to me, to have absorbed the best of psychological anthropology, showing what careful historical scholarship informed by psychoanalytic theory can accomplish. In his works on Spain, Mitchell has explored violence and piety (1988), emotion and society (1990), bullfighting (1991), flamenco song and dance (1994), and the sexual abuse of women and children by the Spanish clergy (1998). These imaginative and well documented studies do not propose a uniform Spanish national character. They do, however, provide an understanding at quite a deep level of many distinctive aspects of Spanish culture, demonstrating their relationship to national institutions, especially the Church, the social class structure, and the differential treatment of male and female children.

For example, in *Blood Sport: A Social History of Spanish Bullfighting*, Mitchell begins by placing bullfighting within the larger pattern of annual fiestas all over Spain. He then turns to the history of this "sport," discussing some of the theories that derive it from antiquity, showing how what had once been a part of local celebrations became professionalized with the breeding of "brave" cattle and the selection and training of masochistic young men.

In his chapter on "psychosexual aspects of the bullfight," Mitchell draws on folklore that reveals the sexual metaphors embedded in the spectacle. He also explores the erotic attraction of the *matador*, arguing that "eroticism is violence and violence is erotic; society must contain and control both [but] desire may secretly caress the notion of murder" (1992:166). (If this seems extreme, consider the news stories about American women who marry convicted killers on death row!) These thoughts lead to his most general conclusions about bullfighting, as relevant to America as they are to Spain:

> For most people, degradation never goes beyond the level of fantasy— if it even gets to that point. In the meantime, culture is there to provide official fantasy gratification as a safe substitute for the real thing. Order must be preserved, after all, even as desire requires some sort of release. One of the fundamental adaptive traits of human culture lies in its paradoxical ability to strengthen taboos by providing for their transgression in carefully designed collective formats of one kind or another. (p. 166)

Furthermore,

> It is extremely difficult for human beings to gaze upon transgression without being aroused in some way. Ironically, even reactions of horror and nausea confirm that *violent spectacle is inherently erotic*. Properly defined, disgust is nothing but negative arousal, caused by the fear of degradation that accompanies the desire to give way to the instincts and surpass all taboos. (p. 171, italics added).

In his detailed consideration of the bullfight and its audience, the *matador* and his admirers, Mitchell convincingly supports these statements. I find it tempting to generalize these ideas to American prizefighting, hockey, and football as well as to most violent films and video games. Remember Freud's analysis of taboos as expressions of *ambivalence*: taboo indicates what is desired and what is, at the same time, forbidden by the superego. Williams James once hoped that sports could become "the moral equivalent of war," but it is not yet clear to what extent "violent spectacle" promotes or reduces actual violence. There is evidence for both views. Perhaps cross-cultural research can help to answer this important question (Ember and Ember 1998; see also Ingham 1996: chapter 8). For an intriguing analysis of the role of ambivalence in culture and motivation, see Nuckolls (1996).

Interlude

The Crisis in Culture and Personality

he year 1950 was an important turning point in the history of psychological anthropology. At about this time, the culture and personality school came under serious attack from several different quarters. These criticisms clearly revealed some of the underlying assumptions of the school, and suggested that these assumptions were invalid or at least unproved. As a result, culture and personality studies went into a brief decline. Many of the founders of the school were now dead (Sapir, Benedict, and—by 1952—Linton). Some studies of modal personality and national character continued to be produced, but the interests of American anthropologists were changing (see Spindler 1978:3). (The major exception to these statements was the cross-cultural approach, to be discussed in chapter 6.)

All of the approaches considered in chapters 3, 4, and 5 have both strengths and defects. I have tried to present each of them in terms of its own logic, emphasizing positive accomplishments. Now, however, it is time to consider the errors and weaknesses of the culture and personality school and to ask what can be done to correct them. Five *basic assumptions* are common to all these approaches. Let us consider each of these in turn.

The continuity assumption This assumption is the notion that early childhood experiences (for instance, nursing, weaning, swaddling, and toilet training) *determine* adult personality. The continuity assumption is relied on to some extent in all culture and personality studies, and especially in those influenced by psychoanalysis. Infantile trauma is assumed to produce fixations, anxieties, and neuroses that form the basis of cultural character and institutions.

109

This assumption was effectively challenged by Harold Orlansky in the important paper "Infant Care and Personality" (1949). Orlansky pointed out that very little evidence really existed to support the assumption that a given pattern of child training necessarily produces a given adult personality. Indeed, different researchers have attributed contradictory effects to identical childhood experiences. Some kinds of early learning are probably important to later behavior, but we have yet to sort out just what is learned in infancy, or to give correct weight to postchildhood experiences.

The proper way to establish continuity between infancy and adulthood is through *longitudinal studies* that follow sets of individuals throughout their lives, starting, if possible, with their prenatal environments. Some such work has been undertaken at Berkeley, Stanford, and the Fels Research Institute, but longitudinal studies are difficult and expensive. For the present we must accept Orlansky's caution that the continuity assumption is still unproved. (See Lomax et al. 1978.)

The uniformity assumption   Virtually all writers on culture and personality assume that each society can be characterized in terms of a single (dominant, basic, or modal) personality type. Despite disclaimers in introductory chapters, the idea that a one-to-one correspondence exists between a culture and a personality is persistent. Even in modal personality studies where the diversity of individuals in the sample is apparent, one is usually left with the impression that the "most frequent" type adequately explains the dynamics of the culture.

Yet, as Lindesmith and Strauss pointed out in their "Critique of Culture and Personality Writings" (1950), most anthropological characterizations of typical personalities are "imprecise and oversimplified," tending to ignore variability and to explain away negative evidence. Furthermore, it is disturbing that "the number of questions that are raised concerning any characterization tends to increase with the number of investigators familiar with the society" (Lindesmith and Strauss 1950:589). (A veritable "scandal" erupted in the late 1940s concerning what the Pueblo Indians are "really like." See Bennett 1946.)

Anthony F. C. Wallace reformulated this critique a decade later in his book *Culture and Personality* (1961). He argued that traditional culture and personality studies had been primarily concerned with the "replication of uniformity," that is, the process by which each society allegedly produced a new generation of individuals who would perpetuate a static culture and conform to an ideal personality type. Such studies, he suggested, must give way to a greater concern with the "organization of diversity." This concept refers to the way in which "various individuals organize themselves culturally into orderly, expanding, changing societies" (Wallace 1970:23). All cultures require a variety of personalities—leaders and followers, artists and shamans, warriors and nurses—if they are to survive. Wallace called for an inductive study of the distribution of personality characteristics within different societies. Similarly, after comparing Rorschach protocols from several cultures, Bert Kaplan (1954) suggested that psychological variation is probably greater *within* any society than it is *between* different societies. In view of these criticisms, we must conclude that the uniformity assumption is false.

The causal assumption   As was noted in chapter 4, a concept such as "basic personality structure" (or "dominant configuration") has the logical status of a hypothetical construct. It is no more *observable* than, say, Freud's "primal horde" or Oedipus complex. Its value (if any) rests in its plausibility: the construct indicates how a variety of observations might make sense *if* the hypothesized basic personality structure were actually shared by the members of a society.

Unfortunately, it is an easy step from formulating such a construct to reifying it into a causal entity. Thus, the anxieties and fantasies that are inferred from cultural institutions are often transformed into the *causes* of those same institutions. Furthermore, when a culture is described by the same persons who formulated the basic personality, fact and interpretation tend to be mixed together. "Psychic entities" that were inferred from overt behavior may later be used to explain that same behavior:

> Whenever it is postulated that a given people have a given trait such as "aggressiveness," "passivity," "withdrawnness," "impulsiveness," as part of their "basic personality structure," it is easy to take the unwarranted step of regarding specific behavior as a manifestation or effect of the given trait. Conclusions of this type are buttressed not so much by evidential proof as by the piling up of illustrations which are unlikely to convince anyone who is not already sold on the underlying ideology. (Lindesmith and Strauss 1950:592)

This whole procedure is circular and scientifically unacceptable. In most cases, the causal assumption is unjustified.

The projective assumption   The emphasis of most culture and personality studies on early, indirect learning and on unconscious motives leads to a heavy reliance on projective tests as a means of validating inferences from cultural materials. (Examples include *The People of Alor, Truk: Man in Paradise*, and many national character studies.) The assumption is that projective tests developed and standardized in one society can be used elsewhere with only minor modifications in content, scoring, or interpretation.

Lindesmith and Strauss objected that the use of projective tests in non-Western societies suggests "an illusory precision," especially if the usual statistical safeguards are not employed. In any case, test results "are not self-explanatory, but must ... be interpreted like other data," and interpretation of the Rorschach is "a matter of controversy" even within Western cultures (Lindesmith and Strauss 1950:593).

Several authors reviewed the use of projective tests in anthropology during the 1950s (for example, Henry and Spiro 1953). The most pessimistic of these was Bert Kaplan, who wrote:

> I have looked for the positive values in these tests and found them very scant. I have looked at the difficulties in their use and found them to be enormous, and have concluded that as these tests are being used and interpreted at present, only a modicum of validity and value can be obtained from them. (Kaplan 1961:252)

Although projective tests have a place within modern psychological anthropology (LeVine 1982: chap. 12), as a general principle the projective assumption is invalid.

The objectivity assumption   This term refers to the implicit claim that anthropologists can take an objective view of alien peoples and, either directly or "at a distance," describe their psychological characteristics as well as their cultural patterns. Yet, as Lindesmith and Strauss suggested, "Western biases must inevitably find expression in the inferences made about the psychological characteristics of a given people" (1950:593). National character studies initiated during wartime are particularly vulnerable to criticism; in retrospect, characterizations of Germans and Japanese appear to have been biased by the historical situation, as were later Cold War descriptions of Russian character and mentality.

It is hoped that anthropologists were never quite as biased as the psychiatrist J. C. Carothers, who once wrote:

> The native African in his culture is remarkably like the lobotomized Western European and in some ways like the traditional psychopath in his inability to see individual acts as part of a whole situation, in his frenzied anxiety and in the relative lack of mental ills. (quoted in Hsu 1961:49)

But anthropologists are *not* free of prejudice and racism just by virtue of their profession. When Francis L. K. Hsu (1973) pointed out the intellectual effects of prejudice in American anthropology, his article was met by an embarrassed silence. Until psychological anthropologists can demonstrate greater independence from political and emotional prejudice, the objectivity assumption will remain highly questionable. (See Dower 1986.)

Perhaps the most telling criticism came from within the culture and personality school itself. Melford E. Spiro (a student of Hallowell's) published a long article in *Psychiatry* called "Culture and Personality: The Natural History of a False Dichotomy" (1951). In it he argued that the school had failed to clarify its two central concepts, and that most culture and personality work was necessarily circular because "the development of personality and the acquisition of culture are one and the same process" (p. 31). Instead of seeking causal relationships between personality and culture, we should try to overcome the "false dichotomy" that separates them into mutually exclusive categories.

We are quite close here to the configurationalist notion of isomorphism, but Spiro is pointing in a somewhat different direction. He insists that *social interaction* is the process uniting individual with cultural phenomena. The existence of a "cultural heritage" is a necessary prerequisite for the emergence of a new human personality, but as a result of interaction with parents and other enculturated persons, "the culture of any individual is incorporated within his personality" (p. 43). One may analytically separate culture from personality (as did Spiro in his later works), and study patterns of interaction apart from the subjective meanings that individuals internalize as a consequence of their interactions. But if we regard culture and personality as aspects of the same learning process, simplistic causal models do not make sense.

What Next?

The ways in which different approaches have characterized the relationship between culture and personality are summarized in table I- 1. For this table, I have borrowed a notation developed by Robert LeVine in his excellent (but highly technical) book *Culture, Behavior, and Personality* (1982). Culture (C) may be viewed as caused by psychological states, motives, or complexes ($P \rightarrow C$); or the two may be considered virtually identical ($P = Q$). In some approaches, personality is considered to be completely determined by cultural or social-structural conditions ($C \rightarrow P$). In others, personality is viewed as *mediating* between different parts of a culture, integrating its customs and institutions $C_1 \rightarrow P \rightarrow C_2$). Finally, in one view, personality systems *interact* with sociocultural

Table I-1   Basic conceptions of culture-personality relations (after LeVine 1982)

Position	Formula	Approaches and leading figures
Psychological reductionism	$P \rightarrow C$	Orthodox psychoanalysis (Freud, Róheim); social motivation (McClelland)
Personality *is* culture	$P = C$	Configurationalism (Benedict, Mead, Gorer)
Anti-culture and personality	$C \rightarrow P$	Cultural determinism (White); materialism (Marx); symbolic interactionism (Goffman)
Personality mediation	$C_1 \rightarrow P \rightarrow C_2$	Basic personality (Kardiner); modal personality (DuBois); cross-cultural correlations (Whiting and Child)
Interaction ("two systems")	$P \leftrightarrow C$	Psychocultural adaptation (Spiro, Edgerton); congruence (Inkeles); neo-Freudianism (Erikson, Fromm)

systems, and relative stability is attained only when psychological needs and social demands are "congruent" ($P \leftrightarrow Q$).

As we shall see, most of the approaches developed during the following decades can still be classified in one of these five categories. But after 1950, it was clear that changes had to be made if psychological anthropology was to continue as a scientific discipline. New methods for cross-cultural comparisons and for the systematic observation of interaction were already being developed. After a brief lull, increasing awareness of the importance of biological, ecological, situational, and linguistic determinants of behavior combined to give renewed vigor to the field. Today, psychological anthropology is alive and well, but the basic assumptions of the culture and personality school are no longer unquestioned. (See Shweder 1980:61–62.)

Continuing public interest in the issues of early psychological anthropology, as well as in the personalities of its founders, was demonstrated in 1983, when an Australian social anthropologist, Derek Freeman, published an attack entitled *Margaret Mead and Samoa: The Making and Unmaking of an Anthropological Myth.* Freeman claimed that Mead's book, *Coming of Age in Samoa,* was riddled with factual and logical errors. For months, newspapers and national magazines were filled with stories and commentary. Symposia were organized at various meetings, and literally hundreds of reviews and articles were published in professional journals.

When the dust finally settled, it was clear that, although Freeman made many valid points, he vastly overstated his case. Mead had indeed claimed that Samoan adolescence was relatively free of conflict and sexual frustration (see pp. 54–55, above). Freeman concluded that she had been misled by her young informants. Samoans, he wrote, experience intense frustration due to the rigid rank system and the "taboo on virginity," and this causes violent criminal outbursts and a high incidence of rape. Freeman did not publish his attack until several years after Mead's death, so we cannot be certain how she would have answered him; his critique, however, neglects Mead's overall *pattern,* picking instead on bits and pieces of her work, often taken out of context. As I wrote in my review of Freeman's book (Bock 1983:337), "The atomistic method is unfortunate, for instead of giving us a *corrected picture* of Samoan behavior and norms, Freeman tends to swing to contrary extremes. Granted that Mead's picture of happy, peaceful, and cooperative Samoans was inaccurate, does it really improve matters to call them frustrated, angry, warlike, or rivalrous?"

Samoan (or American) forms of aggression and sexuality cannot be explained by simplistic appeals to "biology." The proper question today, as in the time of Mead and Boas, is, What does a given society *do* with the variable biological and psychological materials at its disposal? For without an individual organism there can be no behavior, but without a cultural system, behavior has no meaning.

Supplement, 1999

The dangers of unfounded assumptions (of continuity, uniformity and objectivity) continue to haunt psychological anthropology, joined now by premature assumptions about genetic determinism. Fifteen years after his first salvo, Derek Freeman (1999) has produced yet another book criticizing Margaret Mead's research in Samoa for its naïve cultural determinism. Indeed, the Pacific Islands continue to be disputed territories, both politically and psychologically. Bradd Shore (1982) explored the social repercussions of a murder in his book, *Sala'ilua: A Samoan Mystery,* while Catherine Lutz (1988) and Melford Spiro (1997) have passionately debated the nature of emotion using data from their respective studies of the Micronesian atoll of Ifaluk.

Many monographs and collections have appeared in which the question of individualism versus collectivism (under various headings) has been raised. One of the most useful anthologies in *Person, Self, and*

Experience: Exploring Pacific Ethnopsychologies, edited by Geoffrey M. White and John Kirkpatrick (1985). Among the excellent articles we find Catherine Lutz arguing, in effect, that *all psychology is ethnopsychology* and that anthropologists must, therefore, become more aware of the biases inherent in their own concepts. Edward L. Schieffelin describes the place of "anger, grief and shame" in the psychology of a New Guinea people. Other articles in this collection deal with self and emotion in Samoa, Hawaii, the Solomons and the Marquesas islands. In the latter area, Kirkpatrick explores local understandings of shame, action, and identity (pp. 80–120) without, however, any reference to Linton or Kardiner's (1945) writings on these islands.

It now requires an expert to untangle the terminology and concepts regarding self, person, action, agency, and emotion that have come into the literature since 1988. Some newer material will be found in the supplement to chapter 12, Emotions and Selfhood, but even there I cannot bring these topics completely up to date. I will close here by quoting the informed judgment of John W. Bennett on the approaches we have considered in previous chapters.

> One basic difficulty of the culture-and-personality research of the 1940s was that culture on the whole was taken as a static given rather than as a variable. In Kardiner's seminar studies, for example, the "culture" of the various groups was described first, then followed by an analysis of childhood experiences—and of course concordances were found. This seemingly demonstrated the accuracy of the childhood thesis, but what it really did was simply reaffirm or recapitulate the ethnography. . . .
>
> The best of the culture-and-personality monographic studies were similar to Gordon MacGregor's *Warriors Without Weapons* (1946): a straightforward account of the way Plains Indian values underlay the outlook of young men and women, and required them to attempt to perpetuate the aboriginal existence in an environment utterly inappropriate to such behavior. This approach brought attitudes, values, everyday existence, resources, and even some aspects of childhood training, into a synthesis that made considerable sense. In my opinion, it was in these [monographs] that psychiatry and anthropology began to achieve a useful descriptive synthesis. (Bennett 1998:250–251)

I completely agree with this assessment.

Drawing by David Levine. Reprinted with permission from *The New York Review of Books*. Copyright © 1965, NYREV, Inc.

Chapter 6

Cross-Cultural
Correlations

Erik Erikson

As we have seen, the culture and personality school had reached a crisis by 1950. Its fundamental assumptions, methods, and findings were under attack from several directions. Meanwhile, at Yale University, an alternative approach had been developing. Although progress was interrupted by World War II, this new perspective was to become one of the two dominant approaches in psychological anthropology during the 1950s, and it is still influential today. The cross-cultural correlational approach was a product of interaction between psychologists and anthropologists at the Yale Institute of Human Relations, principally Clark Hull, John Dollard, G. P. Murdock, and John Whiting.

The Yale Synthesis

In retrospect, Yale University seems the only place in the country where this particular synthesis of ideas and skills could have occurred. As you may recall, in 1931 Edward Sapir had come to Yale, where he began a series of seminars to study the impact of culture on personality (1932–1933). The Institute of Human Relations was established in part to continue the research Sapir had stimulated. The leading psychologist at Yale was then Clark L. Hull, whose systematic theory of learning had enormous influence in American psychology (Hull 1943). John Dollard was instrumental in applying the behavior theories of Hull to human social learning. In *Frustration and Aggression* (Dollard et al. 1939) and *Social Learning and Imitation* (Miller and Dollard 1941), he showed how Hull's laboratory analysis of *habit* could be extended to complex human behavior.

Dollard was also a psychotherapist, and he wished to integrate Freudian insights into general learning theory. This goal was achieved in *Personality and Psychotherapy* (Dollard and Miller 1950), an elaborate translation of Freudian concepts and mechanisms into the vocabulary of Hull's learning theory. In this book, Dollard's clinical experience was combined with the careful experimental approach of Neil Miller to give scientific respectability to Freudian concepts.

Another key figure in the "Yale synthesis" was George Peter Murdock, an anthropologist with extensive background in sociology and an encyclopedic knowledge of world ethnography. Murdock carried out research on North America, the Pacific, and Africa, and probably knew more facts about more different societies than any other single person. His approach to many anthropological problems rested on worldwide comparisons of technological and social systems. At Yale, Murdock established the Human Relations Area Files (HRAF), a research device that makes available data on hundreds of societies, indexed and cross-listed under dozens of specific topics. (The files have since been duplicated on microfilm and are available in most major university libraries). Together with Clellan S. Ford, Murdock developed analytical methods for testing hypotheses about functional relationships using cross-cultural data from the HRAF. Murdock's *Social Structure* (1949) was the first major study to use these methods to investigate kinship, residence, and sexual relationships.

During the late 1930s, John W. M. Whiting was a graduate student at Yale, where he was strongly influenced by Dollard and Murdock. Whiting became convinced that anthropology lacked an adequate theory of how culture was learned and that anthropologists had failed to gather the kinds of data on which a theory of socialization could be tested. His field research (1936–1937) among the Kwoma, a tribe in eastern New Guinea, aimed at providing some of the necessary data.

In preparation for his fieldwork, Whiting underwent a brief psychoanalysis, but he did not study formal learning theory until he had completed his dissertation. After studying with Hull, Miller, and Otto H. Mowrer, he reanalyzed his Kwoma data; the resulting book, *Becoming a Kwoma* (1941), is in two parts. In the first chapters, Kwoma culture is described as it affects individuals from infancy to adulthood. In the second part, the various "techniques of teaching" Whiting observed in the Kwoma village are examined and discussed in terms of the drives, cues, and rewards identified in Hullian theory (as modified by Dollard and Miller). A final chapter, dealing with the "Inculcation of supernatural beliefs," asks how Kwoma children come to share certain "unrealistic" notions about spirits, sorcery, and taboos and why these beliefs are not "extinguished" by later experience.

The data in part 1 of Whiting's book are rich in individual examples, but the theoretical interpretations in part 2, while often interesting, have a *post hoc* quality. For example, here is one of the explanations of avoidance learning:

> During childhood a Kwoma boy learns to avoid the house tamberan while ceremonies are being held. The drive in this case is anxiety (he is warned that he would die if he did so); the response is avoiding the house tamberan; the cues are the sound of the gong rhythms, the statements of others that a ceremony is being held, the sight of his father, *uncles,* and older *brothers* [classificatory] decorating themselves; the reward is escape from anxiety. (Whiting 1941:176)

Whiting's explanations of the avoidance behavior are plausible, but they were added long after the original observations and no data is offered on individual Kwoma to support these hypotheses.

Whiting published his book on the Kwoma in the hope "that this pioneering attempt will suggest methods of gaining a better understanding of the process of socialization" (p. xix). When he returned to Yale following World War II, he tried to apply Murdock's cross-cultural methods to the study of socialization. This approach seemed to offer a solution to the crisis in culture and personality studies. If cross-cultural data could be used to test hypotheses about the relationship between child training and adult personality, it might be possible to validate the continuity assumption (see Interlude) and to decide between equally plausible theories of causation. Working with the psychologist Irvin L. Child, Whiting set out to formulate hypotheses in learning-theory terms that would be testable using data from the HRAF. In 1953, Whiting and Child's book *Child Training and Personality* appeared, setting forth a new paradigm for research. Let us examine this landmark work in some detail.

Early in the book, Whiting and Child acknowledge the crisis in culture and personality studies. They state that configurational and national character studies are often interesting attempts at "coherent interpretations" of single societies, but that such studies are inherently unable to validate their hypotheses (assumptions). For instance, although Mead's study of Samoa presents evidence that emotional disturbances are not a necessary accompaniment to adolescence, her eclectic methods are not suited to testing more specific ideas. Kardiner believed that his BPS approach constituted a test of Freudian hypotheses, but Whiting and Child suggest that "publications like his seem rather to *use* hypotheses, of whose validity the author has little doubt, as conceptual devices in the interpretation of specific case materials" (Whiting and Child 1953:7; emphasis added).

The authors then state their own ideas of what constitutes "an adequate test of a scientific hypothesis" (p. 8). The hypothesis must be in the form of a statement relating two events, one an "antecedent," the other a "consequent." These events must be isolated from other conditions, and observations must be made to determine if, in a suitable sample of independent cases, the consequent consistently follows (or accompanies) the antecedent. Evidence for the connection should be *objective* in the sense that other investigators following the same procedures will arrive at the same results. (See Jahoda 1982:20.)

The ideal way of testing scientific hypotheses is the *experimental method*. It allows the investigator to control the "other conditions," and repeatedly to verify the consequents of a given set of antecedents. Ethnologists are seldom able to use a truly experimental approach, so they compromise by using other, less well-controlled methods. Among these is the *correlational method,* used in anthropology since the time of E. B. Tylor (1889), and developed by Murdock, but not previously applied to culture and personality. According to Whiting and Child,

> In the correlational testing method the supposed antecedent condition is looked for as it occurs or fails to occur in the natural course of events in a number of cases. Instances are collected of its presence and its absence, or of its presence in various degrees. The supposed consequent condition is also looked for in each of these cases and determined to be present or absent, or present in a given degree. It is then possible to determine whether there is a consistent relation between the two, and thus whether the hypothesis is confirmed or negated. Statistical techniques may be applied [and the] evidence of connection may be based entirely on objective procedures which are repeatable. (p. 10)

Correlations and Customs

Put another way, the correlational method requires a kind of "trait list" (see chapter 3) showing which of the events are present (+) or absent (–) in a suitable sample of societies (table 6-1). A trait list such as that in table 6-1 can easily be transformed into a figure called a *two-by-two correlation display,* showing the association between customs A and B (figure 6-1). When we enter each society into the appropriate cell of the figure, as in figure 6-2, we find that customs A and B "go together" in three societies, and that in the remaining cases A is found twice without B, and B occurs once without A. Both customs are absent in four cases. This sample is too small to have any significance, but a slight positive association is exhibited between the two traits; A and B "go together" in enough cases that one might wish to investigate their association in a larger sample. Let us imagine that we have a sample of one hundred societies and have gathered valid information on the presence or absence of traits A and B in each. A and B could be material items (pottery containers or iron tools), social institutions (patrilineal descent groups, divine kings), or quite specific customs or beliefs (puberty rites for girls, belief in ancestral ghosts, and the like). The possible kinds of two-by-two tables, whatever the trait selected, are shown in figures 6-3 through 6-6.

Table 6-1 Trait list for two customs in ten societies

Customs	1	2	3	4	5	6	7	8	9	10
					Societies					
A	+	+	−	+	−	−	+	−	+	−
B	+	−	−	+	+	−	−	−	+	−

What do each of these tables indicate about the relation between A and B? Figure 6-3 is an ideal demonstration of a purely *chance association;* that is, whether trait A is present or absent seems to have no effect on the presence or absence of trait B, and vice versa. The correlation is *zero,* and even slight departures from this equal distribution of cases among the four cells would make no difference. Since each combination of traits is equally likely, the *null hypothesis* (that there is merely a chance association between A and B) is strongly supported. (Any textbook in elementary statistics will explain these ideas more fully.)

Figure 6-4 is an ideal example of a very strong association between A and B: whenever one is present, so is the other, and whenever one is absent, so is the other. This is called a *perfect positive correlation* (+ 1.00), and is usually found only in cases where A and B are actually aspects of the same trait complex (for example, harpoon heads and shafts) or where they are both effects of some third factor. Even if a few

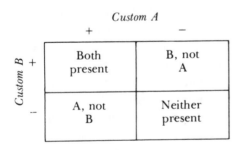

Figure 6-1 The format of a "two-by-two" correlation display.

Figure 6-2 A "two-by-two" equivalent of table 6-1.

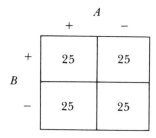

Figure 6-3 Zero correlation (chance association).

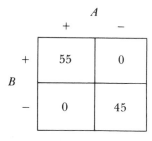

Figure 6-4 Perfect positive correlation.

societies were recorded in the A, not B and not A, B cells, the large number of cases in the "both" and "neither" cells would produce a statistically significant positive correlation. This kind of result both rejects the null hypothesis ("just chance") and lends support to hypotheses that predict the association.

Figure 6-5, with most of the cases in the A, not B and not A, B cells, shows a *strong negative correlation* (about –0.85). A and B are almost mutually exclusive of one another. With only eight exceptions, whenever A is present, B is absent, and vice versa. Such negative correlations can be as important as the positive ones; they enable us to reject the null hypothesis, and they lend support to hypotheses that predict this kind of negative relationship.

Figure 6-6 shows a more typical result of a correlational study. The majority of the cases (66 out of 100) are in the "both" or "neither" cells, indicating a positive correlation; however, more than a third fall into the other cells. Here we need a criterion to tell us whether, for a sample of this size (N = 100), there is a significant departure from the null hypothesis of no association. The methods used to evaluate such cases need not concern us here. It is important to remember that a correlation, no matter how significant, shows only the association between traits, and does not in itself prove anything about a *causal relationship*. Even a perfect positive correlation, such as that shown in Figure 6-4, does not indicate whether A causes B, B causes A, or some third factor causes both. A good theory would provide hypotheses that reliably distinguish antecedent

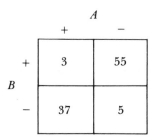

Figure 6-5 Strong negative correlation.

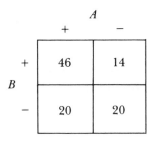

Figure 6-6 Positive correlation.

from consequent events and predict both positive and negative associations.

In *Child Training and Personality,* the authors' hypotheses derive from Freudian theory, restated in behavioral terms. The "traits" that Whiting and Child wish to correlate are customs of two kinds: child-training practices (C_1) and beliefs concerning the causes of illness (C_2). In this approach, child and adult personalities are hypothetical constructs that mediate between two parts of a culture, represent in the formula:

$$C_1 \longrightarrow \underset{\text{personality}}{\text{Child}} \longrightarrow \underset{\text{personality}}{\text{Adult}} \longrightarrow C_2$$

It should be obvious that this is a variant of Kardiner's basic personality approach (chapter 4), in which child-training practices and other primary institutions are related to belief systems and other secondary institutions via basic personality dynamics. Like Kardiner, Whiting and Child present no data on individual children or adults; rather, they examine two kinds of cultural data as reported in ethnographies. From the association between customs in a sample of societies, they infer support for their hypotheses regarding the mediating personality type. As with BPS, this approach assumes that similar childhood experiences will produce similar unconscious fixations and conflicts in a population (the continuity assumption; see Interlude). These neurotic tendencies should be clearly expressed in the society's beliefs about causes of illness, for, in the absence of scientific medicine, folk beliefs are assumed to be projections of shared anxieties.

Whiting and Child divide child-training customs into five universal *systems of behavior:* "oral, anal, sexual, dependence, and aggression—on the assumption that these systems would occur and be subject to socialization in all societies" (p. 54). Children are assumed to derive *initial satisfaction* and/or to develop *socialization anxiety* in each of these behavior systems depending on how (and for how long) their society indulges and/or restricts particular types of behavior. For example, "high oral indulgence" occurs when infants are constantly near their mothers and are nursed whenever hungry or unhappy. Early and/or severe weaning customs are assumed to produce a high degree of "oral socialization anxiety" (especially after a period of initial indulgence). High oral anxiety is hypothesized to produce adult beliefs that illness results from oral behavior: "It must have been something you ate, or said, or someone else said." (The belief that a magical spell causes illness is also considered an "oral explanation.")

Customs that might create oral socialization anxiety in childhood are expected to correlate with oral explanations of illness in the adult culture. A similar explanation has also been offered for the presence of food taboos in a society (Ayres 1967). Traumatic toilet training (anal), modesty discipline (sexual), or severe socialization with regard to dependency or aggression are each assumed to produce characteristic forms of anxiety that should be projected in distinctive explanations of illness. Extreme concern with cleanliness, masturbation, disobedience, or anger as causes of disease should indicate anal, sexual, dependence, or aggression anxiety, respectively.

Whiting and Child base their contention that socialization practices are connected with specific types of anxiety on a combination of Freudian and behavioral theory. Positive correlations between a given type of anxiety-producing socialization custom and the same type of explanation for illness would support the hypotheses. In their sample of thirty-nine societies, one association is positive and highly significant: Oral socialization anxiety (inferred from age and severity of weaning) is strongly correlated with oral explanations of illness (see figure 6-7).

Oral explanations
Present Absent

	Present	Absent
High	17	3
Low	6	13

Oral anxiety

Figure 6-7 Correlation between oral explanations of illness and oral socialization anxiety. N = 39. (After Whiting and Child 1953:156.)

Sexual explanations
Present Absent

	Present	Absent
High	7	7
Low	7	7

Sexual anxiety

Figure 6-8 Zero correlation between sexual explanations of illness and socialization anxiety. N = 28. (After Whiting and Child 1953:159.)

This is the most impressive correlation in the whole book. Other associations are much weaker, ranging down to a *zero correlation,* shown in Figure 6-8, between sexual socialization anxiety and sexual explanations of illness (beliefs that disease is due to improper sexual behavior or contact with "sexual excretions," including menstrual blood).

A crucial question still must be asked: What do the numbers in these tables actually mean? Who *decided* whether the Arapesh or the Chagga had customs that would produce anal socialization anxiety, or if the Siriono had "sexual explanations" of illness? Following procedures developed in social and clinical psychology, Whiting and Child used *independent judges* to evaluate the ethnographic evidence. They chose this method to insure that judges would not know what hypotheses were being tested, and also because the volume of materials to be considered (from the HRAF and other sources) was enormous. Five persons (professionals and graduate students) made literally thousands of judgments, rating each society on dozens of customs, ranking relative amounts of indulgence or severity of restrictions, and evaluating their own confidence in the judgments. Agreement among the five judges was reasonably good, for Whiting and Child provided explicit criteria and eliminated cases for which good data were unavailable or for which the judges lacked confidence in their ratings. Thus, in figure 6-7, the number 17 in the "both present" cell indicates the number of societies for which the judges agreed that oral explanations of illness *and* customs likely to produce oral anxiety were both present. In the book, exact ratings are usually presented for each society, but no consideration is given to spatial, temporal, or intracultural variability (see pp. 94–95, above).

Child Training and Personality contains much more material than I have indicated. The authors provide sophisticated discussions of methodology, including statistical techniques, as well as excellent chapters on positive and negative fixation, the origins of guilt (beliefs about the patient's responsibility for his or her own illness), and origins of the fear of others (various "unrealistic" beliefs in ghosts and spirits). (For his earliest discussion of the latter issue, see Whiting 1941:chapter 8; also Spiro and D'Andrade 1958 for a cross-cultural study of the relationship between child-training customs and adult beliefs in friendly versus hostile spirits.)

Galton's Problem

One annoying problem (acknowledged by the authors) is that some correlations might be due to historical connections among societies in the sample rather than to the hypothesized relationship between child training and adult culture. As Francis Galton recognized over one hundred years ago, correlations lose their significance if the cases are not *independent* of one another. For example, two of the twenty-three societies rated as having oral explanations of illness are the Navajo and the Chiricahua Apache. Since these two societies are known to be closely related historically (speaking similar languages and having quite similar cultures), should they be counted as two cases or as one? Lengthy controversy has ensued over "Galton's problem," and several techniques are now used to select samples that contain a minimum of historically related cases (see, for example, Naroll and Cohen 1970, chap. 47). An example may sensitize the student to the dimensions of this problem.

In 1962, R. W. Shirley and A. K. Romney published a brief cross-cultural study, "Love Magic and Socialization Anxiety." They followed the correlational method, using Whiting and Child's 1953 ratings of sexual socialization anxiety. Shirley and Romney's hypothesis is as follows: if the child-training practices of a society produce individuals with a high level of sexual anxiety, adults might then be expected to use love magic as a means of reducing their sexual anxiety. This is a plausible idea, for it has long been recognized that one function of magic is to reduce anxiety and give people confidence in risky undertakings (Malinowski 1955).

Shirley and Romney never define what they mean by "love magic," but presumably the term covers the use of verbal spells and magical substances to gain the affection of persons of the opposite sex. The authors found a significant, positive correlation between high ratings on sexual socialization, anxiety, and the presence of such customs. Unfortunately, a strong *geographic bias* exists in their sample, which casts doubt upon their conclusions. This bias can be seen in figure 6-9, where presence or absence of love magic (as the authors judged it) is shown to be correlated with major culture areas.

	Love magic Present	Absent
Americas, Africa, or Melanesia	22	3
Other geographic areas	4	10

Figure 6-9 Correlation between "love magic" and geographic areas. N = 39. (Data from Shirley and Romney 1962.)

In the sample of 39 societies, 26 were judged to have love magic while 13 were not. Of the 26 with love magic, 22 are located in North or South America, Africa, or Melanesia (an area of the Pacific including New Guinea and nearby islands); of the 13 societies without love magic, only 3 are located in these geographic areas (Bock 1967:213). What is the significance of this distribution? While it is still plausible that people with high sexual anxiety use love magic to reduce that anxiety, the geographic bias in this sample cannot be ignored. The correlation between love magic and geographic area is actually *higher* than that between love magic and particular child-training practices! (See Driver 1966.)

Another question remains: Why do people in different societies raise their children so differently? This question troubled many people using the cross-cultural approach. After his move to Harvard, where he established the Laboratory of Human Development in the mid-1950s, Whiting began to extend his investigations into the determinants of child-training patterns. He sought an explanation for these "primary institutions" in the environmental adaptations of different societies (cf. Kardiner 1945). This work eventually led to a much more comprehensive theory, in which the "test case" was the widespread custom of male initiation rites.

Male Initiation Rites

Many (but not all) primitive societies carry out puberty rituals for young boys. Whiting and his coworkers wanted to understand why some societies have these customs while others do not, and why the rites range from brief, simple ceremonies to long, elaborate rituals involving isolation, taboos, painful hazing, and genital operations such as circumcision. Most native explanations of the rituals refer to the need to "make boys into men," and many involve symbolism of death and rebirth. What are the psychological motives for carrying out such "bizarre" and bloody rites?

Applying the logic that he and Child had developed in *Child Training and Personality,* Whiting reasoned that certain customs of childhood might produce in young boys such a strong identification with their mothers that traumatic rituals would be psychologically necessary to "make men of them." If the same childhood customs generate hostility between father and son, the fathers might act out their sadistic revenge through circumcision—a symbolic castration in good Oedipal fashion! Antecedent customs that might produce these consequences were

- Exclusive mother-child sleeping arrangements, in which the mother and nursing infant share the same bed for an extended period of time.
- Lengthy postpartum sex taboos, which forbid the father of a young child to have intercourse with the mother for a period of one year or longer.

These two customs were associated in many societies; Whiting hypothesized that they would create both a strong maternal identification in the boy and the likelihood of hostility between father and son. Correlational analysis indicated that, especially in societies where both customs were present and of long duration, the performance of elaborate and painful initiation rites at puberty was highly likely (Whiting, Kluckhohn, and Anthony 1958). Thus, the authors explained the rites "psychogenically"—arguing that these rituals helped to resolve an Oedipus complex that had been made especially severe by specific child-training practices. (Compare Stephens 1962; Cohen 1964.)

Why do some societies have such sleeping arrangements and post-partum taboos to begin with? Here, Whiting invoked the notion of environmental adaptation. He was able to show that these customs were most prevalent in tropical areas where infants' diets would be deficient in essential proteins unless they were allowed to nurse for several years (Whiting 1964). The causal chain was thus extended back to environmental conditions. The full argument took the following form: in environments where long nursing is necessary to prevent protein deficiency, children will tend to sleep with their mothers and a long postpartum sex taboo will develop to guard against premature pregnancy. In such societies, boys develop strong emotional relations (identification) with their mothers, which could lead to an incestuous attachment to the mother and a hostile rivalry with the father unless steps are taken to prevent these results. Puberty rites involving painful hazing, isolation from women, trials of manliness, and genital operations appear to be "effective means" for preventing conflict and incest.

This argument did not go unchallenged. Frank W. Young (1965) responded that Whiting had overlooked the ways in which puberty rites function to dramatize male solidarity. J.-F. Saucier demonstrated that long postpartum taboos correlated with a variety of technological traits and social customs, suggesting that this onerous taboo can be maintained only in specific types of communities (Saucier 1972:263). (For a lively if somewhat rambling discussion of other views, see Brain 1977.)

It is at least plausible that certain childhood experiences could produce excessive identification of boys with their mothers such that many adolescents would have difficulty in fully accepting the adult male role. Harsh initiation rites could be one way that the social group deals with cross-sex identification. However, there is little independent evidence that boys in societies with these rituals actually do identify with the female role (see Herdt 1981). Recent research has tended to focus on the impact of *father absence* on child development. It appears that boys who grow up in female-headed households, even in American society, frequently display "hypermasculine" protest behavior including violent resistance to adult authority later in life. (See Draper and Harpending 1982.)

Besides initiation rites, two unusual customs have been attributed to strong unconscious identification with the mother. Male *transvestism* (discussed in chapter 2) has been taken to indicate a strong cross-sex identification, especially in those cases where a young man adopts both the clothing and behavior of the opposite sex. In our own society, cross-dressing is often attributed to maternal over-protectiveness. Many American Indian societies actually institutionalized such a role. The Crow *berdache* and the Cheyenne "half man/half woman" were individuals who adopted female dress. Often they excelled at women's work, and some were taken as second wives by normal males.

The term *couvade* designates a custom found in various parts of the world in which a man shares with his wife some of the actions and taboos surrounding pregnancy. In a few cases he actually imitates childbirth, but more often he observes restrictions on activity and diet. Robert Munroe (1980) believes that couvade behavior indicates an even stronger unconscious maternal identification than does transvestism. In his sample of forty societies, either transvestism or the couvade were found in twenty-four of the cases, but they never occurred together.

The usual problems of sampling and definition affect this study. For example, should American husbands who attend LaMaze classes with their wives be counted as displaying couvade behavior? And should brief, ritual transvestism (as among the Iatmul or the Tewa) count in the same way as a lifelong role? Cases outside of Munroe's sample where both customs are present are not difficult to find, and Menget (1982) has reported a cluster of South American Indian societies in which couvadelike restrictions are imposed not only on the new father but on other family members and even on the mother's various lovers! In short, identification with the mother (or the female role) has been used to explain too many different kinds of customs or behaviors.

More important than the solution to any of these problems, I feel, is the image of person and culture implied by the correlational approach. Ruth Benedict's conception of cultures as integrated wholes analogous to individual personalities was surely overstated, resulting in highly simplified characterizations. On the other hand, the opposite danger of cultural atomism accompanies the correlational approach. The old trait list has returned, with cultures represented by a series of pluses and minuses, or ratings on a ten-point scale. The names of the societies in correlational studies are frequently omitted from tables, and their geographic locations ignored. Hypotheses and uncertain ratings from one study tend to turn up as established facts in later studies, and correlations are often erroneously interpreted as proof of causation. And, as in basic personality structure studies, no data are presented on individuals.

I am not arguing against determinism, but I do oppose simplistic notions of causation. Correlations are always open to alternative explanations. Ingenious ways may be found to explain cases that do not fit the original hypothesis, and a strong temptation also exists to adjust one's hypothesis after the data are in to give an impression of accuracy (Bock 1967:217). Moreover, reducing a society to a single set of rating leads to neglect of intracultural variability, and this is one form of the uniformity assumption. When the investigators themselves perform the ratings, the objectivity of the correlational method is called into question.

Despite these caveats, the correlational method can be a powerful tool for generating hypotheses. In the hands of knowledgeable and responsible investigators such as Whiting or John M. Roberts, it can lead to fascinating findings. As the HRAF was expanded to cover more than three hundred societies, larger and better samples could be drawn (see Murdock 1957). More suitable statistical techniques were developed and replications of a few important studies were attempted. Large samples do not solve all problems, however, for the quality of ethnographic data on many issues is highly variable. One solution to this dilemma would be to study only a few societies, but intensively and at first hand (see chapter 9 on the Six Cultures project). Alternatively, one might work with existing data from a few particularly well-documented cases. An example of this approach is Robin Fox's cross-cultural study of sibling incest.

Causes of Incest Taboos

Incest taboos have long interested anthropologists and psychologists. Among the theories suggested to account for the widespread prohibition on intercourse between brother and sister are those of Edward Westermarck and Sigmund Freud. Westermarck, a sociologist and anthropologist, believed that the experience of being raised together produced *natural aversion* to sexual contact between brother and sister. He thought that the taboos were an expression of this aversion. Thus his theory can be summed up in the formula:

Childhood nearness → Natural Aversion → Taboos

Freud, as you may recall, traces all taboos to unconscious emotional ambivalence (chapter 2). Pointing out that one does not need taboos (or laws) against actions that people do not want to perform, he insists that family members are the earliest objects of erotic desire. The reason that incest is regarded with such "horror" and punished so severely is that most members of a society have had to *repress* these forbidden wishes. Thus, his theory can be summarized as

Strong unconscious desire → Severe taboos

How can we decide between these two theories? Freud's point about not needing taboos against undesired behavior is certainly valid. Yet many people say, without any trace of conflict, that they are simply "uninterested" in their sisters, or brothers, as erotic objects. Furthermore, while some societies show extreme punitive reactions to the act (or even the suggestion) of sibling incest, other societies show little concern with this offense: people deny in a matter-of-fact way that it occurs very often, and offenders may be punished only with mild ridicule. Indeed, in several societies (ancient Egypt, Hawaii), brother-sister *marriage* was an approved form, at least for the upper class.

In an exemplary small-sample cross-cultural study, Robin Fox (1962) suggested that the theories of Westermarck and Freud are not really incompatible. Together they provide a framework for understanding cultural variation in the *intensity* of incest taboos. Different types of childhood experience could lead to quite different psychological reactions. The "Westermarck effect" is found in societies where siblings are raised in close physical contact: The "natural aversion" is *learned* as a result of the necessary frustration produced by unconsummated sexual experience between young siblings. Placing the two theories together, we are led to ask what kind of childhood experience might give rise to the strong incestuous desires predicted by Freud?

Westermarck: Nearness → Learned aversion → (Mild) Taboos

Freud:??? → Strong desire → Severe taboos

If childhood *nearness* produces a learned aversion to incest, Fox reasons, perhaps childhood *separation* gives rise to strong desires. Cultures that keep brother and sister apart do not permit the natural aversion to develop and thus defeat their own purposes. Especially when alternative erotic objects are absent, Fox reasoned, early separation of siblings could lead to an emotional ambivalence that produces both a strong, unconscious desire for incest and severe, punitive taboos.

The seven societies that Fox selected for comparison include four cases of a nearly pure "Westermarck effect," two examples of the Freudian dynamic, and one intermediate case. The most interesting is the Israeli kibbutz described by Spiro (1958). Here children are raised in coeducational communal nurseries with much physical contact and no prohibitions on sex play. Yet at puberty, members of these peer groups (which include siblings) show no sexual interest in one another. They impose a kind of incest taboo *upon themselves* and seek mates outside the community. A typical comment is that "you can't love someone you sat on the potty with." Arthur Wolf (1970) reported similar findings from his research on extended families in Taiwan.

At the other extreme is a traditional Apache society, where brothers and sisters, although raised together in isolated households, were forbidden to have physical or even verbal contact from about the age of six. Here we find an extreme "horror of incest" with strong taboos and severe punishment: offenders were considered to be witches and were sometimes burned alive. This case seems to combine a maximum of temptation with a minimum of alternatives, leading to a strong "Freudian effect." A similar situation is found in the Trobriand Islands, where, Malinowski reported, the sister is "the centre of all that is forbidden." The African Tallensi and Pondo provide more examples of the Westermarck effect, as do the Mountain Arapesh of New Guinea. An intermediate example occurs on the island of Tikopia, where intimacy between adult siblings leads to temptation (shown in dreams) and occasional acting out. (Offenders, if caught, are expected to commit suicide.)

The advantage of a small-sample approach is that each case can be considered in some detail and the context of various customs specified. Seven cases are too few to be evaluated by statistical tests, but I find Fox's article more convincing than many studies using a hundred or more cases. He concludes that the *"intensity of heterosexual attraction between co-socialized children after puberty is inversely proportionate to the intensity of heterosexual activity between them before puberty"* (Fox 1962:147). There is nothing to stop us from testing this hypothesis on a large sample or from seeking individual clinical data that might confirm or refute it.

Fox adds some intriguing speculations to his findings. For example, if the concept of "learned aversion" is accurate, it may explain why father-daughter incest is empirically much more frequent than mother-son incest. In most societies, fathers have much less physical contact with young children than do mothers. Thus, learned aversion is more likely to develop between mother and son than father and daughter. Since the amount of interaction between brother and sister is highly variable, we would expect to find reactions to sibling incest ranging from "unthinkable" to "strong desire" (Fox 1962:148).

Finally, an interesting series of correlational studies relate aspects of early childhood experience and nutrition to physiological and motor development. Animal experiments have shown that rats who are exposed to stress early in life (rough handling or electric shocks) grow to be longer and heavier than unstressed rats. Few people would advocate deliberately shocking human babies to see if they grow taller, but the cross-cultural method makes it possible to test such a hypothesis, and—surprisingly—the results are positive:

In societies in which infants experience immediate postnatal separation from the mother or are tattooed, scarified, or bathed daily in
scalding water, adult height is greater. The average height of adult
males in the infant-stressed societies exceeds that in societies without these customs by more than two inches. The association between
stress and height was statistically independent of other factors that
might be thought to influence stature, including race, climate, mode
of subsistence, and estimated diet. (Munroe and Munroe 1975:34)

Summary

Despite all its faults, the cross-cultural method will probably continue to
be used in psychological anthropology because it enables us to test
hypotheses that contain both cultural and psychological variables.
Investigators should insist, however, that their samples (large or small)
contain only cases for which high-quality, comparable data are available.
Whether the goal of such studies is to understand causal relationships
or simply to identify areas for further research, it is important to avoid
biased samples and unanalyzed assumptions. (See Hendrix 1985 for a
reanalysis of data from the influential study of Barry et al. 1959.) Most
cross-cultural research uses data from existing ethnographic monographs, but, as we shall see in chapter 9, it is also possible to gather
quantitative data by first-hand investigations of a number of selected
societies. The next chapter, though, deals with some important developments in psychoanalytic anthropology and asks whether these ideas can
help in overcoming the crisis in culture and personality research.

Supplement, 1999

Cross-cultural comparative studies continue to hold a place in psychological anthropology, although the use of the Human Relations Area
Files and correlational methods have become somewhat less important.
The Files are still useful for testing hypotheses, whether the ideas come
from studies of single societies or from the imagination of the researcher,
but most comparative studies today rely on direct observations of behavior and, in some cases, good longitudinal data.

    In an excellent review, Alice Schlegel (1994) distinguishes among
several kinds of behavioral methods. First, she differentiates *closed*
observations, in which the categories are established before the study,
from *open* observations, in which they are developed afterwards. (This
is similar to the difference between multiple choice tests and open-ended

questions.) She then contrasts *intracultural* studies (where comparisons are made between individual or family behaviors in a single society) with *cross-cultural* ones (in which data from several societies are used), pointing out that these two methods can be combined, as in the East African project of U.C.L.A. (Edgerton 1971) and the Six Cultures project (Whiting and Whiting 1963), both discussed in chapter 9.

Schlegel's discussion of the correlational approach (using the HRAF) is also very clear, covering the need to first *operationalize the problem* to be investigated and subsequent steps such as *sampling* from the Files, *coding* the texts, *testing* the findings with appropriate statistical techniques, and *interpreting* the results. Her sections on the correlational studies of the incest taboo, on games in culture, and on other aspects of child socialization (pp. 21–36) are also quite useful, often suggesting further directions for study.

For example, she refers to an article by psychiatrist Mark T. Erickson on the incest taboo in which he suggests that incest avoidance is produced by a process of "familial bonding" that takes place in the first three years of life. In a more recent paper, Erickson (in press) goes further than Westermarck in proposing a Darwinian mechanism underlying this process. He cites data from several studies of *kibbutz* children and from Arthur Wolf's intracultural work in Taiwan as well as recent psychiatric research (see Wolf 1993).

Wolf found that, in cases where the bride in an arranged child marriage moves into her husband's household before she is one year old, the wedding (which takes place in their teens) may never be consummated; if it is, fertility is significantly lowered due to *a learned aversion to sexual contact*. Furthermore, these marriages have high rates of infidelity and divorce. Erickson concludes that "a biologically distinct form of affiliation, characterized by attachment behaviors, altruistic behaviors, and sexual avoidance, is . . . entirely plausible" (in press: 15). He believes that this intrafamilial bonding prevents incest in most cases. As an evolved mechanism to avoid harmful inbreeding, this proposed adaptation is still compatible with cultural explanations for differences in the form of incest taboos in different societies.

An article by Susan Seymour demonstrates the ways in which household structure (e.g., nuclear or extended) and social status may affect the expression of positive emotions between mothers and children. Working in a community in India, Seymour tested ideas about the lack of such expressions using intracultural analysis. She found that "Indian caretakers are less openly warm and affectionate with their children than caretakers in other parts of the world [but] there is extensive intracultural variability" depending on household form and caste status (Seymour 1983:276). In particular, she found more expression of affect in multifamily and extended households than in single-family ones; household status had the strongest effect on emotional expression, with low status families exhibiting significantly more affection than others. These findings should caution us against assuming uniformity of behavior, even within a single village.

As noted above, longitudinal studies are essential to establishing or contesting continuities between child training and later behavior or personality. This is especially true since Judith Harris's book, *The Nurture Assumption* (1998) has gained such popular attention, for she argues that—compared to genetic endowment and the influence of peers—parental actions have little effect in shaping a child's personality. While not directed against her ideas, a series of studies by the Munroes are certainly relevant to such questions.

Starting in 1971, observations were published on a dozen babies (six months to one year of age) in a Bantu-speaking farming community in western Kenya. Follow-up studies were performed when the infants were five and twelve years old. Observations had been made in the first study on the behavior of babies and their caretakers in natural settings, with calculations made of the number of caretakers, the time the baby was held by its own mother, the time it took for caretakers to respond to crying, and the degree to which the infant was protected. A series of papers dealt with how these features related to cognitive or spatial abilities and the expression of affect later in the child's life.

The most recent article (Munroe, Munroe, Westling and Rosenberg 1997) summarizes this work and describes the measures used with the 12-year-olds, concluding that "the child's early ties with the mother were most influential in his or her socioemotional development" though there was little relationship to cognitive variables (p. 369). The authors caution that

> The responses of 12-year-olds cannot be extrapolated to their behavior as adults, but the research results thus far are consonant with the notion that infant attachment styles may be templates for adult relationships. . . . Perhaps in the end . . . continuing to study this sample of Logoli children—who by now would have reached early adulthood—will provide the best evidence for or against the validity of the findings. (Munroe et al. 1997:369)

Readers can certainly appreciate the difficulty and expense involved in carrying out this kind of longitudinal study at a great distance, but the importance of such work cannot be overestimated.

Other topics mentioned in chapter 6 have received further treatment by anthropologists. The early, frequently cited correlational study by Barry, Bacon, and Child (1959) on the relationship of subsistence type to child training for obedience or for independence has been criticized on statistical grounds (Hendrix 1985), and now seems quite oversimplified. Following Herdt's (1981) exposure of homosexual elements in a New Guinea ritual, studies of initiations have taken quite a different tack from the correlational work discussed above (e.g., Ottenberg 1994). Schlegel does a good job of placing these changes in context:

> In recent years, psychological anthropology has witnessed a swing away from "scientific" studies, with their goal of explanation and their methods that require measurement and rigorous testing, toward "humanistic" studies, whose goal is the discover[y] of meaning and whose methods involve the empathetic interpretation of emotions and self-image. But if the behaviorally oriented anthropologists have sometimes forgotten that behavior is the response to reality as the mind has constructed it, the interpretive anthropologists sometimes forget that regularities exist across cultures and cannot be explained by the meaning any particular culture gives to the way its members act. This is an old dialogue in anthropology. . . . It is likely to continue. (Schlegel 1994:36–37)

Chapter 7

The Return of the Repressed

Bruno Bettelheim

I n Freudian parlance, "the return of the repressed" refers to the tendency for repressed psychic materials to crop up later in the life of an individual (or a society). Oedipal strivings forced into unconsciousness during the latency period may reappear later, influencing the individual to choose a mate who in some respects resembles the forbidden parent. Repressed hostile impulses toward a parent or sibling frequently return to trouble the individual in the form of guilt feelings, "delayed obedience," or difficulties with authority. In a parallel manner, it has been argued that problems that a society refuses to face consciously will inevitably return to trouble it, for example, the "specter haunting Europe" (communism) or the "American dilemma" (racism).

As the title for this chapter, the phrase refers to the return of certain problems that were "repressed" by the culture and personality school. Various writers modified the orthodox Freudian framework by selecting and redefining concepts. Frequently, they substituted vague "cultural factors" for the intrapsychic conflicts of psychoanalysis, ignoring ambivalence and equating "internalization" with socialization (Wrong 1961). Many of these neo-Freudians (and here I include such people as Fromm, Dollard, and Whiting) made important contributions to psychological anthropology; however, to the extent that they watered down Freud's tough-minded positions on human sexuality, aggression, and religion, the problems were destined to reappear. This contributed to the crisis in culture and personality studies discussed in the Interlude.

Instinct and Culture

The orthodox Freudian view, in which culture is analogous to a neurosis, had been kept alive by, among others, the Hungarian anthropologist and psychoanalyst Géza Róheim. In his brief monograph *The Origin and Function of Culture,* Róheim undertook to analyze *all culture* as a manifestation of the sexual instincts. Róheim argued for the "fundamental identity of neurosis and civilization," recalling Freud's comparisons of philosophy to paranoia, art to hysteria, and religious ritual to compulsion neuroses. From this point of view, he writes, "we only grow up in order to remain children," that is, to achieve in the real world the fantasies of childhood, though usually in substitute forms (Róheim 1943:31).

Socialization is necessary because of the human being's long infancy, and this process involves an adaptation to reality. However,

Róheim maintains, the dominant adult ideas (configurations) of a society are themselves the products of the infancy situation: not just the "secondary institutions," but such practical activities as trade, agriculture, and pastoralism can be traced to their unconscious roots (1943:40–72). A person's choice of occupation always has a dynamic motive, and the main "professions" of modern society can be viewed as sublimations of infantile impulses. Thus, "a scientist is a voyeur prying into the secrets of Mother Nature, a painter continues to play with his feces—a writer of fiction never renounces his day-dreams, and so forth" (p. 72).

In the final chapter of *The Origin and Function of Culture,* Róheim expands on the concept of sublimation, which, he says, is fundamental to the formation of culture. If sublimation is the "normal" way of dealing with anxiety, it is nevertheless a compromise with and substitute for direct wish-fulfillment. Sublimation is always a compromise that gives the individual some security against the loss of a loved person, since "to be alone is the great danger" (p. 85). Ultimately, says Róheim,

> civilization originates in delayed infancy and its function is security. It is a huge network of more or less successful attempts to protect mankind against the danger of object loss, the colossal efforts made by a baby who is afraid of being left alone in the dark. (p. 100)

Róheim conducted fieldwork in Australia, Melanesia, Africa, and North America, and analyzed the dynamics of particular cultures in such works as *The Riddle of the Sphinx,* first published in 1934. He anticipated Kardiner by suggesting that, in many cases, "the character of a people and their social organization can be derived from their infantile trauma or explained as a defense reaction to an infantile experience" (Róheim 1974:149–150). Róheim was also one of the first anthropologists to make systematic use of data on nonhuman primate behavior in understanding human customs. Outrageous as many of his interpretations first appear, his work contains a number of brilliant insights that are only now being appreciated by anthropologists. He had a knack for grasping the symbolic significance of words and actions. Freud himself acknowledged that Róheim had "extended" and corrected some of the ideas in *Totem and Taboo,* demonstrating the interplay between the biologically universal and the culturally specific elements of human development.

Róheim laid the foundation for "an anthropology that sees cultural institutions as a series of defenses against unconscious drives" (1974:xvii). It would be a mistake to stress the negative aspect of this vision, for he also understood the positive satisfactions provided by culture, and he explored the relationship between the stages of sexual development and cultural evolution. Róheim died in 1953, leaving the task of elaborating these ideas to others, in particular Bruno Bettelheim and Erik Erikson. (For further discussion of Róheim's contribution, see Calogeras 1971; Endleman 1981.)

Symbolic Wounds

Bruno Bettelheim was trained in Vienna as an art historian and, later, as a child psychoanalyst. In his early work with severely disturbed children, he accepted the orthodox Freudian view that neurotic symptoms are caused by intrapsychic conflicts and that they represent unsuccessful solutions to problems rooted in early childhood. A dramatic personal experience, however, led him to modify this view and to take greater account of the role of situational factors in the causation and treatment of mental illness.

In 1938, Bettelheim was suddenly arrested and imprisoned in the Nazi concentration camps at Dachau and Buchenwald. During his imprisonment, he used his psychoanalytic training to understand what was happening to him and the other prisoners. Released in 1939, he came to the United States and, in 1943, published an article in which he set forth his understanding of these experiences. "Individual and Mass Behavior in Extreme Situations" dealt with the impact of the camps on different kinds of people and the long-term effects of imprisonment.

Bettelheim argued that the Nazis systematically set out to destroy the prisoners' will to resist by using forms of punishment that placed the prisoner in a dependent, infantile relationship to the guards. The traumatic experiences of arrest and of torture during transportation to the camps usually produced a reaction of *denial* in the new prisoner: "This can't be happening to me." Those who survived the first few days adapted to the camp situation as best they could, trying to keep their egos intact. Different groups of prisoners (criminal, political, nonpolitical middle-class, and upper-class) reacted in quite different ways, drawing on their earlier experience to support their self-esteem, but all were gradually worn down and forced into increasing dependency (see Bettelheim 1971:108–231).

Eventually, those who had been in the camps more than three years developed a distinctive set of attitudes. They no longer showed concern with people or events outside the camp. Everything that happened since their imprisonment had become "real" to them and many were afraid of returning to the outer world. Most striking was the tendency of the "old prisoners" to mimic the behavior and appearance of the camp guards—punishing other prisoners severely, dressing in pieces of Gestapo uniforms, and even adopting the values of the guards. Bettelheim interpreted this behavior as an example of the Freudian defense mechanism known as *identification with the aggressor.* Just as most boys resolve their Oedipus complex by identifying with the "castrating" father, so these prisoners, who had regressed into a state of infantile dependency, tended to identify with their powerful captors. Bettelheim cautions that this was only part of the story because these same old prisoners who sometimes identified with the Gestapo at other times defied it, demonstrating great courage in helping their fellow prisoners.

The crucial point for Bettelheim was the recognition of how rapidly drastic changes in personality could be produced by such "extreme situations." Much of his later work involved attempts to integrate this realization with traditional psychoanalytic theory and therapy. For example, Bettelheim designed an institution, the Orthogenic School (at the University of Chicago), that could provide a "therapeutic milieu" for autistic and schizophrenic children twenty-four hours a day (see *A Home for the Heart,* 1974). Together with other psychoanalysts, such as Anna Freud, Heinz Hartmann, and Erik Erikson, he came to stress the positive, integrative functions of the ego, rather than seeing it as a passive victim of unconscious processes. Even the mute, autistic child is defending a self, though one that has, tragically, become an empty fortress: "The self is stunted, most unevenly developed, but still seems to function in some minimal way to protect [the child] from further harm" (Bettelheim 1967:92).

In the early 1950s, an event occurred at the Orthogenic School that renewed Bettelheim's interest in anthropology. Three disturbed adolescents (two girls and a boy) banded together spontaneously and created a kind of initiation ritual that expressed their intense ambivalence about growing up. These children both desired and feared the changes that were taking place in their bodies and their lives. The ritual, which was supposed to insure wealth and fame, centered on the girls' experience of menstruation and involved their attempt to impose monthly bleeding on the boy. The children were prevented from carrying out their plans, but the event stimulated Bettelheim to write *Symbolic Wounds,* a study of primitive initiation ceremonies.

First published in 1954 (revised in 1962), this book argues that the unconscious motivation and many "bizarre" details of initiation rites can be understood as expressions of *male envy of female anatomy and reproductive junctions.* This explanation, which also applies to the couvade, reverses the traditional Freudian emphasis on female envy of the male organs ("penis envy"). But Bettelheim documents case after case in which the rituals symbolically assert that men are able to bear children. For both boys and girls, "the human being's envy of the other sex leads to the desire to acquire similar organs, and to gain power and control over the genitals of the other sex" (1962:146).

Symbolic Wounds was written during the period when Whiting and Child were completing *Child Training and Personality* (1953). It is instructive to compare Bettelheim's clinical use of cross-cultural material with the others' hypothesis-testing, correlational approach, even though Whiting's own studies of male initiation rites, described in chapter 6, came somewhat later. Bettelheim uses anthropological materials as Freud did in *Totem and Taboo*. He adopts the psychoanalytic assumption that children, neurotics, and primitives clearly display many processes that are hidden (repressed) in normal, civilized adults (1962:49); however, he proclaims that he is concerned not with "primitive man (a concept I have no use for) but with the primitive in all men" (1962:11). Like Freud, he too makes imaginative use of the best anthropological sources available to him, and his interpretations are guided by analogies with his clinical experience.

Bettelheim emphasizes the positive ego functions served by initiation rituals: They help young people to master their ambivalence toward the opposite sex and toward becoming adults. (Compare Endleman 1967:309–322.) By means of the ritual, initiates achieve new levels of psychic integration:

> Like the spontaneous actions of the children we observed, initiation ceremonies may be meant to foster personal and social integration in a difficult transitional period of life. They should then be understood as efforts of the young, or of society, to resolve the great antitheses between child and adult and between male and female; in short, between childish desires and the role ascribed to each sex according to biology and the mores of society. Whether or not they succeed is another question. (Bettelheim 1962:55)

Several other works of Bruno Bettelheim are relevant to anthropology—in particular, *Children of the Dream* (1969), which is a study of communal child rearing in the Israeli kibbutz. It grew out of Bettelheim's dissatisfaction with Melford Spiro's study (1958) and concludes, essentially, that a good institution is better than a bad family. In *The Uses of Enchantment* (1976), Bettelheim analyzes a series of popular fairy tales and suggests that, like initiation rites, fairy tales perform important positive functions. They offer children support, insight, and reassurance in a context of fantasy, and many children find this safer than more "realistic" literature:

> In the traditional fairy tale, the hero is rewarded and the evil person meets his well-deserved fate, thus satisfying the child's deep need for justice to prevail. How else can a child hope that justice will be done

to him, who so often feels unfairly treated? And how else can he convince himself that he must act correctly, when he is so sorely tempted to give in to the asocial proddings of his desires? (1976:144)

Adults who want to tidy up the traditional tales—making them less violent or overtly sexual—may be depriving children of the most useful parts.

Insight and Identity

The year 1950 is a landmark in anthropology not only for the reasons discussed in the Interlude, but also because it marks the first publication of Erik H. Erikson's *Childhood and Society* (revised edition, 1963). Like Bettelheim, Erikson began in the arts, was trained as a child analyst, and came to the United States to avoid Nazi persecution. His interest in anthropology was stimulated by his association with H. S. Mekeel and Alfred Kroeber, both of whom took him into the field in the late 1940s. Erikson's research on disturbed children, normal students, and famous persons led him to study the individual's developing sense of *identity*. He came to understand both normal and pathological processes in terms of the individual's progression through the life cycle, always modified by the historical context.

Childhood and Society is a complex book containing a great variety of materials. In the first chapter, two contrasting case histories are described, one of a young boy and the other of a Marine veteran. Both patients present bizarre neurotic symptoms. Erikson shows that these cases can be fully understood only if we take into account the interplay among organic, psychic, and sociocultural factors. He stresses the continuing attempts of each patient's ego to cope with its situation, even though it may be periodically overwhelmed by irrational forces of the id or superego. He views society as supporting certain ways of coping, discouraging others, and as building some conflicts into major cultural institutions.

In the second chapter, Erikson suggests an important expansion of Freud's theory of psychosexual stages of development. The oral-anal-genital sequence is retained, but these are labeled *zones,* and each zone is associated with characteristic *modes* of behavior (incorporative, retentive, intrusive, and so forth). Thus Erikson subdivides the psychosexual stages, presenting his scheme in a two-dimensional diagram that he calls an *epigenetic chart* (see figure 7-1). Normal development, in this scheme, is not linear but "step-wise," proceeding from the lower-left zone-mode

Figure 7-1 Part of Erik Erikson's "epigenetic chart."

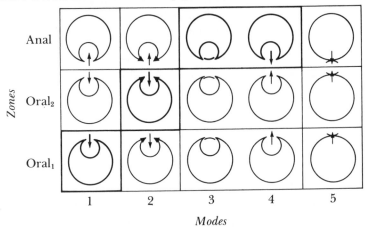

Modes

Source: From *Childhood and Society* by Erik H. Erikson. Copyright 1950. © 1963 by W. W. Norton & Company, Inc., renewed © 1978, 1991 by Erik H. Erikson. Reprinted by permission of W. W. Norton & Company, Inc.

("oral-receptive") to the upper right though some gender differences do occur in the later stages).

The newborn infant starts as a passive receiver of nourishment and stimulation, primarily through its mouth. If its oral-receptive needs are met—in a culturally patterned way—the newborn develops *basic trust* in itself and its social world. Building on this foundation of trust, the child becomes a more active partner in social interaction. By about six months of age, he or she enters the "oral-incorporative" substage, in which biting is the characteristic activity. By actively taking and holding onto objects (including other people), the child can further build its trust and confidence. However, if the pain of teething is aggravated by too-early weaning or separation from the mother, this trust can be undermined, resulting in a deep-seated rage or infantile depression. In Erikson's scheme, a child may become *fixated* at a given zone and/or mode; thus, the wish to remain a passive receiver or an active "taker" may be established very early in life, and these modes may be generalized to zones other than the oral.

Erikson associates the anal zone with retentive and eliminative modes—hanging on and letting go—and he includes in these stages the child's development of muscular control that makes possible a sense of *autonomy*. Toilet training is only one example of the interplay between social restrictions and a toddler's need to act on his world, but it is a crucial one, since the child who does not (or cannot) learn to control his bowels may suffer shame and doubt of a pervasive kind (compare Bettelheim

1967:33–39). Again, fixation can take place in zone and/or mode, so that enduring "anal" character traits may be established at this time. For Erikson no simple formula connects severe toilet training with miserliness or sorcery. What is at stake is the ego *strength* necessary for making mature choices, including the ability to cooperate with others:

> If outer control by too rigid or too early training insists on robbing the child of his attempt gradually to control his bowels and other ambivalent functions by his free choice and will, he [is] forced to seek satisfaction and control either by regression or by false progression. In other words, he will return to an earlier, oral control—i.e., by sucking his thumb and becoming whiny and demanding; or he will become hostile and intrusive, using his feces as ammunition and pretending an autonomy, an ability to do without anybody to lean on, which he has by no means really gained. (Erikson 1963:82–83)

Stepwise progression (at least for males) leads to the "genital-intrusive" stage, usually toward the end of the third year of life. By this time, mastery of locomotion has also taken place and the child begins to show real *initiative* in his dealings with others. His learning is "intrusive" in the sense that "it leads away from him into ever new facts and activities; and he becomes acutely aware of differences between the sexes" (p. 86). The boy's infantile genitality is destined to be repressed as part of the resolution of the Oedipus complex; but at this stage, depending on how the conflicts are handled in the family and larger society, initiative can either be encouraged or stifled by guilt. The ultimate achievement of mature, adult genitality also requires the development of a capacity for intimacy and a concern for *generativity*—the procreation of and care for a new generation. (See Kegan 1982 for a further elaboration of this scheme.)

One can best appreciate the subtlety and eloquence of Erikson's formulations by reading them in the original. However, we can examine here how he used these concepts of psychological development to understand cultural differences. In two concise essays in *Childhood and Society*, one on the Sioux Indians of South Dakota and the other on the Yurok of northern California, Erikson brings out the connections between patterns of childhood experience and adult character as expressed in cultural institutions. He makes use of his developmental scheme to understand how each society provokes and then exploits particular childhood conflicts to produce adults who will be motivated by needs that sustain the culture. (In this effort his goals are quite similar to those of the basic personality approach, but Kardiner's influence, if there was any, is not acknowledged.)

The Sioux were the best-known mounted warriors and bison hunters of the Great Plains—they were nomadic, generous, brave, and proud of their freedom. Erikson shows that their self-confidence and initiative were grounded in childhood experience (pp. 133–147). He also discusses the conflict between traditional Sioux character and the conditions of life imposed on them by military defeat, economic dependency, and restriction to the reservation. (Some of their psychological reactions are like those found in "old prisoners" in concentration camps and may be due to a similar identification with the aggressor.)

By contrast, the Yurok were sedentary river-dwellers who lived in a highly circumscribed universe, fishing for salmon and trading for goods or shell money. "The acquisition and retention of possessions is and was what the Yurok thinks about, talks about, and prays for. Every person, every relationship, and every act can be exactly valued and becomes the object of pride or ceaseless bickering" (p. 167). Where the Sioux value strength and assertiveness, the Yurok are concerned with "purity," and they engage in compulsive rituals and avoidances to insure success in fishing, hunting, and trade: "Only once a year, during the salmon run, are these avoidances set aside. At that time, following complicated ceremonies, a strong dam is built which obstructs the ascent of the salmon and permits the Yurok to catch a rich winter supply" (p. 168).

Erikson relates these ceremonials and the Yurok concerns with purity and accumulation of wealth to early conflicts regarding the retentive mode (though not exclusively the anal zone). The annual closing off of the river is a dramatization of the tendency to "hold on" to people, property, and feces. The corresponding Sioux ceremony was the annual Sun Dance, which enhanced the prosperity of the entire tribe through individual sacrifice and self-torture. Erikson offers a dynamic interpretation of this last feature by suggesting that the infantile rage of the "biting stage" is turned by the Sioux child against himself, and acted out in their masochistic rites (pp. 148–149).

In these two essays, Erikson's approach is quite similar to a traditional culture and personality approach, but he insists that he is dealing with the "mutual assimilation of somatic, mental, and social patterns which amplify one another and make the cultural design for living economical and effective" (p. 156), rather than with "simple causality." The relationship between historical pattern and individual identity is complex and circular: If culture creates neurosis by exploiting infantile needs, it also gives *meaning* to the compulsions it has created (p. 185). And there is no way for human beings to forge a valid identity outside of a particular historical situation. Similar themes are explored by Weston LaBarre in his fascinating book, *The Ghost Dance* (1970).

Psychohistory and the Interpretation of Myth

The concept of ego identity continued to gain importance in Erikson's work as he turned to the study of exceptional persons in the context of their times. Freud wrote an early essay, "Leonardo da Vinci and a Memory of His Childhood," and his final book was *Moses and Monotheism.* But Erikson is the real founder of the enterprise known as *psychohistory.* His studies of Luther, Gandhi, Jefferson, and Hitler are landmark works whose relevance to psychological anthropology is still to be evaluated and made explicit.

Young Man Luther (1958) and *Gandhi's Truth* (1969) focus on revolutionary figures who changed their respective worlds. In Erikson's framework, they were able to do this because (for a variety of reasons) they felt the contradictions of their times more keenly than others, and because (again, for many reasons) each achieved a new and more comprehensive identity, which enabled him to lead an entire society into a new era.

Not many anthropologists have followed Erikson's lead, although those who study comparative socialization, life cycles, or innovative leadership could certainly profit from his insights. Most of Erikson's followers are psychotherapists who are strongly concerned with social issues. Outstanding among these are Robert Coles and Robert Jay Lifton. Coles, who wrote a biography of Erikson (1970), has systematically applied Erikson's ideas to a number of neglected groups within American society. In a series of books called *Children of Crisis,* he has studied the children of Southern blacks, of migrant workers, of sharecroppers, and of other disadvantaged groups. At the other end of the life cycle, *The Old Ones of New Mexico* (1973) is a brief, sensitive study (with superb photographs by Alex Harris) of aged couples living in the small Spanish-American villages of northern New Mexico. Coles manages to reveal the great dignity of these people despite their poverty, and he probes the social and psychological sources of their strength.

Lifton has written on women in America (before this topic was popular), on "thought reform" and the Cultural Revolution in China, and on the survivors of Hiroshima. He is also the author of numerous articles on psychohistory, many of which are collected in *History and Human Survival* (1970). Like Coles, Lifton is a superb interviewer with a deep commitment to studying contemporary social problems. Like Erikson, he is able to enter into very different cultural traditions. Lifton writes that

> what is unique to Erikson's approach (particularly in *Young Man Luther*) is his ability to maintain an individually oriented depth-psychological perspective while simultaneously immersing himself and

his subject in the ideological currents of the period under study. (Lifton 1970:296)

This kind of work requires extraordinary qualities of scholarship and insight. With contributors such as Erikson, Coles, and Lifton, psychohistory could become "a means of bringing psychoanalysis and history together in a way that does justice to the richness of human experience" (Lifton 1970:296; see chapter 12).

Lifton's most recent book, *The Nazi Doctors* (1986), examines the way that many ambitious German doctors were seduced into cooperation with the Nazi regime and how they became agents of torture and death in Hitler's concentration camps. Combining interviews with other historical research, Lifton concludes that people trained to heal came to murder through a series of stages, and that a process of psychic "doubling" enabled them to separate their medical selves from the part of them that killed innocent adults and children. I believe *The Nazi Doctors* is a particularly important book at this moment in history, for as the AIDS epidemic spreads the medical profession worldwide will be drawn into complex political decisions involving testing, treatment, and perhaps isolation or destruction of affected individuals. The stakes, both financial and moral, will be enormous, and Lifton's study of Nazi doctors offers important warnings about the consequences of such medical decisions for doctors and for the rest of society.

The interpretation of myth and legend is another area in which psychoanalysis has continued to be influential. Anthropologists and other scholars have used Freudian concepts to analyze folk tales from both familiar and exotic cultures (for example, Jacobs 1959; Bettelheim 1976). One of the most interesting of these analyses is Alan Dundes' study of the "earth-diver" myth (1962). In this widespread North American creation myth, a small animal dives deep into the primeval sea to bring up some dirt, which then rapidly expands to become the earth. Often in these tales a number of other animals try unsuccessfully before the earth-diver rises to the surface, nearly dead from his effort, with a bit of mud beneath his claw. (Compare Genesis 8:7–11.)

Dundes' interpretation of this tale at first seems bizarre, but it does account for many details. He argues that, like many children today, early people held a vague theory of "cloacal birth," that is, the notion that babies and feces come out of the same body opening. (See Erikson 1950:21–34 for a case study of a young boy who refused to defecate because he believed himself pregnant.) If we add to this notion the recognition that males frequently envy female reproductive powers (Bettelheim 1962), we can begin to understand the motives that lie behind this myth: the earth-diver's achievement is the symbolic excretion of the world by a male.

Freud's colleague, Sandor Ferenczi, had noted the intense interest that children have in the waste products of the body—nasal mucus, feces, dead skin—but he thought that most adults repress or sublimate this interest. As Dundes writes,

> the common detail of the successful diver's return with a little dirt under his fingernail is entirely in accord with Ferenczi's analysis. The fecal nature of the particle is also suggested by its magical expansion. One could imagine that as one defecates one is thereby creating an ever-increasing amount of earth. (Dundes 1962:1041)

In short, this analysis views the earth-diver myth as a creation of the male who simultaneously sublimates his interest in feces and fantasizes great reproductive powers by identification with the hero. Psychological studies like this one supplement but do not replace analyses of the geographic distribution and formal structure of myths. (Compare the discussion of clothing at the end of chapter 2.)

Psychosocial Adaptation

The most recent attempts to synthesize psychoanalytic and anthropological theory are found in the works of Melford E. Spiro and Robert A. LeVine. These scholars have been trained in both disciplines, have had extensive clinical experience, and have carried out ethnological fieldwork. Each has tried to develop a conceptual framework in which psychological and cultural variables will play a part in explaining human behavior. Both of their syntheses emphasize the *adaptation* of individuals to their social environments, by intrapsychic or societal means, while noting the interaction between these alternative modes of adaptation.

In a widely discussed article, Spiro argues that many stable societies provide institutionalized modes of adaptation for people who suffer from *typical* forms of emotional conflict. For example, although Burmese men with "idiosyncratic" conflicts may, under prolonged tension, become psychotic, those who suffer from typically Burmese conflicts (including features such as extreme defensiveness, withdrawal from emotional situations, fear of women, and strong self-preoccupation) have available a culturally valued alternative to ordinary life. Such men can enter a Buddhist monastery and, in this setting, "resolve their conflicts with a minimum of distortion" (Spiro 1965:109). Religious institutions in many societies provide similar alternatives, enabling individuals to reduce their tensions and to achieve an adequate level of social and cultural functioning. Following Hallowell (and, more distantly, Benedict), Spiro claims that

> as a culturally constituted defense, the monastic institution resolves the inner conflicts of Burmese males, by allowing them to gratify their drives and reduce their anxieties in a disguised—and therefore socially acceptable—manner, one which precludes psychotic distortion, on the one hand, and criminal "acting-out" on the other. Hence, the monk is protected from mental illness and/or social punishment; society is protected from the disruptive consequences of antisocial behavior; and the key institution of Burmese culture—Buddhist monasticism—is provided with a most powerful motivational basis. (Spiro 1965:109; cf. Endleman 1967:497–526)

LeVine's more ambitious synthesis also hinges on the concept of adaptation, which he defines as "the shaping of the organism's response potentials toward fit with environmental conditions" (1982:5). Drawing on the work of Spiro and of John Whiting, LeVine argues for a Darwinian view of personality processes, in which variations in "personality phenotypes" are subject to selection by the environment, and the likelihood of survival of the best-adapted types is thereby increased (1982:113). Farther on, he presents a "cost-benefit analysis" of research on psychosocial adaptation.

LeVine's emphasis on populations and their variability is useful, as is his discussion of alternative strategies for personality study. However, his mixing of metaphors and of frameworks is troublesome. "Personality phenotype," "response potentials," and "cost-benefit analysis" are uneasy bedfellows. *Culture, Behavior, and Personality* is less a new synthesis than an eclectic attempt to salvage the culture and personality approach. One passage shows how little progress we have made since 1951, when Spiro identified the "false dichotomy" between culture and personality. LeVine writes:

> If internal motive and environmental demand lead to the same response, as they do in the case of adaptive fit, *observed responses can be attributed either to psychological disposition or immediate environmental pressure* according to the theoretical inclination of the investigator. (LeVine 1982:286–287; emphasis added)

True enough! But LeVine seems to imply that *if only our diagnostic methods were better* we could make the attribution (to personality or to culture) with certainty. Yet this kind of implicit dualism is exactly what prevents a fuller understanding of the relationship between person and institution (see Watts 1969; Sisk 1970; Bateson 1972; Levy 1973). In the chapters that follow, we shall discuss some of the attempts that have been made to overcome this dilemma.

Summary

What is the present relationship of psychoanalysis to anthropology? Psychoanalysts are still concerned with social and cultural problems, but many contemporary anthropologists are uninterested in (or unaware of) their contributions. Both reasoned and impassioned attacks have been made on psychoanalytic therapy and theory; critics claim that the former is ineffective and the latter implausible. Such claims are part of a general reaction against psychoanalysis, which many social scientists now regard as reactionary and privatistic or as radical and dangerous, depending on the critic's political orientation.

Clearly, psychoanalysis is a total worldview that one adopts out of a kind of conversion experience rather than as a cool, detached, rational decision. But the view of humans as cool, detached, rational creatures is precisely what psychoanalysis has undermined in this century. We are just realizing the extent to which *all* our actions are overdetermined. All human knowledge is "personal knowledge" for, as Michael Polanyi says, "Our believing is conditioned at its source by our belonging" (Polanyi 1964:322). Humans cannot escape from history, even if they view it as a nightmare from which they struggle to awaken.

The late George Devereux repeatedly cautioned anthropologists against thinking that they fully understood their own motives—what I have termed the "objectivity assumption." Devereux (like Spiro and LeVine) was both an anthropologist and a practicing psychoanalyst. He wrote several challenging works on "ethnopsychiatry" (see chapter 11), including the provocative book, *From Anxiety to Method in the Behavioral Sciences* (1967), where he argues that our scientific methods and instruments should be viewed as defenses against our unconscious fears. Devereux suggests that these ostensibly "objective" methods actually blind us to the most valid and useful data available: our own "subjective" responses to the behavior and feelings of other peoples: "In short, behavioral science data arouse anxieties, which are warded off by a countertransference inspired pseudo-methodology; this maneuver is responsible for nearly all the defects of behavioral science" (Devereux 1967:xvii; for a striking illustration of this process, see Tobin 1986).

Psychoanalysis insists on what we apparently most wish to deny: that we were all tiny, dependent babies once; that our lives are forever entwined with our early loves and hates, identifications and disappointments; and that virtually any human action may carry a great load of symbolic significance. So long as we repress these truths, they will return to haunt us and to upset our tidy theories and methods. If for no other reason, anthropology needs the psychiatrist.

Supplement, 1999

Psychoanalytic anthropology has had its ups and downs over the past two decades. Attacks on Freud and on psychoanalytic therapy have been frequent and often justified, though some of them seem motivated more by animus than science (F. Crews; J. Masson). At the same time, the need for a culturally sensitive approach to mental illness has become increasingly clear. For example, Arthur Kleinman has written that "the neuroses represent the medicalization of socially caused psychophysiological syndromes of human misery" (1986:61), and he calls for a rethinking of psychiatry in cultural terms.

Many anthropologists continue to use some version of psychoanalysis in their research and writings. In a highly sympathetic review of psychological anthropology, John Ingham (1996) states that

> Classical and post-Freudian psychoanalysis offers the most comprehensive and anthropologically useful framework for thinking about personality. Implicitly dialogical, it can accommodate the observations of other dialogical perspectives. It is also more suggestive than other psychologies when it comes to interpreting and theorizing about the motivational underpinnings of social relations and the symbolic content of myth, ritual, folklore, and other cultural practices. (p. ix)

I agree with Ingham on this, provided we beware of the loose logic that can "accommodate" almost any findings to Freudian theory.

Regarding the material in the present chapter, it is appropriate to mention a complex biographical study of Bruno Bettelheim by Nina Sutton (1996). My admiration for Bettelheim goes back to my time as his student in the mid 1950s. Though I was not a disciple, he was certainly one of the most inspiring teachers I ever had contact with. Following his death, many negative stories circulated about his deceitfulness and his arbitrary use of authority at the Orthogenic School, but he had as many defenders among former students and patients as he had detractors. The Sutton biography puts all of this material into perspective, revealing a complicated, often tormented individual, whose ideas and methods still deserve to be evaluated on their merits (*pace* Richard Pollak, whose less sympathetic biography stresses the negatives of Bettelheim's life and career.)

For example, behavioral and drug therapies are now available for the partial treatment of autism, but these do not cancel out the value of his "milieu therapy" at the time Bettelheim developed it (especially as contrasted with the cattle prods advocated by some doctors for shaping behavior of difficult children) or the heuristic value of his ideas for anthropology. I, for one, find his analysis of *some* male initiation rites as showing men's envy of women's reproductive functions quite plausible. As with any explanation, the danger is that it may be generalized to *all* such rites without adequate evidence. (For a challenging analysis of circumcision rites in a Uganda tribe, see Heald 1994.)

Melford Spiro has continued to write in an orthodox Freudian vein, defending, for instance, the universality of the Oedipus complex (though in a modified form). His recent Boyer Prize-winning book, *Gender Ideology and Psychological Reality* (1997) makes several important distinctions regarding motivation and the internalization of cultural ideologies. As Spiro notes, most theorists agree that Oedipal fantasies "originate in early childhood in connection with the boy's interaction with parents and other significant adults" (1997:160n).

Two U.C.L.A. anthropologists (Johnson and Price-Williams 1996) recently produced a major study of world folklore in which they detected Oedipal themes (broadly defined) in virtually every society under consideration. Unlike many speculative works, these authors present most of the folktales discussed in translation so the reader can judge the validity of their analysis.

The psychodynamic analysis of "myth, ritual, folklore, and other cultural practices" (Ingham 1996) as well as the visual arts and music, is still mainly the province of Freudian inspired scholars. Anthony Seeger's fascinating book, *Why Suyá Sing* (1987) is not explicitly Freudian, but the insights he gains into the psychology of this South American people by careful study of their songs and rituals is clearly informed by a dynamic psychology. My own studies of contemporary music in Yucatan (Bock 1992) and of a poem by Shakespeare (Bock 1993) are concerned, respectively, with the role of music in maintenance of a regional identity and with the use of ego psychology in the analysis of a highly ambiguous text, "The Phoenix and Turtle."

Many writers on myth and literature combine formal analysis with Freudian insights (e.g., Fox 1994). A fascinating example is Mario Vargas Llosa's (1986) study of *Madame Bovary*, which he calls "the first modern novel." His discussion of time, narrative and emotion in the novel sounds quite anthropological, as is his comment that the "dividing of self of the human being, in order to satisfy his or her desires without violating the social conventions, is something that [Flaubert's] characters do instinctively" (1986:162). Don't we all rationalize and "compart-mentalize"?

An outstanding advocate of psychoanalytic anthropology is Howard F. Stein who, in a series of books and articles, has drawn attention to many hidden themes in American culture, e.g., alcoholism as a metaphor for loss of self-control (discussed in chapter 11) and, recently, the existence of "Holocaust imagery" in the narratives of victims of corporate "downsizing" (Stein 1997). His many other books and anthologies demonstrate that sensitive Freudian interpretations of contemporary society can be both powerful and important to our self-understanding. (e.g., Stein 1994; 1998.) Whether or not you agree that *culture is the neurosis of humanity*, psychoanalytic anthropology has important lessons to teach about the behavior of others—and ourselves.

Chapter 8

Social Structure and Personality

Karl Marx

The approaches to be considered in this chapter share one important feature: they all reject the uniformity assumption—that a one-to-one relationship exists between a culture and a typical personality or character type. The authors of many of the works discussed are sociologists and social psychologists, not anthropologists. Nevertheless, their work is highly relevant to the development and future of psychological anthropology.

I have chosen the term *social structure and personality* to distinguish this school of thought from psychoanalytic anthropology and from culture and personality (see table 3-1). Within the social structure and personality school, I recognize three major approaches: *materialist, positionalist,* and *interactionist.* Each approach has its distinctive concepts and methods. The three are united by the fact that they all address the psychological characteristics of classes or roles within a society or across several societies rather than characteristics alleged to be typical of entire societies.

Materialist Approaches

The materialist view of the relationship between society and personality goes back at least to Karl Marx. In a famous passage in the *Critique of Political Economy*, Marx states:

> The mode of production of material life conditions the social, political, and mental life-process in general. It is not the consciousness of men that determines their being, but, on the contrary, their social being determines their consciousness. (Marx 1904:11)

Marx is asserting the primacy of material (economic) conditions as the source of a group's ideas and values and rejecting Hegelian idealism, in which the world is viewed as a product of immaterial (spiritual) forces.

Throughout his works, Marx insists that social classes and class conflict are the dynamic basis of historical change. The "ruling class" in any complex society is the group that controls the means of production—land, machines, and other forms of capital. The beliefs and values of the ruling class are generally appropriate to its material interests, that is, to maintaining and increasing its power. Ruling-class ideology also includes elements contributing to the "mystification" of the masses, for the workers must be convinced that the ruling group *deserves* its position of privilege. Under the influence of the rulers and their accomplices, the lower classes are kept ignorant of their true (revolutionary) interests. They often develop a "false consciousness," which actually corresponds to the interests of the rulers, accepting their subordination as being the "will of God."

Ultimately, say the Marxists, *all psychology is class psychology* (Bukharin 1969:213). Individual differences within classes are unimportant; to a Marxist, what really matters is how people will behave in situations of class conflict, including revolutions. Especially at these times, material interests emerge as the real determinants of behavior. (Marx was, of course, more concerned with revolutionary action than with dreams or neuroses.)

What produces class psychologies and the ideologies that are their systematized forms? The primary force is awareness of shared *material interests*. This awareness is facilitated by certain *conditions of work*. For example, in their daily interactions with one another, industrial workers realize both the fact of their exploitation and the power that solidarity with fellow workers can bring them. The factory that draws hundreds or thousands of workers together in the production process inadvertently promotes class consciousness among them. Industrial workers differ in this respect from peasants, who work in isolation from one another and who own small amounts of property. (See the discussion, below, of "peasant personality.")

A great deal of Marxist analysis is devoted to the psychology of the *bourgeoisie*—the class of capitalists who exploit the labor of the working class to produce commodities and to accumulate more capital. The bourgeoisie are much more mobile and innovative than the conservative feudal landholders whom they replaced as the ruling class in Western Europe and America. This is due to their conditions of work, which produce the following psychological characteristics: "*individualism*, a result of the competitive struggle, and *rationalism*, a result of economic calculation," together with a "*liberal* psychology . . . based on the 'initiative of the entrepreneur'" (Bukharin 1969:291). It follows that, as economic conditions change, class psychology also changes. Marx believed that "feelings, illusions, modes of thought, and views of life" were the *superstructure* that each class creates "out of its material foundations, as well as out of the corresponding social relations" (quoted in Bukharin, p. 292).

Marxist analysis cuts across the usual cultural units considered by anthropologists. From this perspective, it matters little if one is a Russian, a Japanese, or a Nigerian. What does matter is whether one is an industrial worker, a peasant, or a petit bourgeois (small-scale merchant). One's position in the social (class) structure largely determines one's beliefs and actions. As we shall see, positionalists and interactionists assume related points of view.

As noted earlier, some contemporary materialists believe that psychological concepts and personality variables are simply irrelevant to the understanding of cultural process. Most materialists do take account of individual differences in perception, motivation, and cognition, although they treat these distinctions as dependent variables to be explained by material factors. For example, a key concept in Marxist analysis is *alienation,* the estrangement of individuals from the material world and from themselves. Alienation is the result of a class structure that deprives individuals of access to the necessary means of production: "This separation from their work and the products of their work results also in their being alienated from nature and from themselves" (Lang 1964:19). The psychological state of alienation is thus a result of material conditions.

Much discussion of alienation is highly speculative, but some empirical studies help to clarify the significance of this phenomenon. One such work, *The Hidden Injuries of Class,* by Richard Sennett and Jonathan Cobb (1973), provides rich data from long, sensitive interviews to illuminate the effects of the class structure on American blue-collar workers. Although their sample is small, the authors convincingly portray the deep ambivalence of their subjects toward their jobs, the possibility of mobility, and themselves:

> One aerospace worker pinpointed the paradox in the situation very well, in reflecting on his own daydreaming at work. The more a person is on the receiving end of orders, he said, the more the person's got to think he or she is really somewhere else in order to keep up self-respect. And yet it's at work that you're supposed to "make something" of yourself, so if you're not really there, how are you going to make something of yourself? (Sennett and Cobb 1973:94; compare Garson 1977)

An excellent critical overview of cross-cultural research on alienation is found in an article by George M. Guthrie and Patricia P. Tanco (1980). The authors believe that the concept of alienation has been vaguely defined and poorly measured in most studies. They also feel that is has been used to explain too many things (alcoholism, addiction, delinquency, unconventional sexual behavior, etc.). Simply asking people to rate their feelings on "alienation scales" that have been translated into the local language may prevent a genuine understanding of the relationship between cultural change and individual stress. Their own studies in the Philippines indicate that

> there is, among those who could be expected to be alienated, evidence of optimism, a preservation of norms, and a cultural continuity that is counter to the behavior one would expect. [Philippine society]

would appear to disprove the inevitability of alienation under conditions of severe disruption of traditional patterns. (Guthrie and Tanco 1980:53)

Perhaps their findings could help us to understand the Philippine revolution of 1986.

Positionalist Approaches

Positionalism denotes a body of research that shares with Marxism the materialist assumption that one's behavior is strongly influenced by one's position in the social structure. However, positionalist studies treat social class as only one of a number of social positions that influence individual behavior. Ethnic group, social role, age, occupation, and even birth order are among the positions that have been studied from this perspective.

While using the concepts of material interests and conditions of work as explanatory principles, positionalists extend these ideas to nonmaterial interests and to general conditions of living. They also suggest that the principal mechanism through which material conditions affect personality characteristics is *differential socialization*. This phrase refers to the hypothesis that behavioral and personality differences found in members of various groups and performers of different roles can be traced back to specific socialization practices in childhood and in later life (Cohen 1961; Krake 1978).

Applied to social classes, the hypothesis of differential socialization suggests that a class psychology cannot simply be inferred from shared interests and conditions of work. The socialization practices characteristic of each class must be studied empirically and their consequences for adult behavior traced. For example, Urie Bronfenbrenner, whose comparison of Russian and American child rearing was mentioned in chapter 5, has also examined class differences in socialization within the United States. He summarizes a number of different studies indicating that

> middle class parents especially have moved away from the more rigid and strict styles of care and discipline . . . toward modes of response involving greater tolerance of the child's impulses and desires, freer expression of affection, and increased reliance on "psychological" methods of discipline, such as reasoning and appeals to guilt, as distinguished from more direct techniques like physical punishment. At the same time, the gap between the social classes in their goals and methods of child rearing appears to be narrowing, with working class

parents beginning to adopt both the values and techniques of the middle class. (Bronfenbrenner 1967:190)

Within each social class, however, Bronfenbrenner found that girls are exposed to more affection and less punishment than boys. Similar differences are found in the treatment of first-born versus younger children in a given family. Great use of "love-oriented techniques," although highly efficient in producing conformity with parental wishes, entails the risk of "oversocialization" of girls and eldest children, often producing individuals who are "anxious, timid, dependent, and sensitive to rejection" (p. 193). Differences in socialization of the sexes are most pronounced at lower-class levels; they decrease as one moves upward in the social structure where "patterns of parental treatment for the two sexes begin to converge" (p. 195).

Bronfenbrenner's studies (together with more recent ones, which seem to confirm his general findings) depart from the uniformity assumption by recognizing (1) class differences within a society, (2) sex differences within the same class, and (3) changes in socialization practices over time. However, the positionalist approach is also applied to social categories that cut across cultural boundaries, for example, in studies of *peasant personality*. Oscar Lewis, in his work in a Mexican peasant community (1951), and Herbert Phillips, in his analysis of Thai peasant personality (1965), concentrated on the peasantry of a single nation or region. Other investigators have attempted to establish psychological characteristics common to *all* members of the peasant class.

The best known of the anthropological characterizations is that of George M. Foster (1965). Foster argued that peasants in all societies share a common "cognitive orientation," which he calls the *image of limited good*. This is the shared (though usually unverbalized) assumption that the good things of life—wealth, health, land, prestige, and even pleasure—are strictly limited in quantity. Since nothing can be done to increase the resources that peasants divide among themselves, one person's gain is inevitably another's loss. (See the discussion of Benedict's description of the Dobu in chapter 3.)

Foster claims that this shared cognitive orientation accounts for a great deal of otherwise puzzling peasant behavior. (For a similar argument, see Banfield 1958.) For example, people who believe that good is limited will understandably be secretive about their own successes and envious of others'; they will avoid cooperative work situations for fear of being cheated; and they will resist innovations that, in their view, cannot increase the available good. Foster argues that peasants as a class *are* secretive, envious, uncooperative, fearful, and tradition-oriented, regardless of their specific culture. He also believes that this "image" often persists into an era in which cooperation and acceptance of modern techniques could lead to a better life for all. Peasant communities have strong sanctions against innovation: "The villager who feels the need for Achievement and who does something about it, is violating the basic, unverbalized rules of the society of which he is a member" (Foster 1965:309).

John G. Kennedy (1966) questioned Foster's assumptions and thus his interpretations of peasant personality. He believes that Foster underestimated cultural differences among peasant communities, particularly with regard to familistic values, degree of stratification, and types of relationships with the elite class. According to Kennedy, "economic differentiation and differences in social ranking not only exist in some peasant societies, but . . . they are associated with status-striving and achievement orientations" (1966:1217). Steven Piker (1966) and many others have offered quite different interpretations of peasant behavior, but continued controversy has failed to resolve any of the basic questions about peasant personality: Does it exist at all? If so, what is it like? Is it the result of a cognitive orientation, a culture of poverty, a rational ethos, or differential socialization?

Recent research emphasizes the capacity of peasants for rapid change and their eager adoption of innovations when new opportunities in a developing economy make change clearly beneficial. It has been argued that a person's economic position and ability to take risks determine whether he or she will accept an innovation or participate in a revolution, and that peasant "personality" is irrelevant to these decisions (Cancian 1967; Scott 1976). As a result of these studies, some anthropologists have been drawn to a more materialist position—one that allows for a certain amount of "lag" between economic change and psychological change, but that emphasizes the ultimate dependence of psychological phenomena on material conditions.

Positionalists have also studied the personality types associated with various social roles and the socialization of adults for role performance. Classic studies by Max Weber and Robert Merton of the "bureaucratic personality" are examples of this concern. In Merton's formulation, the typical bureaucrat has chosen an occupation that offers security through conformity. The individual advances by avoiding conflict with superiors and by passively achieving seniority. Passing "objective tests of competence," usually involving knowledge of bureaucratic regulations and procedures, may also be necessary for advancement. Bureaucratic careers thus *attract* a certain type of person, but they also *reinforce* tendencies toward conformity and a narrow view of life. Under these circumstances, it is not surprising that bureaucrats are often more concerned with adhering to the rules than with getting a job done or satisfying a client (Merton 1957:123–124).

Unfortunately, few studies include many data on individual peasants, workers, or bureaucrats. To this extent they are open to the same criticisms leveled at culture and personality studies: inferences made about personality from institutional data are not verified independently. Also, we cannot know whether timid, conformist, authoritarian individuals are attracted to bureaucracies or whether these traits are created by bureaucratic careers unless we have reliable data on individuals before, during, and after their acceptance (or rejection) of bureaucratic positions. Both mechanisms are probably involved. Some evidence, however, suggests that children are socialized somewhat differently in families where the father has a bureaucratic position than in families where he is an independent entrepreneur. (See Miller and Swanson 1966.)

Only a few psychologically oriented studies of occupations provide rich individual data. Outstanding among these are the studies of eminent American scientists conducted by Anne Roe (summarized in Endleman 1967). Roe used projective tests, life-history interviews, and comparisons with other groups to understand the personalities of highly successful natural and social scientists (Nobel Prize winners and the like). She found that members of this group shared some background characteristics and psychological tendencies. For example, a large number of individuals in the group had been firstborn children. Many of the scientists had experienced early loss of a parent (through death or divorce), and almost all reported a sense of personal isolation early in life. TAT protocols revealed notable differences among subjects in various disciplines, and Rorschach responses indicated that

> all of the types of eminent scientist show unusual capacity to see things in ways that are out of the ordinary and share a considerable load of anxiety, probably reflecting underlying insecurities which are presumably connected with their drive toward unusual achievement and the strength and persistence of their immersion in their work. (Endleman 1967:374)

Intermediate between general studies of class psychology and studies concerned with specific roles lies an area where relatively little research has been done, yet it was in this area that one of the most significant studies of social structure and personality was attempted. Building on data collected in earlier research, John Rohrer and Munro Edmonson directed a careful, interdisciplinary study of New Orleans blacks. Their work was first published as *The Eighth Generation* (1960), a title referring to the eight generations since the first slaves were brought to Louisiana. The study has many interesting features, including its sampling and interviewing methods; however, I am concerned here with the ideas that Rohrer and Edmonson developed to account for continuities between childhood experience and adult psychosocial adaptations. To understand these ideas, we must review the history of the study.

Allison Davis and John Dollard carried out fieldwork in New Orleans during the 1930s, when "white supremacy" was still strong in the South, and when all Americans were feeling the effects of the Great Depression. These investigators argued that *social class was more important than race* in the experience of many blacks, and they demonstrated the influence of class on child training and school experience. Their staff interviewed nearly two hundred adolescents and in most cases the children's families as well. Their book, titled *Children of Bondage,* contained rich case studies of several youths from each social class.

Rohrer and Edmonson introduce their follow-up study with a detailed history of class and race relations in New Orleans, describing the many kinds of groups that exist within "New Orleans Negro society," such as families, churches, schools, unions, and lodges. They next look at the ways that people *relate* to the groups available to them. The central thesis of *The Eighth Generation* is that individuals develop a series of role identifications—that is, they organize conceptions of their "selves" in terms of the role or group that has greatest importance to them at a given time of life. Furthermore, they become highly "ethnocentric" about their choices and hostile to opposed groups.

People may be aware of alternative identities (and may even choose differently later in life), but Rohrer and Edmonson found that they could specify a *primary role identification* for most subjects, and that this identification was an essential part of the individual's psychic integration. Furthermore, they observe,

> these commitments are not unique or idiosyncratic but are characteristic of groups of individuals. For one group the primary role identification was with the middle class, and was suffused with the values associated with that class. For another it was the maternal role in the matriarchal family, and in this group sex becomes a more basic fact— even socially—than class. For a third group the primary identification was with older boys and men in more or less age-graded peer groups—gangs; while for a fourth being a family member was the most important of all roles and the family became not only a focus but almost the total sphere of social life. (Rohrer and Edmonson 1964:299)

The authors argue that a clear role identity and a sense of individual ego identity (in Erikson's sense) are both necessary to achieving an adult level of personality integration. Rich case studies with longitudinal data going back twenty years support these interpretations, showing remarkable stability in the identifications achieved early in life. There was also a consistency of *marginality* in certain individuals:

> As would be expected, not all individuals are able to evolve unequivocal identifications of this type; some have only vague or conflicting role identifications. There is a corresponding diffusion or lack of mature integration in the psychic functioning of such individuals. (1964:299)

The approach developed by Rohrer and Edmonson, with its combination of cultural and individual data compiled by interracial and interdisciplinary teams, holds much promise. The authors criticize Davis and Dollard's overemphasis on class, and also take issue with a study of Negro "basic personality" (Kardiner and Ovesey 1951), arguing that both approaches oversimplify the complexity of black personality and adaptation. The concept of primary role identification is, I believe, especially important as a way to synthesize individual and social data. It has been neglected, partly because many psychological anthropologists are unfamiliar with the study, but also because having the kind of background data provided by the Davis and Dollard study is unusual. (See McClelland et al. 1978 for a preliminary report on a longitudinal study of the effect of child training on adult personality.)

Interactionist Approaches

The studies discussed in this section start from the positionalist assumption that one's place in society is the major determinant of behavior and carry this assumption to its logical conclusion: *the self is an entirely social product.* Interactionists go beyond concepts such as *class psychology* and *primary role identification* to insist that one's sense of identity is continually constructed from ongoing interactions. They are more concerned with the effects of one's *immediate situation* on behavior than with alleged *continuities* of intrapsychic structures. Writers in this tradition seldom use such terms as *personality* or *character,* preferring such concepts as *social self* or *personal identity,* (Carson 1969).

The speculative background of interactionism is found in the sociological works of Georg Simmel, Émile Durkheim, W. I. Thomas, and C. H. Cooley. American interactionism is also derived from the teachings of the University of Chicago social philosopher George Herbert Mead on the development of the self (1934). Fundamentally, Mead argued that we learn who we are only by observing how others respond to our actions and by "taking the role of the other" toward ourselves. This idea is similar to the Freudian concept of the superego as an "internalized parent," but Mead emphasizes the continuous operation of this process. Unlike the superego (which is formed in childhood), the self is constantly being modified by interaction with *significant others* as part of what we would today call a system with positive and negative feedback. Even when no one else is physically present, says Mead, we still take the attitude of a *generalized other* toward our own actions, approving or disapproving, and keeping ourselves in line. For Mead, the self is a *process,* not a "thing."

An empirical offshoot of this Chicago tradition took the form of intensive field studies of occupations. During the 1950s, under the guidance of Everett C. Hughes, a generation of University of Chicago graduate students studied taxi drivers, furniture salesmen, dance musicians, and funeral directors at first hand. These investigators were less concerned with general "conditions of work" than with the concrete interaction situations that each job created and with the interpersonal dynamics of these situations.

Fascinating as some of these studies are, it remained for someone to synthesize them and spell out their relevance to the problems of individual and society. This person was the late Erving Goffman. For nearly thirty years, in a series of books and articles, Goffman stimulated thought and research on a variety of topics, offering an important challenge to psychological anthropology and to many other disciplines. I believe that Goffman's work is as important to the study of interaction as Freud's has been to the study of dreams and the unconscious. (The parallel is deeper than most people realize; see Bock 1988.)

The title of Goffman's first book, *The Presentation of Self in Everyday Life* (1959), has many resonances. The "self" referred to is, like G. H. Mead's concept, a constant process of creation rather than a stable entity. Its "presentation" is a dramatic one, entailing the realization of a role in relation to an audience and in cooperation with backstage teammates. The title probably alludes to Freud's early work *The Psychopathology of Everyday Life,* which, like Goffman's book, builds an elaborate interpretive framework out of mundane experience.

Taking his cue from Simmel (1950:307), Goffman points out that people who enter into "the presence of others" (that is, any social situation) are faced with a problem of information control. As in a theatrical performance, certain data must be revealed and others hidden. Each performer in a social situation implicitly claims to be a certain kind of person and expects to be treated as such (whether as a doctor, a cabdriver, a faithful spouse, a skilled mechanic, or an innocent bystander). He or she "projects a definition of the situation" in which these claims should be honored. Yet we know that claims to a social identity can be false, and terms such as "quack," "con man," or "traitor" are common labels for fraudulent performers in American culture.

Given the possibility of fraud, Goffman asks what the implications of deception are for everyday social interaction. Since people are not always what they claim to be, even legitimate performers must put on a kind of show to convince their audience that they are genuine. Real doctors and faithful spouses have the same *dramaturgical* problems as do quacks and faithless spouses. Indeed, the frauds may be more skillful than the legitimate performers at presenting a believable self! This is why Goffman uses many concepts and terms from the world of the stage and the confidence game.

Most of our everyday life with others is indistinguishable from a staged performance, including moments spent "backstage" with team members (people like our barbers, tailors, doctors, and spouses), who help us prepare our public presentations. This fact has important consequences for the relation of self to society. In several of his works, Goffman shows how social norms penetrate every aspect of individual behavior: whether we wish to be considered authoritative, threatening, harmless, or just "normal," we must take constant care that a momentary slip doesn't "spoil the show," causing others to get the "wrong impression."

People who are very obviously not "normal," and people who have something to hide—the discredited and the discreditable, in Goffman's terminology—are excellent subjects for study from this perspective. In *Stigma* (1963), Goffman analyzes the situation of stigmatized persons (for example, the physically handicapped, the mentally retarded, ex-convicts, or ex-mental patients). He argues that the differences among kinds of stigmas are less important than the common dilemma faced by all stigmatized persons when they interact with "normals." He calls such interaction situations the "primal scene of sociology" (another Freudian allusion), and he documents the similarities among organized groups of stigmatized persons, from Alcoholics Anonymous to the NAACP.

Another significant Freudian parallel is found in Goffman's treatment of the relationship between persons who share the same stigma, whether or not they are organized into a political action group. Goffman characterizes this relationship as highly ambivalent: stigmatized persons feel a common bond with their "own," yet they also want to be accepted by normals. Whether blind, diabetic, retarded, or born into a despised minority, they are torn between social identities, sometimes wishing to "pass" as normal, and at other times militantly defending their fellow sufferers. There is no solution to this dilemma. Stigmatized persons who become leaders of their "own" groups end up spending much time interacting with normals who consider them "different" from those they represent and/or "a credit to their people."

To me, the most fascinating point in *Stigma* is Goffman's demonstration that organized groups of the stigmatized rest, ultimately, on their *shared guilt*. Members of these groups frequently feel that they have done something terrible to deserve their stigma. They may also feel guilty about their ambivalence toward their "own" and may try to compensate by working for the cause or proclaiming pride in their handicap. Goffman comes close to suggesting that, since we are all stigmatized relative to some category of "normals," *guilt lies at the basis of all social organization* (1963:124–128). If Goffman had accepted my analysis, this least Freudian of sociologists would have found himself advocating a position very like that expressed in *Totem and Taboo:* that participation in a "primal crime" is the precondition of human social cooperation (Brown 1966:13).

Goffman's other works deal with a wide variety of topics, but he always returns to the interpretation of interaction in specific social situations. In *Encounters* (1961a), he is concerned with the ways in which people express their involvement in, or distance from, the roles they perform. *Relations in Public* (1971) suggests how certain ideas developed in the study of animal behavior (ethology) can be fruitfully applied to human interaction. In *Frame Analysis* (1974), he borrows concepts from literary criticism and symbolic anthropology to analyze the ways in which people "frame" their experiences in order to attribute meaning to them. There are also several collections of essays (1961b; 1967; 1969) whose topics range from the situation of mental patients to behavior at the gaming tables of Las Vegas, and an analysis of sexual symbolism in advertising (1979). Goffman's work is important to psychological anthropology as a demonstration of the complex ways in which social norms influence behavior quite apart from "intrapsychic" (personality) factors. He has led many ethnographers to focus more carefully on details of interaction and discourse (Goffman 1981).

Several other kinds of interactionist studies can only be mentioned briefly here. The term *symbolic interaction* has been applied to a variety of approaches that, like Goffman's, seek to interpret the meaning of social behavior in concrete situations (Blumer 1969). A closely related approach goes by the rather awkward title of *ethnomethodology*. As developed by Harold Garfinkle and others, ethnomethodology focuses on details of behavior and written texts that reveal social actors *creating* the categories and rules that they live by, and *negotiating* their interpretations of what has happened. (See Turner 1974.)

A particularly clear example of this approach is found in Jack D. Douglas's book *The Social Meanings of Suicide* (1967). There is a long tradition in sociology of studying the official rates of suicide in various social groups (classes, religions, nationalities) and then interpreting the social causes of these rates. For example, Protestants appear to have higher suicide rates than do Roman Catholics; this differential has been attributed to the Protestant emphasis on individual responsibility for sin as well as the alleged lack of forgiveness for individual failings in Protestant communities.

Douglas argues that such interpretations are invalid because the classification of a given death as suicide is strongly influenced by community attitudes. Actual rates of self-destruction may be the same for Protestants and Catholics, but the strong condemnation of suicide by the Roman Catholic Church probably leads families, doctors, and other officials to classify uncertain cases as "accidental" or "natural" deaths. Differing suicide rates are thus seen as the result of *negotiated decisions,* not as objective *social facts.*

Ethnomethodology raises questions about all studies that rely on official statistics. In particular, the method of *epidemiology,* used to analyze possible causes of physical and mental illness, must be critically reviewed. Epidemiology involves identifying social groups that have different incidence rates for a particular disease, and then inferring the contribution made by factors such as diet, stress, custom, or climate to the rates. The method is extremely useful in tracing the causes of clear-cut physical illnesses such as heart disease or tuberculosis, but serious problems arise when it is applied to mental illness, for which the official statistics are less reliable.

For example, if one uses the rate of admission to mental hospitals as a measure of illness, some strong correlations between psychosis and social class are revealed. But what happens when we ask (as Douglas did of suicides) *who decides* whether a given patient will be admitted (or committed) to a mental hospital? It is now well established that upper-class sufferers tend to receive private psychotherapy and to stay at home (or in private "rest homes"), whereas lower-class sufferers with objectively similar symptoms often get into trouble with the law and end up being committed to state institutions. Thus, some of the correlations between illness and social class disappear when we determine the *meaning* of official hospital statistics.

One significant study in social psychiatry clearly showed the danger of relying on official statistics. The Hutterites are members of a large, communal Anabaptist sect that settled in western Canada about a hundred years ago after centuries of persecution in Europe. They are highly conservative in speech, dress, and customs, though they accept modern agricultural techniques and have become successful farmers (to the envy of their neighbors). Because few Hutterites entered mental hospitals, it was long believed that Hutterite society had an extremely low rate of mental illness; this characteristic was usually attributed to the stability and security of their way of life.

Intensive, first-hand studies by anthropologists and psychiatrists, however, revealed that rates of mental illness in Hutterite society were *not* very different from those in neighboring communities (Eaton and Weil 1953; Kaplan and Plaut 1956). The low rate of hospital admissions can be explained by Hutterite cultural values, which encourage sheltering and supporting afflicted persons rather than expelling them from the community (cf. Cumming and Cumming 1957). For example, a common form of adult depression, called by the Hutterites *Anfechtung* ("temptation by the devil"), is met with sympathy and emotional support. Afflicted persons are patiently counseled by Hutterite ministers, who assure them that many people experience similar temptations. In most cases, the depression passes and the person resumes a normal pattern of life.

Social psychiatry is a rapidly growing discipline in which anthropologists often play important roles. Whether they are carried out in large urban centers (Srole et al. 1962) or in depressed rural areas (Leighton et al. 1963), within a single society or across several cultures, studies of mental health and illness often benefit from the specialized knowledge and interviewing skills of anthropologists. A survey of this field by Ransom J. Arthur (1971) indicates the range of topics it embraces. In addition to epidemiology, Arthur discusses social class and psychiatric disorder, social factors in the onset of disease, studies of mental hospitals, community psychiatry, and transcultural psychiatry (see also Kiev 1972). Although the two share many interests and methods, social psychiatry and psychological anthropology differ in that practitioners of the former are oriented toward *healing* as well as research. But many anthropologists have participated in cross-cultural studies of mental illness, and others have described mental disturbances specific to certain societies or regions (see Barnouw 1985:353–388; Bourguignon 1979:270–297). I shall return to these topics in chapter 11.

Summary

We have seen that the social structure and personality school presents an alternative both to psychoanalytic anthropology and to culture and personality. Materialist and positionalist approaches reject the uniformity assumption, looking rather at the psychological correlates of social classes, roles, and occupations that are not limited to single societies. Interactionist approaches reject the continuity assumption, and focus instead on factors in the immediate situation that produce regularities in behavior. In this view, the self is a continual creation of social interaction; its apparent consistency is due to the fact that people tend to play the same interaction "games" throughout life (Berne 1964), but when placed in unusual, or "extreme," situations, much of this consistency disappears (Bettelheim 1943). In the next chapter, we examine some recent anthropological studies that also de-emphasize the concept of personality in favor of empirical observations of behavior in the "here and now."

Supplement, 1999

A number of newer approaches in psychological anthropology take issues of class, gender, and occupational role seriously (see chapter 13), but they seldom connect with what we have termed "social structure and personality." The writings of James Scott (1985) inspired interest in the concept of "resistance," though not in the standard psychoanalytic sense. Scott noted the numerous ways (some subtle, some not) in which peasants and other exploited classes *resist* the power of landlords and of the state. Forms of resistance range from "self-protective deference" and "sullen non-compliance" (phrases borrowed from John Updike) to acts of sabotage and outright rebellion. For a while, every ethnographic study discovered some form of resistance among oppressed peoples living in colonial situations or internal to modern states. Helen Horowitz (1987:118) argued that college students are "a subject people" who have "much in common with workers, slaves, and prisoners" and who often resist requirements imposed on them by professors and administrators! However, more general considerations of *power* seem to have replaced this still valuable concept.

Nancy Scheper-Hughes contributed a stunning book on child neglect in a shantytown of northern Brazil to follow up her earlier article on this topic (1985, discussed in chapter 9). In *Death Without Weeping* (1992) she demonstrates the reasons for the relative "detachment" of poor mothers who make difficult choices, perhaps unconsciously, about which of their infants are least likely to survive. These babies suffer severe neglect and frequently die so their more favored siblings may live. But Scheper-Hughes is neither a Darwinian nor an "extreme ethical relativist" (a fictional anthropologist who supposedly believes that whatever exists in any culture is, therefore, acceptable). Rather, she is outraged by the political and economic situation that makes such maternal detachment a necessary protection against despair.

A similar study of poor women and their difficult choices was carried out in the "back streets" of Cairo by Unni Wikan in fieldwork extending over thirty years. *Tomorrow, God Willing* (1996) documents the life and attitudes of the urban poor. As in her studies of Oman and Bali, intimate knowledge of people combines with fluency in the local language to produce striking results. Many of the Cairo poor are of peasant background and their position at the bottom of the urban social structure produces a combination of envy and gossip directed at holding back anyone who seems to be getting ahead. Wikan writes:

> From my first day in the back streets people cautioned me "Don't get involved with people . . . it just leads to trouble. The people here begrudge others everything they have!" Over the years these warnings have taken on a semblance of truth for me. Not because it is true that nobody wishes anybody else well, but because the people themselves are so convinced of the veracity of the statement that they live their lives accordingly. (p. 117)

This sounds a great deal like the "cognitive orientation" that George Foster called the Image of Limited Good (discussed above). Though the situation in Egypt's largest city differs from that in Mexican or Italian peasant villages, the similarities produced by humble position and grinding poverty are striking (see Farley 1998).

Wikan focuses on women and children, but she also reveals a great deal about adult gender relations. Despite the poverty and many associated health problems, the book testifies to the warmth and capacity for friendship of these Egyptian women. In Cairo, the anthropologist found her hostesses unwilling to accept any return other than occasional gifts of clothing for their children.

> I never paid for anything, not even my food. The hospitality of the people is such that it would have been an affront if I had offered to. . . . I simply gave my friendship. Nor was I ever asked for money, not even a loan [although] I have been a burden on their meager resources with my comings and goings through the years. And yet they always made me feel that I could not come often enough, or stay long enough. (p. 330)

The apparent contradiction between generosity to an outsider and fierce envy of relatives and neighbors is not easy to reconcile, but we must take this talented scholar's word that it exists, even though it complicates, for the better, our view of human behavior.

Elsewhere, writing of the Balinese, Wikan (1990:32) comments on their "careful and comprehensive self-monitoring of behavior, thought and affect" that seems, especially for women and low status men, to be a constant part of their public life. If we recall Goffman's analysis of "presentation of self," especially of stigmatized persons, we may be able to view such Balinese conduct as a function of people's position in a complex social structure rather than as being due to a pathological personality.

Also relevant to the study of social structure and personality is much of the work of Arthur Kleinman and his students on the social and cultural framework of mental illness in different societies. Some of this research will be considered in chapter 11, but here we should note the stresses imposed by social upheaval and migration as well as those that come with membership in a low status group or social class (Kleinman 1988:chap. 4). We know, writes Kleinman, that "the rates of depression and other neurotic conditions are elevated in refugee, immigrant, and migrant populations owing to uprooting, loss, and the serious stress of the acculturation process" (1988:38), and he calls for a culturally sensitive social psychiatry that will learn from similarities and differences across cultures. (See Westermeyer 1989.)

Finally, what of *slavery*, an institution that defines whole classes of people as less than fully human, exploits them for their labor and sexuality, and subjects them to being bought, sold, tortured, and killed without recourse? It is hardly surprising that slaves might share a "psychology" common to their class, whatever the dominant culture, or that this class psychology would involve hatred of their "masters," sullen resistance, and other features that appear peculiar to more fortunate people.

For example, Patricia J. Williams has written about "Kate," a slave who was involved in an 1835 court case when her Louisiana owner returned her to the seller because she was "crazy." She had *burned her master's bed* and run away! "Like a mad dog or a wild horse, she wouldn't make good property in a system that envisioned property as the extension of the owner's will" (Williams 1998:10).

The seller argued that Kate was not crazy, only (expectably, for a slave) "stupid." However, Williams suggests that "she was neither stupid nor crazy but very, very smart." It was her resistance to doing her master's will that branded her as crazy. As with women in Brazilian shantytowns and Cairo back streets, slaves and their stigmatized descendants may be stereotyped as abnormal. But, Williams asks, "What does it mean . . . when whole communities are effectively dismissed as crazy by the use of such a term as 'culture of pathology' [or] when the mere look of a person is enough to trigger the limitations on liberty we license by saying someone has a 'suspect profile'?" (Williams 1998:10). I think it means that stereotyping and stigmatization are at work, and that the point of view advocated in this chapter is essential for understanding our world.

Chapter 9

Focusing on Behavior

Bronislaw Malinowski

S tarting in about 1960, several new approaches in psychological anthropology were developed based on the *intensive observation of human behavior in natural settings.* Some of these developments were responses to criticisms of the cross-cultural approach (chapter 6). Others were stimulated by naturalistic studies of animal behavior (ethology), while some showed the influence of interactionist theories, especially in their emphasis on situational variables and their questioning of the continuity assumption.

Similar interactionist tendencies appeared in popular psychotherapies of the same era. Gestalt therapy, transactional analysis, and related movements all encouraged patients to deal with their feelings and conflicts by focusing on "the here and now" rather than by reliving the past or probing the unconscious. In these theories, neurosis and character structure were no longer viewed as entities but as interaction "games" that people play, sustained by the responses of other people (Berne 1964). All these factors contributed to the development of the approaches surveyed in this chapter.

Six Cultures

One way of meeting criticisms of cross-cultural studies was to train investigators in observational methods and have them collect firsthand data on a diverse sample of societies. These data could be used to test hypotheses concerning the effect of variables such as age, sex, child training, or culture type on behavior, eliminating the need to infer measures from ethnographies collected for other purposes (see chapter 6). In the "Six Cultures Project," directed by John Whiting and his wife, Beatrice Whiting, six pairs of investigators (most of them husband-wife teams) were used to observe six communities, widely distributed from Africa to Okinawa. Special attention was given to the behavior of children between three and eleven years old as they interacted with peers, infants, and adults.

The theory guiding the project derived from the earlier cross-cultural work of Whiting and Child (1953). It differs from this approach mainly in its emphasis on the children's *learning environment,* which is viewed as mediating between cultural institutions and personality (see figure 9-1). As John Whiting did in his study of the Kwoma (1941), Whiting and Whiting wished to discover exactly how culture impinged on children's lives.

The findings of the project were published in three major books. In *Six Cultures* (B. Whiting 1963), brief ethnographies of the communities were presented together with the "Field Guide for a Study of Socialization" used by the investigators to make their observations more comparable. *Mothers of Six Cultures* (Minturn and Lambert 1964) was based primarily on data from questionnaires administered to mothers in each community. It reveals the diversity of cultural norms regarding child rearing in the six societies (for example, adult attitudes toward child obedience, responsibility for chores, treatment of aggression, and discipline). Finally, *Children of Six Cultures* (Whiting and Whiting 1974) presents data on child behavior in relation to selected variables. As the authors note,

> We try to combine cross-cultural and intracultural approaches. The same children were compared with other children within their culture as well as those of different cultures. It must be admitted that with but six cultures and sixteen to twenty-four boys and girls in each varying from three to eleven years in age . . . we had the barest minimum of cases to test our hypotheses. . . . Despite this defect, the opportunity . . . of testing the same hypotheses both within and across cultures . . . makes up to some degree for the inadequacy resulting from small sample size. (Whiting and Whiting 1974:2–3)

This project differed from earlier cross-cultural studies in several other ways:

- It relied on direct observation of child behavior in natural settings. Precautions were taken to avoid bias in observations. A total of at least fourteen five-minute observations were made on each child; the ethnographer recorded general interaction and a bilingual assistant transcribed all verbal communications.
- Behavior was used as an "index of personality." Projective tests were not employed, and inferences from "projective-expressive systems" to adult personality were avoided. No assumptions were made about continuity from early experience to later character.
- Child behavior was observed in different settings (home, garden, and school), during various kinds of activities (play, work, learning), and when different kinds of groups were present.
- Quantitative data on intracultural variability as well as intercultural differences were preserved and published. Independent judges were used to classify reported behaviors into categories for statistical analysis, but subjective ratings by judges as to presence, absence, or intensity of customs were not necessary.

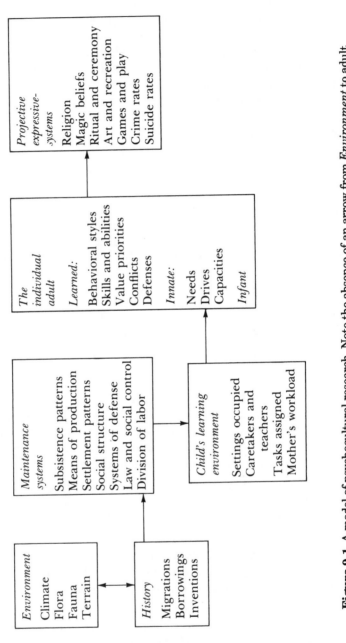

Figure 9-1 A model of psychocultural research. Note the absence of an arrow from *Environment* to adult behavior. (From *Children of Six Cultures* by Beatrice Whiting and John W. M. Whiting. Cambridge: Harvard University Press. Copyright © 1974 by the President and Fellows of Harvard College.

Despite all these methodological improvements, the results of the project are disappointing. The six ethnographies are presented in uniform style for easy comparability, but they are not really that easy to compare. The categories and procedures used by the judges to classify behavior frequently seem arbitrary. For example, as any parent knows, it is often difficult to distinguish behavior that "seeks help" from behavior that "seeks attention," and such actions can also be confounded with behavior that "seeks dominance"; yet these are three of the twelve categories used in the analysis. Reliability of the original observations must be questioned when we read that, "since only one [bilingual] assistant was available at any one time at a field site, it was impossible to make simultaneous observations; hence the question of reliability must be taken *on faith*" (p. 42; emphasis added).

The conclusions of the Six Cultures study hold few surprises. Age, sex, setting, and culture type (for example, whether agricultural or pastoral) can all be shown to affect child behavior under certain circumstances. A given child's behavior shows variation depending on the setting and whether the child is interacting with infants, peers, or adults, but enough consistency is present to indicate a "personality" factor at work:

> Above all, the findings of this study suggest that none of the traditional theories alone can account for the social behavior of children. That boys are more aggressive and less nurturant than girls cannot be completely explained by either a biological or a cultural model. The children of each culture are unique in some respects but indistinguishable in others. Differences in learning environments produce differences in children's social behavior; despite this all children seek help and attention from adults and offer help and support to infants. (pp. 184–185)

This conclusion does not really represent a great deal of new information, considering the time, effort, and expense such an undertaking requires.

In another use of intensive on-site observation, adults in four East African societies were studied by members of the UCLA Culture and Ecology Project. Because each society had both farming and pastoral populations, the investigators were able to make comparisons among the four societies and also between farmers and pastoralists across cultures. An elaborate test-interview was conducted with a total of 505 men and women, but despite considerable methodological ingenuity, the results of this project are also rather disappointing (Edgerton 1971). What are the problems with these approaches and where can we look for alternative methods of study?

Human Ethology

One of the problems in any observational study of behavior is finding the appropriate language to describe what one observes. Even when high-quality video tapes are available for repeated viewing, at some point the analyst must describe what is happening. This usually means breaking up the continuous "stream of behavior" into *units* that can be classified, counted, and compared.

In the Six Cultures Project, a subset of English verbs and adjectives was used, and these terms were later classified under twelve categories, from "acts sociably" to "assaults." Similar classifications have been used for many years in experimental studies of small-group interaction and in psychological studies of behavior. Unfortunately, the use of ordinary English for behavioral description introduces a cultural bias, because actions that can be most easily named (codified) are most easily noticed or remembered by the observer. Some categorization is surely necessary, but it should not be arbitrarily imposed upon the data.

Faced with these problems, many anthropologists have looked to ethology, the scientific study of animal behavior, for ideas. In defining the field of "human ethology," Robin Fox and Usher Fleising state:

> The essence of the ethological approach is the acceptance of the synthetic theory of evolution as the master paradigm for the analysis of all life processes, including such uniquely human processes as language and culture. Human behavior then, like the behavior of any life form, must be analyzed in terms of its evolution and patterns of adaptation. (Fox and Fleising 1976:265)

Human ethologists use concepts and methods developed in the study of animal behavior. For example, child ethologists try to identify a list of objectively defined behavior units and then study their organization and development in a sample of children (Blurton Jones 1972; McGrew 1972). Because the quantity of data in such studies can be enormous, mathematical techniques such as sequence and factor analysis are employed to discover relationships and identify causal factors.

Some of the most impressive results of human ethology have been achieved by Paul Ekman and his associates in their cross-cultural studies of *facial expression*. They wished to test ideas first suggested a century ago by Charles Darwin. Darwin believed that facial expressions were universal in the human species, and that they had evolved from muscular responses of lower animals. However, many anthropologists who were impressed with the way culture could shape nonverbal behavior argued against Darwin's views. Some took the extreme position that all expressions of emotion were learned—that smiles, frowns, grimaces, and gestures were culture-specific. Others, while not denying the contribution of universal biological factors, pointed to the role of culture in shaping or "masking" the expression of joy, anger, or grief. That is, in every society some emotions are subject to *display rules*, "norms regarding the expected management of facial appearance" (Ekman 1973:176).

Ekman and his colleagues developed a "judgments task" in which they showed a standard set of photographs to people in various societies to find out "whether people from different cultures will judge the same emotion when viewing the same facial appearance" (p. 188). The investigators found remarkable agreement within and across five literate societies (the United States, Brazil, Chile, Argentina, and Japan) in judgments of photos representing six basic emotions. More than 85 percent of all subjects agreed on the photos showing happiness, disgust, or surprise, and a large majority also agreed in their judgments of sadness, anger, and fear. Furthermore, when asked to "rate each facial expression on a seven-point intensity scale," no significant differences were found between North American and Latin American subjects. (The Japanese were not tested on this scale.)

Although members of literate cultures made similar judgments of emotions one "loophole" remained: the similarities might be due to common visual experiences (for example, in the mass media). After all, "I Love Lucy" is a great favorite on Japanese television! But where can one today find people who are "visually isolated" from these ubiquitous stimuli? To overcome this problem, they went to New Guinea to study the Fore, a society that until a few years ago had been isolated from Western influence. They carefully selected only Fore subjects who had "seen no movies, neither spoke nor understood English or Pidgin, had not lived in any of the Western settlements or government towns, and had never worked for a Caucasian" (p. 211).

A form of the judgments task suitable for nonliterate people was administered to 189 Fore adults and 130 children. On most of the photographs, high levels of agreement with the other samples were found, although the Fore had some difficulty distinguishing "fear" from "surprise." Conversely, video tapes of Fore adults posing the basic emotions were accurately judged by American college students. These studies led Ekman to declare the need for a *neurocultural* theory to "account for both the universal elements (neurally determined) and the culture-specific (learned) element in facial expression" (p. 219). Universal elements do exist, and some of them have now been objectively measured. But we have yet to understand their adaptive basis or to discover the display rules that mask or distort them in specific societies. (For additional research on emotion, see chapter 12.)

Attachment, Separation, and Crowding

Clues to important behavioral regularities in human interaction have also been revealed by studies of nonhuman primates (apes and monkeys). These sources include the famous experimental studies conducted by Harry Harlow and the well-known field studies of Jane Goodall. Many less well-known works may be important to our understanding of human socialization. For example, studies of macaques (a genus of Old World monkeys) have shown a typical sequence of mother-infant interactions:

> At birth and for some time thereafter . . . the mother and infant are very close, physically and otherwise. A stage follows in which the infant makes efforts to disengage from the mother, but these efforts are frequently thwarted as the mother attempts to keep the infant close. Following this, however, there is a progressively greater apartness of the pair, which the mother either encourages or allows. The infant spends more and more time away from the mother, involved in play, increasingly with peers, as it develops autonomy and acquires the skills of its species and gender. (Kaufman 1975:133)

This general developmental sequence obviously bears strong similarities to mother-child interaction among human beings. Intensive studies of two macaque species by I. Charles Kaufman and his colleagues have demonstrated that, although the bonnet macaque and the pigtail macaque share many behaviors (including those described in the extract above), these species differ in three major ways:

- Bonnets tend to huddle in close physical contact with one another, even when sleeping, whereas pigtails do not often touch one another unless involved in social interactions such as grooming, mating, or fighting.

- When a mother macaque of either species is removed from the pen containing her four- to six-month-old infant, the infant becomes "agitated." Bonnet infants are quickly comforted and cared for by other adult females or by their own fathers. Pigtail infants seek comfort but receive no attention from other females or their fathers, and they may even be abused by the adults. Within a day or so, these infants show signs of intense depression similar to that displayed by human infants separated from their mothers. When the pigtail mother is returned to the pen, "there is usually a very intense reunion with increased closeness between mother and infant lasting for as many as three months after reunion. The reunion behavior is much less intense when a bonnet mother is returned" (Kaufman 1975:134).

• When groups of macaques are observed for several generations, it becomes apparent that pigtails interact much more with their "clanmates" (descendants of the same female ancestor) than do bonnets. This probably follows from the exclusive and intense contact between pigtail infants and their own mothers. Bonnet mothers, on the contrary, allow unrelated females to interact with their infants; while they provide good care of their infants, "bonnet mothers are less restrictive and more tolerant, that is, they allow infants to go and to return" (p. 138).

These observations suggest that the bonnets develop greater security than the pigtails because of the "multiple mothering" that is part of their social structure. Apparently, their feelings of security make it possible for them to move away from the mother sooner and to establish "initiative" and "autonomy," though they also display some emotional "shallowness" in reunions (cf. M. Mead 1949; Erikson 1950). Kaufman himself relates the species differences to some of Margaret Mead's ideas regarding styles of mothering and their consequences for child development, though he cautions us not to take monkeys too literally as models for human behavior (pp. 139–140).

It is much easier to carry out many hours of detailed observations on penned monkeys than on free humans, yet a few anthropologists have managed to collect behavioral data of great richness. For example, Patricia Draper has spent many months in the field intensively observing social interaction among the !Kung Bushmen of southern Africa. Fortunately for the anthropologist, these hunter-gatherers live mainly in the open, using their small brush shelters only for storing food, skins, and tools:

> Each hut, with its own hearth, is a marker signifying the residence of one nuclear family. Typically huts are so close that people sitting at different hearths can hand items back and forth without getting up. Often people sitting around various fires will carry on long discussions without raising their voices above normal conversational levels. (Draper 1973:302)

Despite the extremely low population density of the !Kung territory (approximately 1 person per 10 square miles), Draper found that the Bushmen choose to crowd together in their camps, using an average area of only 188 square feet per person (compared with the 350 square feet minimum recommended for Americans by the American Public Health Association). Furthermore, the !Kung showed none of the symptoms of stress usually produced by such crowding: "Blood pressures are low and do not rise with age, and serum cholesterol levels are among the lowest in the world" (p. 302).

Bushman children sometimes accompany their parents on foraging trips, but more often they are left at the base camp where they can be supervised by adults who are not working that day. Draper comments that "the single most striking feature of !Kung childhood is the extraordinary close association between children and adults" (p. 302). Her detailed observational data make possible statements such as the following:

> In a series of 165 systematically collected, randomized spot observations of 30 children living in the bush, girls (14 years and under) showed an average score of .77 on being inside the circle of huts. (In this usage, a "score" for each child is the proportion of spot observations during which the given behavior was observed.) Boys of the same age range had an average score of .50 on being inside the circle. One or more adults . . . was always present with the children within the village circle. (p. 303)

Spot observations of physical contact revealed that all !Kung touch each other a great deal. This characteristic is most pronounced in children: girls were touching at least one other person in 57 percent of the observations, while the average for boys was 35 percent. (See also Konner 1976.)

While Bushmen can evidently live in close quarters without experiencing stress, it should be remembered that they are still located in the "wide open spaces" of the Kalahari Desert and that, if tensions develop in a camp, any !Kung family can easily move to a different camp containing friends and relatives. Much of Draper's later work deals with behavioral changes that occur when Bushmen abandon the nomadic life and congregate in sedentary villages. She has shown the enormous impact of this situational change on socialization, findings of great importance to our understanding of the human condition in a rapidly urbanizing world.

Related studies have been carried out in other disciplines. The British psychiatrist John Bowlby (1973) has written eloquently of mother-child interactions, and especially of the traumatic effects on human children at certain ages of separation from the mother. In research combining psychoanalytic theory with ethological methods, Mahler, Pine, and Bergman (1975) established substages in infant development as indicated by the child's responses to brief separations from the mother.

Observational studies, then, can help us to understand the effects of different types of child care upon behavior. For example, James Chisholm's important book, *Navajo Infancy,* allows us to evaluate the role of prenatal experience, infant temperament (as measured during the first weeks of life), and cultural influences (such as the use of the cradle board) in producing behavioral regularities (Chisholm 1983).

One significant comparative study of attachment is that by Mary Ainsworth, who made careful observations of maternal behavior in Africa and the United States. Her early work among the Ganda (1967) indicated the importance of breast-feeding and body contact to the development of infant attachment. Ainsworth devised ingenious indices and measurements of behavior which she later applied to a sample of mothers in Baltimore, Maryland. Despite the vast difference in the incidence of breast-feeding (27 out of 28 in the African sample but only 4 out of 26 in the U.S.), Ainsworth found that maternal availability and responsiveness to infant signals were clearly related to the growth of "secure" attachments in both samples. Her detailed data also suggested that "a relatively large amount of physical contact of good quality in early infancy facilitates rather than hinders later development toward independent exploration and self-reliance . . . contrary to the fear of many [American] mothers that such treatment 'spoils' children" (Ainsworth 1977:146).

Less systematic in its observations but equally important in its social implications is Nancy Scheper-Hughes's (1985) study of maternal *detachment* in a Brazilian shantytown. Scheper-Hughes found that under conditions of extreme poverty and high child mortality, mothers tend to neglect passive and undemanding babies even though these "character traits" are usually signs of chronic malnutrition. Women in the shantytown rationalize their selective neglect with statements that some babies lack a strong drive to live. These are not cases of "child abuse" in the usual sense. These mothers pity their weak offspring and despise the idea of infanticide; they feel, however, that resources (including their own strength) are limited. They agree that "it is best if the weak and disabled die as infants . . . without a prolonged and wasted struggle" (1985:304).

Scheper-Hughes uses her data to question overstatements about maternal-infant "bonding" in the early days of life. She points out that infant life and death "carry different meanings, weight, and significance" to poor women in the shantytown than to the kinds of mothers generally studied in bonding research. Although the birth environment in Brazil appears "optimal for intense, early bonding to occur, mother-infant attachment is often muted and *protectively distanced*" (p. 311). That is, the mother develops an emotional "estrangement toward the infant that is protective to her but potentially lethal to the child" (p. 313).

Despite the many physical conditions (bad water, infectious disease, malnutrition) and cultural assumptions that contribute to infant death in the shantytown, Scheper-Hughes points out that some babies survive early neglect and eventually develop close, supportive relations with their mothers. Her conclusions sound an important message:

> That there must be a biological basis to human emotions is not disputed. It is argued, however, that the nature of human love and attachments is a complex phenomenon, socially constructed and made meaningful through culture. (p. 314)

We shall return to this point in chapter 12.

Sociobiology

The past fifteen years have seen the development of a challenging new approach to behavior called *sociobiology* (Wilson 1975). Although first used in the study of insect societies, sociobiology is now applied to all species, including humans. It shares with ethology the careful observation of behavior, usually in natural settings, and the assumption that genetic selection is responsible for behavioral adaptations as well as anatomical ones. Sociobiology interprets observations by means of evolutionary biology, asking in each case what a given form of behavior contributes to the *reproductive success* of the organisms involved (the number of offspring or genes they contribute to the next generation). All kinds of behavior—aggressive or altruistic, parental or possessive—are demonstrated (or at least claimed) to be adaptations to present or past environments (see Barash 1982).

For example, parental behavior varies greatly among even closely related species of animals. Some species produce a great many eggs but leave the young to fend for themselves; others produce few offspring but "invest" a great deal of time and energy into care and protection of the developing young, often at risk to their own lives. One or both parents may be involved in the parental effort. Which of these "reproductive strategies" is adopted by a species can be shown to depend on a number of ecological factors (resource distribution, predators, disease, etc.), and the strategy is viewed as an evolved adaptation to that situation, though not necessarily as the *best* adaptation. Similar explanations are given for the size of social groups, competition for territory, food preferences, cooperation among related individuals, and so forth.

This is not the place to consider the claims or criticisms of sociobiology as applied to human affairs. (See Alexander 1979 for broad application of sociobiology to human behavior; Sahlins 1976 presents an impassioned critique.) To the extent that evolutionary theory makes clear and testable predictions about behavior such as parental investment or courtship, it provides an important and stimulating alternative to other approaches. But like human ethology, sociobiology may fall into a trap when it comes to categorizing forms of behavior (for example, "rape" among mallard ducks, or "adultery" among bluebirds) and assuming equivalence of meanings. Some studies use the methods of cross-cultural correlational analysis with all the questionable assumptions and dubious data of that approach. As Jerome Barkow (1984:377) has cautioned, the failure of sociobiologists to be explicit about their psychological assumptions "leads to the repetition of the archaic errors of logic of the old culture-and-personality school."

We should also recognize that sociobiology is a *materialist* approach. It views human social behavior and culture as determined by the composition of a population's gene pool, which changes in response to material conditions that provide new opportunities to enhance one's reproductive fitness. According to Barash (1982:45–46), the *central principle of sociobiology* states that "individuals will tend to behave in a manner that maximizes . . . their success in projecting copies of their genes into succeeding generations." From the viewpoint of the "selfish gene," all else is superstructure (Dawkins 1976).

It is ironic that Marxists, who also reduce cultural differences to material interests and conditions of work (chapter 8), have been among the strongest critics of sociobiology, on both scientific and political grounds. In general, sociobiology has appealed to political conservatives who tend to interpret group and gender differences as innate and relatively unchangeable. But to say that behavior is genetically influenced is not necessarily to say it cannot change, and a synthesis of sociobiology with, say, historical materialism, is not an impossibility (see Irons 1979). However, like the decision to take the interpretive stance of psychoanalysis or Marxism, the adoption of a sociobiological view of the world has many of the characteristics of a religious conversion, and it frequently extends outward to cover all aspects of experience, resisting integration with other ideologies (see Dawkins 1982).

Psychological anthropologists can no longer afford to be naive about human biology and genetics. Imaginative studies of the behavior of primates and other animals are both challenging and suggestive: the ethological approach can, with care, be extended to human beings, and it may help us to understand emotional expression and the consequences of different forms of child care. Sociobiology offers a longterm, adaptational perspective on a range of important topics. But each of these research traditions has weaknesses as well as strengths, and it would be premature to capitulate to any of them. For the concerns of psychological anthropology cannot be reduced to objective measurements of behavior, nor can ancient moral dilemmas be resolved by labeling certain behavior patterns "natural" or "adaptive" (Oyama 1986:87–92).

Human actions are embedded in a web of social meanings and individual self-awareness. In the tension between social norms and individual acts, each constantly modifies the other. As Robert Murphy put it,

> The relationship between mind . . . and society is not . . . unilaterally causal, but is one of interplay and conflict. In this oppositional setting, neither mind nor society emerges wholly victorious, for each is a product of the struggle and neither is completely reducible to the other. Social life is not a mechanism, or even an organism, but a dialectic. (Murphy 1971:85)

Language plays an essential part in our articulation of experience and our communication of constructed meanings to others. In the next chapter, I turn to several comparative studies of human thinking, most of which use language as an essential clue to understanding the relation of culture to cognition.

Supplement, 1999

Bronislaw Malinowski, whose picture adorns the opening of this chapter, was a great observer of "natives" and of himself. His contributions to psychological anthropology included his insistence on extended "participant observation" and linguistic fluency, together with the attempt to understand the *functions* of seeming irrational behaviors (i.e., what strange customs accomplished in terms of satisfying personal and social needs). His encounter with Freudian psychoanalysis is detailed in an article by George W. Stocking, Jr. (1987), together with a description of the extraordinary *resistance* of orthodox psychoanalysts to observational data. A posthumous work by Ernest Gellner (1998) examines philosophical influences on Malinowski's thought.

Behavioral observation sounds simpler than it is. For example, McGrew and Marchant (1994) have discussed the difficulty of deciding whether different species of apes and monkeys display "handedness" such as all humans do. Following many hours of careful observations and comparative studies, they were able to suggest the existence of "strong hand preferences and weak task specialization in other primates, at least for tool use tasks in chimpanzees, but no compelling signs of manual specialization or handedness" (1994:176). (In human populations, the percentage of observed or reported *left* handedness ranges from under 5 percent in two studies in Africa to about 10 percent in

American and Japanese studies. The highest yet reported is over 22 percent in a Native American group. No one knows what kind of selective pressures might produce such differences.)

In the same volume, Ruth and Robert Munroe discuss methods for field observations of behavior with special attention to observations of "child life." The advent of inexpensive video recording has made possible "a more fine-grained observational approach," while, as they point out, future research needs "to integrate observational approaches with other sources of data" such as interviews with parents (1994:264–265).

At some point, of course, if data is to be treated quantitatively, someone must decide into what category a given sequence of actions falls, and this is the crucial act that gives *meaning* to observations. It is also the point at which cultural or theoretical bias can most easily enter. For instance, where is the "line" between teasing and hostility, or between flirtation and "unwanted sexual overtures"? And can we validly make such discriminations in our own society, much less an alien one?

Human ethology and sociobiology continue to be important sources of ideas, some of which are discussed in the final chapter of this book under the heading of "Evolutionary Psychological Anthropology." Edward O. Wilson has recently claimed a central position for biology in the understanding of human behavior. His concept of *consilience* refers to a bringing together of information from different disciplines to create a single, unified science. Within this reductive scheme, anthropology will take its proper place, for, as Wilson writes, "Nothing fundamental separates the course of human history from the course of physical history, whether in the stars or in organic diversity" (1998). He views evolutionary biology as the bridge from the natural sciences to the social sciences and humanities. Wilson may be right, but he may also be indulging in the wishful thinking for which our species is famously adapted.

Research on attachment and separation in animals and humans suggests that there are critical periods of development during which organisms can be helped or harmed by caretakers. As Rogoff and Morelli (1994:237) observed, in many cultures, "adults guide children in carrying out activities that are beyond the children's individual skills, and this joint problem solving provides children with information appropriate to stretch their individual skills." But this is not always the case, for child abuse can be passive as well as active. (For a history of the study of human development in anthropology, see Harkness 1992.)

Current controversy revolves around the claims made by Judith Harris in *The Nurture Assumption* (1998), that parental behavior is much less important to child development than previously thought. Harris contends that genetic dispositions and experience with peers account for most of one's adult personality and she cites, with other evidence, studies of identical twins raised apart who resemble each other psychologically in quite amazing ways. Such twin studies had given pause to psychologists for some time.

The weak points in Harris's argument have to do with her assumptions about the independence of genetic features from environmental conditions and the absence of any real data on the peer groups that children either enter or admire from afar. (On the interaction between genes and environment see Oyama 1994.) American psychologists have probably overestimated the influence that parents can exert on their children, especially during adolescence, but before we throw the parents out with the bathwater, it would be wise to ask where "peer culture" comes from. Who or what creates, perpetuates, reproduces, and changes the cultural environment? And do we dare to take American experience at the end of the twentieth century as a model of what happens in families throughout the world?

There is a further fallacy built into the reasoning that because two children who are "raised the same way" often turn out differently, parenting hardly counts. Genetic differences are surely part of the story, but the key phrase is "the same way." Having older or younger siblings, coming into a family (and a society) at a different point in its development and, above all, responding differently to subtle differences in parental treatment may account for very different outcomes. It is a tempting mistake to blame one's parents for whatever goes wrong in one's life, but it is equally fallacious to say that they had no influence on or responsibility for one's successes!

These considerations bring us back to the important question of perception: Do you see (or otherwise experience) what I see? Culture provides us with standard "categories of experience" as well as "plans for action" in response to these categories (Bock 1974), but *culture does not determine our behavior.* The ability to think "outside the box" is recognized as the essence of creativity. Neurobiology is beginning to explain how the brain operates and the part that social and personal "representations" play in our perceptions (Worthman 1992). Indeed, this is an area of research that holds great importance for the future of psychological anthropology. Once again, the Gestalt principle holds true that any perception is always part of a larger pattern.

Chapter 10

Cognitive
Anthropology

Claude Lévi-Strauss

The final goal of ethnography, according to Bronislaw Malinowski, should be "to grasp the native's point of view, his relation to life, to realize *his* vision of *his* world" (1961:25; original, 1922). Many anthropologists have expressed interest in "how the natives (both male and female) think." But to what extent can cultural differences be explained by differences in the thought processes of individuals in diverse societies? If such cognitive differences exist, are they due to biological or environmental factors? To what degree are they modifiable by experience? And what can cross-cultural studies of cognition teach us about our *own* habits of thought?

In chapter 1, we considered the views of Tylor, Frazer, Lévy-Bruhl, and Boas on the question of "primitive mentality." Like Boas, Malinowski believed that language was an important key to understanding native thought: both men stressed the importance of collecting extended texts in the native language. Paul Radin, a student of Boas, collected texts of American Indian myths, to which he applied ideas derived from Jungian psychology. In 1927, Radin wrote an influential book, *Primitive Man as Philosopher,* in which he demonstrated the speculative and logical powers of so-called primitives.

One modern heir to this approach was the late Dorothy Lee. Her sensitive essays suggested ways that differences among languages affect the individual's sense of self, of time, and of causation (Lee 1959). Her style of writing and her attempts to synthesize data of various types are reminiscent of Ruth Benedict and Edward Sapir; however, like Irving Hallowell and Paul Radin, Lee fits into no particular school or approach. Her influence has been mainly transmitted by a small group of students.

Although other issues dominated the field after World War II, interest in primitive thought never completely vanished from American anthropology. Starting in the mid-1950s, however, concern with human thought processes reappeared in several different quarters, leading to the emergence of a school of cognitive anthropology (Tyler 1969). In the following sections, we shall trace the emergence of this school and its relation to developments in other disciplines.

Ethnosemantics

For many decades, American linguistics was a formal, descriptive science concerned largely with sound systems and syntax to the neglect of semantics. Anthropologists trained in this discipline used language as a practical research tool, and some improvised ways of using the native language to explore unique cultural meanings (see Hymes 1964). When new methods were developed in linguistics for analyzing semantic relationships, anthropologists were quick to take an interest in and to use these methods for their own purposes.

This approach to understanding native systems of meaning through language became known as *ethnosemantics*. In the hands of skilled ethnographers such as Harold Conklin, Ward Goodenough, and Charles Frake, a variety of topics were studied. Ethnosemanticists set themselves the goal of understanding how cultural knowledge is organized (Spradley 1972). They systematically investigated *semantic domains* (areas of meaning) such as kinship terms, disease categories, and color terminology, carefully defining individual terms and showing each term's relationship to other terms in the domain. They also compared the structure of semantic domains within and across languages, and sought to understand how people *use* such cultural knowledge to interpret behavior and make decisions.

Even the simple task of "getting names for things" turned out to be much more complicated than had been suspected. The ethnosemanticist must learn to ask the right kinds of questions if the informants' answers are to be really meaningful. As Frake observed,

> an ethnographer should strive to define objects according to the conceptual system of the people he is studying. [One should] look upon the task of getting names for things not as an exercise in linguistic recording, but [as] a way of finding out what are in fact the "things" in the environment of the people being studied. . . . The analysis of a culture's terminology will not . . . exhaustively reveal the cognitive world of its members, but it will tap a central portion of it. (Frake 1962:74–75)

One technique used in the study of semantic domains is called *componential analysis*. This technique helps us to discover the "dimensions of meaning" that differentiate the terms in a domain and to display the relationships of contrast and hierarchy among the terms. For example, the English subject pronouns contrast in terms of the dimensions of *person* (first, second, third), *number* (singular, plural), and, in one case, *gender* (masculine, feminine). This differentiation is schematized in table 10-1.

French subject pronouns use these three dimensions, extending the gender contrast to the third person plural pronouns (*ils, elles*). The French pronouns also include two different forms for second person singular (*tu, vous*), which introduce an additional dimension of meaning, usually called *intimacy* (familiar, formal), as shown in table 10-2. This display is quite similar to the previous one, for English and French are

Table 10-1 Subject pronouns in English

Number	Person and gender		
	First	Second	Third
Singular	I	You	He (m.), She (f.)
Plural	We	You	They

Table 10-2 Subject pronouns in French

Number	Person, intimacy level, and gender		
	First	Second	Third
Singular	*Je*	*Tu, Vous*	*Il* (m.), *Elle* (f.)
Plural	*Nous*	*Vous*	*Ils* (m.), *Elles* (f.)

closely related languages; nevertheless, there are significant differences between them. In some languages (including classical Greek) there is also a *dual* number so that the second person pronoun indicates whether one is speaking to one, exactly two, or more than two persons.

The "components" of a componential analysis are the semantic values of a term on each relevant dimension of meaning. For example, the components of *she* are third person, singular, and feminine on the dimensions of person, number, and gender, respectively. Anthropologists have used componential analysis to discover the dimensions of meaning in the domain of kinship terms (see Tyler 1969). In English, for example, the terms *grandfather, father, son,* and *grandson* contrast with one another on the dimension of *generation*, and the entire set contrasts with the terms *grandmother, mother, daughter,* and *granddaughter* on the dimension of *sex*. These eight terms may be displayed to bring out their contrasts and similarities as in table 10-3; however, it is only when they are contrasted with all the other English kin terms (including *cousin* and *sister-in-law*) that the full range of components is realized. In other languages, quite different dimensions and components may be used to contrast kinship terms (see Burling 1970; Frake 1980).

Besides contrasting on one or more dimensions of meaning, many terms in a semantic domain stand in *hierarchical relations* to one another. For example, a *father* is a kind of *parent*, and a *parent* is a kind of *relative*. This relationship of class inclusion can be displayed in a tree diagram such as figure 10-1, where the general terms are above and connected by lines to the specific terms they include. (For a formal method of generating such trees and their components, see Bock 1968.) Terms

Table 10-3 Contrasts among some English kinship terms on two dimensions (generation and sex)

| | Sex | |
Generation	Male	Female
+2	Grandfather	Grandmother
+1	Father	Mother
−1	Son	Daughter
−2	Grandson	Granddaughter

on the same horizontal level in such a diagram contrast with one another on dimensions of meaning (sex, generation, and the like), but terms on different levels do not directly contrast with one another. Instead, lower-level terms are related to higher-level terms as species to genus, part to whole, ingredient to mixture, and so forth, depending on the specific domain.

Ethnosemantic studies of anatomy investigate cultural conceptions of the human body, its parts and their functions. These studies have shown that not all societies divide up the body in the same way. Our notion of what constitute body parts (for example, shoulder, hip, or foot) and of how these parts relate to one another (*finger* is part of *hand*, which is part of *lower arm*) are far from universal. For example, the Kewa of New Guinea have terms for body parts that we would roughly translate as *back*, *chest*, and *arms*, but these parts are considered parts of a unit called kádésaa, a term that has no simple English equivalent (Franklin 1963). Kewa body parts are also associated with distinctive physiological and spiritual functions peculiar to Kewa culture. (See Bock 1984, chapter 10.)

One of the most interesting studies of this domain is the Navajo anatomical atlas compiled by Oswald Werner and his colleagues, a work that demonstrates the remarkable amount of anatomical knowledge accumulated in traditional Navajo culture. It specifies hundreds of dif-

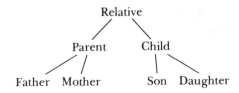

Figure 10-1 Hierarchical relations among some English kinship terms.

ferent terms (some for minute bodily structures) and complex relations among them. This Navajo ethnoscience is in error only where the Navajo have transferred to human anatomy structures that they learned about in butchering sheep and other mammals. (These are exactly the kinds of errors that persisted in European anatomy books for hundreds of years, including the centuries when dissection of human cadavers was forbidden by the Roman Catholic church. In the Navajo case, the traditional fear of corpses contributed to lack of direct knowledge.)

Another area of continuing interest is the ethnosemantic analysis of *color terminology*. Each language has a set of terms that partitions the domain of color, but languages differ in the number of basic terms and the range of colors to which each term refers. In reaction against ethnocentric notions about "primitive languages," American anthropologists usually argued that the size of a color lexicon was unimportant, since all such systems were arbitrary and one way of partitioning the visible spectrum was as good as the next.

During the late 1960s, however, anthropologists at the Language Behavior Laboratory at Berkeley began to uncover a fascinating pattern in the color terms found in hundreds of languages. When one examines the *basic* color terms (words such as *red* or *blue,* but not *scarlet,* or *cerulean*), it appears that the number of such terms in a language is closely related to the kinds of colors they designate. Brent Berlin and Paul Kay published an exciting study, *Basic Color Terms* (1969), suggesting that color terminology evolves from simple to complex, with new terms being added in a fixed order. In the few languages that have only two basic color terms the domain is simply divided into "light" and "dark," but languages that have three basic color terms *always* refer to white, black, and red. Five-term systems always have these first three plus yellow and green, and the sixth term added is always blue, which takes over some of the hues formerly included in black and green. In seven-term systems, brown is added, and this term is found only in systems that have at least six other terms. There are four other basic terms (gray, pink, orange, and purple), but these do not appear to be added in any particular order.

Minor modifications have been made in the Berlin and Kay analysis since it first appeared, but controversy continues over its significance. What produces these regularities in color lexicons? Could they be due to biological universals? The regularities are too widespread to be entirely accounted for by the historical diffusion of words or ways of categorizing. Furthermore, an undeniable correlation exists between size of color lexicon of a language and level of social and technological complexity of its speakers. As summarized by Robbins Burling, languages with two terms are confined to people with the simplest level of technology, such as the New Guinea Jalé. At the other extreme, the only languages known to have terms for all eleven [basic colors] are from Europe and east Asia where the people have long histories, and great complexity in their culture and technology. Between these extremes are people like the Tiv, a rather simple African tribe of Nigeria with three terms, the Hanunóo tribe of the Philippines with four, the Eskimo with five, some rather complex African tribes with six, the Malayalam of southern India and the Burmese with seven. (Burling 1970:48)

Other studies suggest that there may be a physiological basis for the distribution of color terminologies. Marc H. Bornstein (1975) draws on recent work in color vision that indicates that people with dark retinal pigmentation have impaired vision in the blue-green part of the spectrum, whereas light-eyed people are relatively more sensitive to color differences. Bornstein demonstrates that societies with small color lexicons cluster in the latitudes near the equator, where populations with high frequencies of dark eye pigmentation are found. Melvin Ember has recently shown that latitude and level of social complexity appear to interact (statistically) in determining the size of color lexicons:

High societal complexity predicts large basic color lexicon *only* in the relatively higher latitudes . . . and high latitude predicts a large basic color lexicon *only* where social complexity is high. [These facts] suggest that we have an example here of cultural and biological factors interacting as determinants of a semantic domain. (Ember 1978:366–367)

The color-term controversy will doubtless continue for many years. It is a good example of the way in which ethnosemantic studies can lead to hypotheses about human cognition. We cannot *assume* that differences among languages correspond to group differences in perception or thinking, but imaginative ways are being found to test ideas about these topics. Intensive field studies of native systems of classification ("folk taxonomies") have focused on plants, animals, body parts, color terms, and classifications of everyday objects (Conklin 1972; Rosch 1975). All such studies can contribute to our understanding of human thought, but they must be interpreted with great caution.

An anthology of works on cognitive anthropology (Dougherty 1985) illustrates some of the recent changes that have taken place in ethnosemantic studies. In particular, the article "The Utilitarian Factor in Folk Classification," by Eugene Hunn, suggests that we have focused too exclusively on the formal and intellectual character of folk taxonomies. In his own studies of New World plant classification, Hunn discovered the relevance of *practical criteria* to the complexity of taxonomies. American Indians, he argues, possess elaborate classifications of plants that are useful (as food or raw materials) and of those that are dangerous or easily confused with useful species, but they simply disregard many other species. Plants that have no practical significance may be lumped together under a label meaning "just a grass" or "some shrub" (similar to the English category "weed"). However, the labels for these residual categories may be mistaken by interpreters for names of general classes (such as our terms "mammal" or "bird"). When this happens, practical native taxonomies may be forced into the hierarchical model of Western biology. Hunn (1985:118) writes, "We have unduly stressed the disinterested intellectualism of our informants, and as a consequence have taken for granted their practical wisdom. . . . To properly appreciate the achievements of folk science, we need to investigate its practical significance as assiduously as we have its formal order." (See Werner and Schoepfle 1987.)

Cognitive Development: Stages, Styles, and Maps

A second group of approaches in cognitive anthropology is concerned with development and functioning. Most of them address differential development of thought processes in various cultures and environments. Topics studied range from perceptual learning to mathematical and moral reasoning, but all have been influenced by the work of the great Swiss psychologist Jean Piaget.

Piaget's studies of cognition began in the 1920s and include major books on play, imitation, and the development of moral judgment as well as children's conceptions of time, space, number, and logic. Piaget is best known to American psychologists and educators for his work on stages of intellectual development. His concepts of *sensory-motor schema* and *operational intelligence* have become as popular in some circles as Freudian concepts once were. Much of contemporary cross-cultural psychology is intended to validate or modify Piaget's ideas.

Essentially, Piaget holds that knowledge is not a "passive copy of reality" but rather an active construction that the individual achieves in the course of time:

> Knowing an object does not mean copying it—it means acting upon it. It means constructing systems of transformations that can be carried out on or with this object. . . . Knowledge, then, is a system of transformations that become progressively adequate. (Piaget 1971:15)

Piaget believes that there are *universal stages of cognitive development.* Children learn about reality first by perceptual and motor exploration of their world and then by acquiring mental operations, such as seriation, conservation, and propositional thought, that enable them to transform their experience without actually manipulating the environment. All normal children are said to master these operations in the same order, though at somewhat different ages (Murray 1972).

Claims about universal cognitive stages must be validated by cross-cultural research. Piaget was fully aware of this, and in *The Child and Reality* he posed these important questions: "Does the life cycle express a basic biological rhythm, an ineluctable law? Does civilization modify this rhythm and to what extent? In other words, is it possible to increase or decrease this temporal development" (Piaget 1973:1–2)? Most research on these questions has been carried out by cognitive psychologists rather than by psychological anthropologists, but the results are highly relevant to anthropological problems (see Dasen 1972). We wish to know whether Piaget's stages are indeed universal and, if so, how they are modified by social experience (culture).

A great deal of attention has been devoted to Piaget's concept of *conservation,* that is, the child's recognition that some things remain "the same" despite transformations of physical properties. For example, to study conservation of volume, the experimenter may pour liquid from a short, wide beaker (A) into a tall, narrow one (B). Children can see that all the water in A has been poured into B, but up to the age of about six they will usually insist that there is a different amount of water in the second beaker. When children learn to judge the volume of water to be equal despite the transformation of shape, they are said to have mastered the concept of conservation of volume.

A number of studies seem to indicate significant cultural differences in the mastery of such basic concepts. For example, conservation concepts that most American children learn by age seven (when they have entered elementary school) may be learned several years later by non-Western children, especially in societies that have no formal educational institutions. However, as Cole and Scribner comment, even within a single society, "performance depends on how the task is presented and the particular past experiences of the subjects (as for instance, whether they live in a rural town or the city, and whether or not they attend school)" (Cole and Scribner 1974:151). Before leaping to conclusions about primitive mentality, we must carefully consider such factors as the content of tests and the familiarity of test materials.

Another of Piaget's conservation tests involves two identical balls of clay. When one of the balls is rolled out into a long "sausage," children who lack the conservation concept report that the amounts of clay are now different. To assess the effect of familiarity with test materials on outcome, Douglass R. Price-Williams, W. Gordon, and M. Ramirez (1969) went to a Mexican village where many families of potters lived. They tested seventy-six children between six and nine years old, half from potter families and half from nonpotter families. As might be expected, children of potters did much better on the tests using clay than did the other children. (They also did somewhat better on other conservation tests.)

It has been difficult to correlate performance on conservation tests with other cognitive skills; however, as in Piaget's original work, many valuable data do not appear in the summaries of results. Piaget developed subtle ways of interviewing that reveal the *kinds of reasoning* that lie behind a child's actions or judgments. The Piagetian method of inquiry has as much to offer to psychological anthropology as do the proposed developmental stages. (The same might be said of psychoanalysis.)

The French anthropologist Claude Lévi-Strauss is another European scholar who has written about universals of human cognition. Like some psychoanalytic anthropologists, Lévi-Strauss works from cultural rather than individual data, attempting to infer properties of the human mind from myths and from social structures.

In his best-known book, ironically titled *The Savage Mind,* Lévi-Strauss asserts that no significant differences exist between the mental capacities of civilized and primitive peoples. He argues, rather, that many preliterates employ a "style of thinking" in which the *sensible* qualities of objects and organisms (size, color, odor, and the like) are used in the construction of categories and the performance of logical operations, rather than the *abstract* qualities that Western science has found useful (mass, frequency, acceleration, and so on). Use of this style, Lévi-Strauss argues, is not evidence of confused thinking. Magic and mythical thought have a logic as rigorous as that of science, and they are based on "a complete and all-embracing determinism" (Lévi-Strauss 1966:11). The accomplishments of mythical thought are also to be admired: the development of pottery, weaving, agriculture, and animal domestication all "required a genuinely scientific attitude, sustained and watchful interest and a desire for knowledge for its own sake" (p. 14).

In the same book, and from a perspective closer to Piaget's than Freud's, Lévi-Strauss takes up the topic of totemism and its relationship to food taboos. He suggests that totemic societies use food taboos to *deny man's animal nature* (p. 108). Taboos function to support essential distinctions between categories: human versus animal, man versus woman, friend versus enemy, and so forth. Lévi-Strauss shows that mythical thought encounters exactly the same intellectual problems that have troubled Western philosophers for centuries in trying to comprehend the mystery of human origins and our place in the universe.

The phrase *cognitive style* is most closely associated with H. A. Witkin's theory concerning general modes of psychological functioning. Witkin (1967) argued that individuals differ in their approaches to cognitive and perceptual tasks: People with a "global" style respond to the general characteristics of a situation, whereas those with "articulated" styles are more able to differentiate component features of their environments. (For an early discussion of global versus differentiated perception, see Murphy 1947:331–361.)

Witkin also introduced the concepts of *field-dependence* and *field-independence* to denote the perceptual abilities of global and articulated thinkers, respectively. Field-dependent people have difficulty picking out geometric forms embedded in complex figures, whereas field-independent people are better at decomposing such configurations. Both environmental and cultural factors (child training) have been shown to contribute to cognitive articulation. (See Cole and Scribner 1974:82–90; Berry 1976; Serpell 1976:51–54.)

The concept of *cognitive maps* is somewhat less elusive than the notion of cognitive styles. It was first formulated by Edward C. Tolman in the classic paper "Cognitive Maps in Rats and Men" (1948). Tolman noted a number of behavioral phenomena that the mechanistic behaviorism of his time could not explain. For example, hungry rats who had run through a maze ten times without receiving a food reward at the exit seemed to learn very slowly compared with rats who were rewarded. However, if the first group was rewarded on the eleventh trial, they showed a sudden marked improvement in performance from then on. Tolman argued that the unrewarded rats had nevertheless built up cognitive maps of the maze while exploring it on the first ten trials; when the reward was offered and incentive provided, these maps enabled them to perform quickly and with few errors.

Other experiments seem to confirm the idea that organisms develop maplike concepts of their environments and that these maps include many features they have never been rewarded for learning. Cognitive maps are not just narrow "strips" showing starting point, route, and destination, but are often broad and "comprehensive." Tolman (1958:261) lists four factors that induce narrowness in rats and humans:

- Brain damage
- Inadequate environmental cues (what we would today call an "impoverished environment")
- Overlearning by repetition in early training
- Overmotivation or intense frustration

Assuming that one favors broad, comprehensive knowledge, these points have obvious implications for child training and education. Tolman also suggests that the Freudian defense mechanisms of regression, fixation, and displacement are instances of people adopting (or returning to) extremely narrow cognitive maps under conditions of strong motivation or intense frustration.

The concept of cognitive maps was used and reinterpreted by a number of anthropologists in the 1960s. In ethnosemantic studies the term refers to the contrastive and hierarchical relationships among the categories of a semantic domain. For example, the use of one term rather than another in a given context (*she* rather than *he*, *bush* rather than *tree*) allows the ethnoscientist to discover "the category boundaries on a culture's cognitive map" (Frake 1962:77).

Anthony Wallace stayed closer to Tolman's meaning; he incorporated the term into his own concept of the *mazeway*, defined as "the sum of all the cognitive maps which at any moment a person maintains" (1965:277). Wallace argued that even simple tasks such as tending a fire or driving to work require a high level of cognitive complexity, including action plans and rules, control operations, monitored information, and organization. (George Foster's "image of limited good," discussed in chapter 8, is also a kind of cognitive map that can be used to account for peasant behavior.)

Kevin Lynch, an architect at MIT, used the map concept quite literally in his book *The Image of the City*. His detailed interviews with the inhabitants of three cities revealed systematic differences in the cognitive maps these people had of their respective urban environments. There were differences in the degree to which each group cognized its city by means of landmarks, districts, paths, edges, or "nodes," and in their use of these elements to orient themselves when traveling (Lynch 1964:46–90). Dean MacCannell (1976) used a similar approach to study the role of *tourism* in the development of people's cognitive maps of the modern world.

The most useful recent treatment of this topic is Ulrich Neisser's book *Cognition and Reality* (1976:108–127). Neisser argues that cognitive maps are not just passive images of the environment; rather, they are active, information-seeking structures that *direct* our perceptual exploration of the world. Guided by our general maps and the specific "perceptual schemata" embedded in them, we *sample* the information present in the environment; this process frequently leads us to *modify* our conceptions of the world. Our new conceptions then direct renewed exploration, creating a continuing cyclical process (see figure 10-2).

Neisser's treatment of cognitive maps and perceptual schemata is highly compatible with my own views on the relation of culture to behavior.

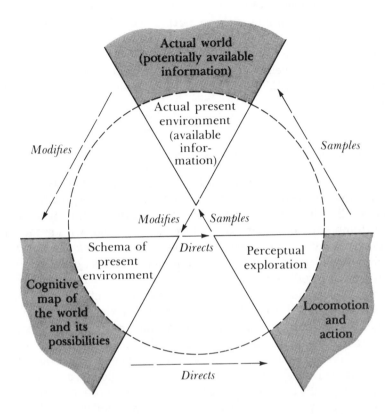

Figure 10-2 The "perceptual cycle," showing schemata embedded in cognitive maps, directing perceptual exploration of the environment, and being modified by the results of that exploration. (Neisser 1976).

For many years I have argued that culture consists of *categories of experience* associated with *plans for action* (Bock 1974). We can infer the existence and structure of these categories and plans from the regularities of verbal and nonverbal behavior they produce. The capacity to learn the conventional categories and plans of one's community is fundamental to a human level of existence.

These cultural structures *influence* but do not completely determine behavior, and they can be modified by experience. Furthermore, I believe that the *meaning* of a cultural element, be it a word, a social role, or an artifact, is defined by its contrastive relations with similar types of elements and by the types of situations in which it is expected to occur

(Bock 1986). This theory of culture is "psychological" in that it explicitly presupposes that all humans share certain cognitive capacities. I fully endorse Neisser's statement that "actions are hierarchically embedded in more extensive actions and are motivated by anticipated consequences at various levels of schematic organization" (Neisser 1976:113). See Smith and Medin (1981) for a useful discussion of the process of categorization.

Race, Culture, and Intelligence

All normal people do acquire the basic cognitive skills necessary for social life in their respective cultures. This fact does not logically exclude the possibility of significant group differences in mental capacity, but most attempts to document such differences have met with great difficulties. Since investigators now agree that *there is no such thing as a culture-free test of intelligence*, any claims about ethnic, class, or racial differences in intelligence must be examined with great caution. For a brief and thoughtful discussion of the issues, I know of no better source than Price-Williams' essay, "The Cultural Relativism of Intelligence" (1975:51–64). I shall draw heavily on this essay in the following pages.

To avoid the problem of defining intelligence, many psychologists subscribe to the circular statement "Intelligence is whatever intelligence tests measure." But no intelligence test can do more than *sample* the cognitive abilities of those who take it. Furthermore, an intelligence test is itself the product of a particular cultural tradition in which certain cognitive styles and skills are valued while others are disparaged. Even within a complex society some groups may place more emphasis on skills such as rote memory or rapid arithmetical calculations than do other groups. Are any of these skills valid indices of intelligence for all people?

Using tests constructed for and validated on Western populations to assess non-Western peoples introduces enormous problems of interpretation. Cross-cultural studies must be especially sensitive to the multitude of factors that can influence performance (see "Perception, or 'Do You See What I See?'" in chapter 1). According to Price-Williams,

> psychologists seem to have followed just the wrong sequence in probing other cultures. Instead of first exploring the social environment of the tested and examining cognitive skills such as classification, sorting and discrimination, and then constructing tests to accommodate such background knowledge, the tendency has been to impose tests already constructed for another culture. Then the researcher finds out what should have been modified, excluded or otherwise al-

tered in the tests, and only afterward does he look around for influencing social factors. (1975:55)

Social change is another factor that may interfere with attempts to measure intelligence. Industrial technology makes certain demands on the populations that use it, and in the process of meeting these demands for literacy and "linear" thinking, school systems in developing countries become increasingly homogeneous. Western intelligence tests assess readiness for this type of schooling—indeed, that is what they were invented to do. For this reason they may be of use in industrializing societies, but this does not mean that they measure any *general capacity* of individuals. In fact, there is little evidence that IQ scores bear much relationship to occupational success or creative achievement in our own society.

Remember that the dominant Anglo-American culture is exceptionally individualistic in its values and practices (see "The Lonely Crowd," chapter 5). In consequence, we evaluate intelligence with a strong individualistic bias. However, we should be aware that

> many societies do not go about solving problems individually but in groups; that tackling artificial tasks in the abstract is an alien challenge; that methods of instruction and the subsequent learning process are not to be differentiated from the rest of living; that the notion of doing something within a predetermined time, let alone with haste, is again foreign. (Price-Williams 1975:58)

There are, then, different styles of intelligence and perhaps even qualitatively different kinds of intelligence.

The concept of intelligence is itself a social product. An ethnosemantic investigation of this domain might begin with the analysis of words used in different cultures to refer to cognitive abilities. For example, the exceptionally intelligent child in American society is usually said to be "bright," while the exceptional French child is described as "wise" *(sage)*; the corresponding term in Mexico means "ready" *(listo)*. In the Shona language of Zimbabwe the word closest to our "intelligence" is *ngware*, but this term also carries the connotations of "caution, prudence, and wisdom, particularly in social matters" (Price-Williams 1975:60).

Even at this superficial level we seem to be dealing with four quite different conceptions of intelligence. This observation does not mean we should abandon cross-cultural research, but it should put us on guard against "a facile comparison, based on category schemes that are not sufficiently representative of the cognitive domains of any one of the cultures being compared" (Price-Williams 1975:64). These cautions also apply to research on racial and ethnic differences within a complex society.

In the mid-1980s, then, cognitive anthropology appears to be alive and well. The big questions about "how the natives think" remain unanswered, but we do have some new methods for approaching them. We have gained a fuller understanding of the content and processes of folk classification in domains such as plant names, color terms, and artifacts (Casson 1981; Dougherty 1985). The works of Jean Piaget continue to stimulate research into cognitive development, free now of the assumption that a universal sequence of stages is already established. And a healthy skepticism accompanies the search for transcultural criteria of intelligence, for we now acknowledge the intellectual achievements of the Navajo singer, the Nuer herder, the Papuan big man, and the Hawaiian genealogist, whose memories (and creativity) far surpass those of many literate city dwellers.

Much remains to be done, but psychological anthropology is beginning to form a synthesis between cognitive and dynamic approaches. Whether such a synthesis can take place is a question that will have to wait until we have considered recent work in the areas of culture and mental health, mental illness, and the social construction of the body and the self. It is to these topics that we turn in the remaining chapters.

Supplement, 1999

The original contrast between the terms "cognition" (thought) and "conation" (will or motivation) has returned to haunt us. Anthropologists in the 1990s have tried to bring the two back together. It seems obvious that thinking without action is fruitless, but it is also true that undirected drives or instincts do not exist. Evolution has seen to it that, normally, desire is canalized toward an appropriate goal. Animals eat foods that are suitable for their digestive systems and attempt to mate (usually) with others of their species and of the opposite sex. But in human communities, culture has constructed local concepts of the desirable, and these patterns influence some people more than others.

Cognitive anthropology continues to borrow many ideas from cognitive psychology, computer science, linguistics, and philosophy in its attempts to understand the nature and diversity of human thought. A history of mainstream research in cognitive anthropology has been provided by one of its best known practitioners: Roy G. D'Andrade's book, *The Development of Cognitive Anthropology* (1995), is a clear guide to one tradition of research in the United States. As noted elsewhere, I found this history rather narrow in focus. Its practitioners have surely made "essential contributions to cognitive anthropology . . . in the areas of ethnographic semantics, schemata, and consensus theory," but a broader approach that dealt with "cognitive maps or styles, studies of intelligence or of cognitive development" would, I think, have been more useful (Bock 1996:361). (For a brief overview of this type of research see Casson 1994.)

Bradd Shore has written about a variety of "cognitive models" and related phenomena (schemata and scripts), using them to understand everything from American baseball to modular furniture. In his very rich treatise, *Culture in Mind* (1996), he suggests that we rethink culture in terms of models, stating that "the work of culture in meaning construction may be understood to involve the use of shared models to produce a kind of collective memory" (p. 326). In a section on "model genres" (pp. 56–68) he lists dozens of specific types under several general headings: Linguistic and Nonlinguistic Models are followed by functionally different Orientational Models (Spatial, Temporal, Social, and Diagnostic), Expressive/Conceptual Models (Classificatory, Ludic, Ritual, and Dramatic Models and Theories), and Task Models (including Scripts, Recipes, Checklists, Mnemonic and Persuasion Models). Whew!

Shore uses some of these concepts to illuminate such anthropological puzzles as Kwakiutl animal symbols, Murngin ritual, and Samoan spatial concepts. In a late chapter he explores what happens "when models collide," arguing that *ambivalence* is the result of contradictory models within the same system. He examines four cases of such conflicting models within Samoan culture, showing that in three cases truly incompatible models exist "for the same domain of behavior [while] in the remaining case, a cultural model conflicts with and blocks the expression of deep personal needs" (p. 284). Conflicting models (or "norms" in an earlier terminology) can produce comedy, tragedy, or simple deadlock, e.g., in arguments as to what constitutes an "impeachable offence." However, I suspect that some types of ambivalence are pre-cultural although, like Oedipal conflicts, they are given different forms in specific societies and historical periods.

A similar attempt to bring abstract cognitive models together with motivation is found in the collection edited by D'Andrade and Strauss (1992). All of the articles struggle with the problem of how linguistic models or "cultural meaning systems" acquire "directive force" in the lives of those who learn them. (In a popular vocabulary, these authors are trying to explain "the power of ideas.") For example, in Naomi Quinn's discussion of the ways that women come to understand and perform the role of "wife" in American culture, she analyzes lengthy interview data to learn how this role concept acquires "motivational force" (her preferred term):

When particular ideas about human relations, about role obligations, or about types of people have force for us, rather than just being possible interpretations of the social world, it is because as children and young adults we have been socialized by means of appeals to these very ideas. We have been taught it is our role, our nature, the way we should be treated and treat other people. (Quinn 1992:121)

Whether called internalization, naturalization, ideology, or hegemony, the actual psychological processes that produce conformity in some instances, resistance or rebellion in others, still needs to be clarified (Wrong 1961). By refusing to commit itself to any particular motivational theory, much talk of cultural models gains in flexibility, but loses in strength. I have recognized this as a problem in my own work on formal descriptive models (Bock 1986). A recent attempt to connect "gender ideology" with psychological reality is found in a book by Melford Spiro (1997) where a discussion of different types of beliefs is joined with a psychoanalytically informed understanding of internalization. This seems to be a step in the right direction.

An even more ambitious attempt to connect beliefs with motives is found in Charles W. Nuckolls's book, *The Cultural Dialectics of Knowledge and Desire* (1996). Unfortunately, the argument of this work is too involved to present here, but advanced students will profit by studying his combination of dialectical philosophy with a thorough ethnography of a south India fishing village. I find his account of ambivalence in Jalari kinship quite convincing, and he supports Spiro's position when he argues that: "There is no principled theoretical reason for the ethnopsychological rejection of depth psychology. Nothing in the cognitivist account is threatened by it, and indeed, a much richer account of motivation could be developed if it were incorporated" (Nuckolls 1996:6). So, once again, the repressed returns!

Chapter 11

Shamans, Alternative States, and Schizophrenia

R. D. Laing

Prior to the spread of Western scientific medicine early in the twentieth century, most illnesses—physical and mental—were treated by "home remedies" such as rest, hot drinks, or medicinal applications. Only if an illness was painful or persistent would a healing specialist be called in to diagnose the meaning of symptoms and to treat the cause of the problem. Folk curers relied primarily on their practical knowledge of the effects of herbs or on manipulative techniques such as massage or bone-setting, but their treatments usually had ritual aspects as well (for example, prayer, sacrifice, and imposition of taboos on the patient and his or her family).

One ancient type of folk healer is known as a *shaman*. (The word is from the Tungus language of Siberia.) The shaman diagnoses and heals with supernatural aid. In most shamanic performances, the curer enters a deep trance during which he (or she) contacts specific spirits and uses their power to discover the source of the illness and to combat it. Within a given society, this ability may be limited to a few individuals or it may be widely shared. For example, among the !Kung of southern Africa, most adults take part in periodic healing rituals, although a few are recognized as especially gifted. As described by Richard Katz, about four times each month a !Kung healing dance begins at nightfall:

> The women sit around the fire, singing and rhythmically clapping. The men, sometimes joined by women, dance around the singers. As the dance intensifies, *num* or spiritual energy is activated in the healers, both men and women, but mostly among the dancing men [and] they begin to *kia* or experience an enhancement of their consciousness. While experiencing kia, they heal all those at the dance. (Katz 1982:34)

The music gradually becomes more spirited and the dancing more serious. As midnight approaches, some of the healers begin to shudder violently, the whole body convulsing in pain:

> The experience of kia has begun and the healers who are in kia go to each person at the dance and begin to heal. They lay their fluttering hands on a person . . . pulling out the sickness. . . . Then they shake their hands vigorously toward the empty space beyond the dance, casting the sickness they have taken from the person out into the darkness." (1982:40)

Shamanic performances are often highly dramatic events. Shamans may swallow or inhale dangerous substances (including tobacco smoke); they dance, chant, or play a drum to induce trance, and finally they contact spirits who may act or speak through them. Many shamans claim to be able to send the spirits they control against the human source of an illness (a sorcerer or witch) or to do battle with angry spirits (including ancestral ghosts) who may feel offended and who may be responsible for the sickness. Shamans may cure by laying on hands (as do the !Kung), or they may extract intrusive objects from the patient's body by sucking and sleight of hand, depending on the native theory of disease. Navajo "singers" create complex symbolic altars and elaborate potions, which, together with lengthy chants, restore the patient to health. (See Lamphere 1986.)

Shamans are rarely full-time curers. Although paid for the services they render, they generally carry out subsistence tasks as well. Shamanism is often believed to be a "vocation" whose call cannot be resisted without spiritual endangerment. The curer is obligated to respond whenever called, even if the payment offered does not compensate for time lost from other activities.

A persistent question among students of shamanism has been whether people who become shamans are psychologically normal or if they suffer from a mental illness. This is a sensitive issue since even in our own society there are thousands of "faith healers" whose performances include claims of contact with the supernatural, direct "seeing" of disease entities, and curing while in a trance state, yet whose actions are viewed as entirely normal and highly desirable by members of their congregations.

Some anthropologists feel that the irrational beliefs and bizarre behaviors of shamans indicate a severe psychological instability that has been channeled by their cultures into an acceptable social role (in Freudian terms, a useful "sublimation"). Others believe that the average shaman is no more (or less) mentally disturbed than are successful curers in our own society (including faith healers, medical doctors, and psychotherapists—roles that attract people of many personality types and all degrees of pathology). These anthropologists stress shamans' practical skill and familiarity with the individuals they treat, including intimate knowledge of sources of stress in family and local conflicts. Some interpreters go even further, affirming the empirical validity of folk medicines and the efficacy of shamanic cures (Harner 1980).

The late George Devereux was one anthropologist who argued that the shaman is always *abnormal*. His firsthand studies of "ethnopsychiatry" in Southeast Asia and in several American Indian societies (e.g., Devereux 1961) convinced him that the bizarre behavior of most shamans indicates serious disturbance and that, even allowing for cultural influence on symptoms, psychiatrists would recognize the shaman as a neurotic or a psychotic in temporary remission. "Briefly stated," writes Devereux, "my position is that the shaman is mentally deranged" (1980:15). However, he continues,

> Unlike the "private" neurotic or psychotic, [the shaman] does not have to evolve most of his symptoms spontaneously. He can express, control, and redirect his impulses and conflicts by using . . . devices that each culture places at the disposal of those whose conflicts are of the "conventional" type [for often] his conflicts are simply more intense than those of other members of his group. . . . This explains why the normal members of the tribe echo the shaman's intrapsychic conflicts so readily and why they find his "symptoms" (ritual acts) so reassuring. (1980:17)

Devereux's views were highly unpopular among American anthropologists, especially during the 1960s, when many people looked to drug experiences and exotic societies for alternative models of social life, religion, and healing. These concerns of the "counterculture" contributed to the enormous popularity of the works of Carlos Castaneda, from *The Teachings of Don Juan* (1968) to *A Separate Reality* (1971), *Journey to Ixtlan* (1972), and *Tales of Power* (1974). These four books purported to be accounts of Castaneda's apprenticeship to a Yaqui Indian shaman, "don Juan." Over several years, don Juan allegedly taught Castaneda how to experience an alternative reality and how to take charge of his own life—to live as a "warrior" and a man of knowledge.

Many anthropologists questioned the authenticity of Castaneda's account, but even those most knowledgeable about Yaqui culture seemed reluctant simply to call it a fraud (Beals 1978). The reaction of the profession as a whole was one of "silence and uneasiness" (Maquet 1978:362). In an earlier work, I suggested that Castaneda had "imaginatively transported a Japanese Zen master to the Sonoran desert, presenting parables as real events and *koans* (Zen riddles) as the wise sayings of an old Indian" (1980:220), but I lacked the background to prove this was the case. Castaneda's descriptions of his experiences with peyote, datura, and psychotropic mushrooms did correspond with the experiences of many of his readers, including many of my students.

Also in 1980, however, the psychologist Richard de Mille published *The Don Juan Papers,* in which he and his fellow authors document at length the falsehoods and plagiarisms in Castaneda's books. They demonstrate, at least to my satisfaction, that Castaneda's "fieldwork" was actually done in the U.C.L.A. library and in conversations with trusting colleagues—many of whom mistook his plagiarisms for confirmations of their legitimate findings! (See Bock 1981.) I entirely agree with de Mille (1980:168) that "The don Juan books deserve to survive as an ingenious and instructive hoax, but they will never be literature or sacred texts."

Alternative States of Consciousness

The revelation of Castaneda's work as a scientific hoax should make us cautious, but it should not discourage careful investigation into shamanism or other aspects of folk medicine, for we still have much to learn from different traditions of healing. For example, independent researchers in Central and South America have confirmed the importance of certain drugs in New World shamanic practice. In particular, the writings of Michael Harner on the use of hallucinogens by the Jívaro contribute to our understanding of alternative states of consciousness. Jívaro Indians regularly take large quantities of a drug called *nätema (Banisteriopsis sp.)*, and Jívaro shamans learn by using this drug to summon and control animal spirits. These spirits can be used to kill or to cure and may also protect their master against attack from other hostile spirits. According to Harner,

> any adult, male or female, who desires to become such a practitioner, simply presents a gift to an already practicing shaman, who administers the *Banisteriopsis* drink and gives some of his own supernatural power to the apprentice. These spirit helpers . . . are the main supernatural forces believed to cause illness and death in daily life. To the nonshaman they are normally invisible, and even shamans can perceive them only under the influence of *nätema*. (1973:17)

In their drawings, Jívaro men show considerable agreement about the appearance of the spirits; some appear as jaguars, others as snakes or birds, and the shaman's head appears to others who have drunk *nätema* as surrounded by a halolike crown. Cultural expectations concerning the animal spirits doubtless affect the drug-induced fantasies, but it also seems possible that certain drugs produce specific kinds of visual, auditory, and kinesthetic effects. Harner, who took these drugs, reported experiences very like those described by Jívaro shamans, as did a number of non-Indian Peruvians who knew nothing about the usual effects of the drug (Harner 1973:151–190).

The careful reader may have noticed that I use the phrase *alternative states of consciousness* rather than the more usual *altered states*. I do this to avoid the presumption that our (my) everyday way of experiencing the world is "unaltered" or normal in any absolute sense. Our sense of "ordinary reality" is socially constructed. We do not really know what the world is like to people with very different cultures or to people who speak radically different languages. Nor, for that matter, do most of us know how the world might appear if we fasted for four days. Many American adults have large quantities of nicotine, caffeine, alcohol, or other less legal drugs circulating in their bloodstreams. What would our consciousness be like without these chemicals or without the constant crowding and noise pollution of urban life? We cannot yet answer these questions, but studies of brain functioning and of "meditative states" indicate that ordinary waking consciousness is just one of several alternative mental states available to humans, with or without the use of drugs (Sugerman and Tarter 1978; Prince 1982).

The most common of these alternative states is *dreaming*. Anthropologists have long known that societies attribute different kinds of importance to dreams. A few representative examples of social attitudes were summarized by Dorothy Eggan as follows:

> Huron Indians believed that dreams were a revelation of the secret and hidden wishes of the soul, while the Trobriand Islanders reversed this belief and thought that magically induced dreams could *produce* a wish in the dreamer, and thus influence his waking conduct. The Naga of Assam dismissed much of the manifest content and looked for symbols. Other groups, such as the Hopi and Navaho Indians, treated the manifest content at face value, interpreting it loosely, depending upon the dreamer's emotional and physical reaction on awakening. . . . The Navaho treated a bad dream as they did any illness, by religious ceremony and native medicine. (1961:553; see also Wallace 1958.)

Documenting such cultural differences is an important part of psychological anthropology, but many problems of theory and method remain. Should cross-cultural analysis of dreams attempt dynamic interpretations, combining "the couch and the field" (LeVine 1982)? Or should it deal only with manifest dream content? To what extent are dreams personal and to what extent are they shaped by cultural expectations or universal symbolism? Since dreaming appears to be universal in human experience, what are its adaptive functions for the individual and the group? (See Kennedy and Langness 1981.)

Freud, Róheim, Devereux, and other psychoanalytic anthropologists used dream material in their cultural studies. But while dreams provide special kinds of information about an individual, to attempt to collect a representative sample of dreams may present great difficulties. Such a task calls for close rapport between the anthropologist and the dreamers, a willingness on the part of the dreamers to record or tell their dreams, an avoidance by the collector of "cultural standardization" of the contents of the dreams, and a sensitivity on the part of the collector to linguistic and symbolic meanings. For example, the Hopi believed that "a bad dream required immediate confession and action, while a good dream had to be remembered but not told until it came true" (Eggan 1961:567). Obviously, this attitude might bias the sample of dreams available to researchers. Nevertheless, with persistence and imagination, a great deal can be learned from dream analysis. Dorothy Eggan's own work with the Hopi and George Devereux's extended case study of an Indian man (1969) are examples of what can be accomplished in this area.

Abundant evidence exists to show that intense mental activity goes on during sleep. Solutions to personal or intellectual problems often come in dreams, as do poems, melodies, and visual images that may be developed into works of art (Dement 1974:95–102). These facts should make us aware that not all learning can be accounted for by mechanical stimulus-response connections. Some types of learning appear to have quite special characteristics.

Anthony Wallace has called one of these special types *ritual learning*. This refers to the rapid reorganization of experience under conditions of stress, resulting in far-reaching cognitive and emotional changes (1966:239–242). Such learning may take place in tribal initiations, individual conversions, and in the restructuring of behavior that often accompanies someone's recruitment to a messianic cult (Katcher and Katcher 1968). Some people would argue that becoming a nuclear physicist, a communist, or a Freudian involves a similar reorganization of experience under stress. The techniques of "thought reform" developed in the People's Republic of China and methods of intensive persuasion (such as those used in Reverend Jim Jones' People's Temple) combine situational and interpersonal factors to produce special kinds of learning (Lifton 1961; Holloman 1974). One does not have to approve of these methods to recognize their potency.

Ritual learning is often accompanied by music, and it frequently involves the belief that people can become "possessed" by spirits, holy or demonic. In his recently translated *Music and Trance* (1985), Gilbert Rouget explores the relationships among shamanism, spirit possession, and various states of consciousness that are induced and maintained by music. His detailed study concludes that different types of trance make use of music in different ways. For example, the shaman, whose "adventure" is primarily "an individual affair," always makes his own music. "Possession trance, on the contrary, consists in a change of identity [that] would be meaningless if it were not recognized by the group. . . . This is why the music is provided by the group" (p. 325).

Rouget denies that music in itself has any mysterious power over mental states: its effects can be understood only in terms of particular cultural patterns of symbols and behavior. Anthropological studies of alcohol intoxication have come to similar conclusions, for similar levels of blood alcohol appear to produce very different behaviors depending on social expectations. Japanese businessmen entering a bar after work, for example, are reported to exhibit a typical form of "drunken comportment" even before purchasing their first drink. Situational factors always play a role in the display and interpretation of behavior "under the influence" (MacAndrew and Edgerton 1969). The combination of alcohol intake with loud, rhythmic music is characteristic of most places of adult entertainment in America; together with the shared expectations brought by patrons, these factors help to induce and maintain an alternative state of consciousness that is familiar but not well understood.

A recent essay by Howard F. Stein (1985) serves to remind us how little we really understand about our own culture. Stein points out that the American fascination with "the alcoholic" functions to "*deflect* our attention from others whose official pathologies are not supposed to be noticed" (p. 208). According to Stein, "Alcoholism will be fully understood only when we can begin to accept the fact that . . . dryness and wetness, workaholism and alcoholism, social control and social violation are states and often social roles that complement, require, and presuppose one another" (p. 208). Stein argues that focusing our attention on alcoholic aggression and drunk driving enables us to ignore and deny the out-of-control aggression and intoxication with power exhibited by our political leaders in foreign policy and the nuclear arms race.

Alcoholism has become a central *metaphor* in American society, used to organize our thinking about loss of self-control. Stein claims that alcoholism has the character of a "secularized form of possession" in which people are influenced by the "spirits" in the alcohol and thus freed of responsibility for their sexual and violent actions (p. 212). He points out that one of the cultural rituals for curing alcoholism (detoxification) is similar to exorcism (p. 215). He further argues that alcohol and drugs are among the many "toxins" that Americans now fear are "polluting the body politic, sapping vitality, and making the national group feel impotent." Other such threats include the deliberate poisoning of foods and medicines, the infection of the nation's blood supply by herpes and AIDS viruses, and the dangers of "such substances as sodium salt, refined sugar, caffeine, saturated fats, and tobacco [which] represent loss of control in all areas of psychosexual functioning" p. 232, n.2).

Mental Illness and Society

Stein's account of American character in the 1980s makes us sound even more "paranoid" than the Dobu in Ruth Benedict's (1934) configurational analysis. But hasn't psychological anthropology moved away from such simple psychiatric characterizations of whole cultures?

Haven't we learned the dangers of the "uniformity assumption" and other pitfalls of the culture and personality school? If so, why do I have the impression that Stein is saying something really important about our national "state of mind" even if he is generalizing from limited clinical evidence using "old-fashioned" Freudian theory? (See Bettelheim 1982.)

One of the main themes of this book has been the *recurrence of ideas* in the human sciences. Concepts and methods that have been abandoned and even ridiculed by one generation often reappear in the next, although their sources are not always known or acknowledged. Richard Shweder (1980) calls for a "neo-Tylorean anthropology"; Rodney Needham (1965) writes an "appreciation" of Lévy-Bruhl; and the much-abused Boas finds his ideas vindicated by such luminaries as Dell Hymes, George Stocking, and Claude Lévi-Strauss. Abram Kardiner receives a belated tribute (Spindler 1978:23; also, Manson 1986). And when Margaret Mead is attacked soon after her death by Derek Freeman (1983), a host of young anthropologists rally to her defense (see *American Anthropologist,* December 1983).

Freud's influence, as mediated by Jacques Lacan and other contemporary thinkers, is probably greater today than during his lifetime. (See Paul 1976.) Because of Freud, we now see the compulsive attack on one's intellectual ancestors as a kind of Oedipal project—a declaration of academic independence. The solidarity between alternate generations is only partly due to the "return of the repressed" (see chapter 7). The passage of time allows us to appreciate the ways of our ancestors more fully. But if we are not simply to repeat the errors of the past, our appreciation must be critical, aimed at preserving what is true and useful while avoiding what I have termed *banalysis,* that is, "research that merely goes through the motions of scientific analysis" (Bock 1980:246).

A wonderful example of how the best ideas of the culture and personality approach can be revitalized by critical intelligence is the book *Saints, Scholars and Schizophrenics: Mental Illness in Rural Ireland* by Nancy Scheper-Hughes (1979). Focusing on the unusually high incidence of schizophrenia in several of Ireland's conservative western counties, Scheper-Hughes does more than "probe" the Irish psyche (or genome) in her effort to understand why so many middle-aged males from these locales are hospitalized with the illness. She places her study in a historical framework that goes back to the Christian conversion of Ireland, examining the social and religious past, the centuries of English domination, the impact of the famine and emigration, patterns of family interaction, and the great cultural changes since World War II.

Using a combination of social history, ethnographic fieldwork, psychiatric interviews, and projective tests (TAT), Scheper-Hughes draws a striking portrait of Irish family dynamics. On many of western Ireland's isolated farms, late marriage and high rates of celibacy interact with church doctrine and patterns of child care to put enormous stress on certain individuals—especially last-born males. Scheper-Hughes successfully synthesizes a modal-personality approach (providing rich data on individuals) with a social structure and personality analysis (combining positionalism with interactionism). It is impossible to summarize this provocative book, which all serious anthropologists should read, but a few sentences may give some idea of its conclusions:

> The tentative diagnosis of the schizophrenia-evoking factors in rural Irish society has focused on the breakdown of traditional patterns of Irish familism, its symptoms: the steady decline in marriage and birth rates and the proliferation of consanguineal and independent nuclear households; its causes: the spread of a secular world view and an individualistic ethos of rural capitalism; and its consequences: a demoralizing spirit of anomie. The emotional isolation, loss of self-esteem, and uncertainty and confusion about roles expressed by villagers—both young and old—has reference to several related sociocultural interpretations of mental illness.... (Scheper-Hughes 1985:190)

She goes on to discuss several epidemiological theories that attempt to link high rates of mental illness with specific environmental and social variables. Epidemiology, discussed in chapter 8, above, deals with "the distribution of diseases in space and time and the factors which account for these distributions." Epidemiologists "try to find populations with differing rates of illness and then try to compare their respective environments in the hope of discovering possible causes of disease" (Arthur 1971:12).

Psychological anthropologists have been especially intrigued by forms of mental illness that appear to be restricted to specific societies, and they have worked with epidemiologists and psychiatrists to understand such culture-bound syndromes. (See the discussion, in chapter 8, of the phenomenon of *Anfechtung* among the Hutterites; also, Lindenbaum 1979.) Anthropological approaches to these disturbances have ranged between two polar types: a *relativistic* approach that tries to understand each disorder in its unique cultural context and a more *universalistic* approach that tries to relate similar disturbances to one another across cultures. The former usually interprets symptoms as symbolic communications about stress within the social system, while the latter usually looks for genetic and physiological causes of classes of illness.

Philip Newman's (1964) discussion of the Gururumba "wild man" exemplifies the relativistic approach, for Newman shows how the bizarre symptoms of this apparent psychotic episode related to the pressures on a young married man in this particular New Guinea society. On the other hand, Anthony Wallace (1960) suggested that the disease called *pibloktoq* by the Eskimo is probably caused by the same dietary calcium deficiency that produces similar "arctic hysterias" in other northern groups (cf. Foulks 1972). Most recent studies recognize both culture-specific and universal biological factors as affecting the onset and course of mental disturbances. For example, all human populations include a few individuals who, probably for neurological reasons, are particularly easily startled; but only in certain Asian societies has this tendency been culturally elaborated into a recognized illness with standardized symptoms and folk therapies. Ironically, the recognition and labeling of this behavior pattern as an illness may accentuate the problem and make it difficult to cure (see Szasz 1961).

The Culture-Bound Syndromes (1985), an excellent collection of articles edited by a psychiatrist, Ronald C. Simons, and an anthropologist, Charles C. Hughes, includes both relativistic and universalistic articles, though the compilers seem to favor a biocultural synthesis that links related syndromes into seven classes of illness ("taxons") with more or less evident neurophysiological elements. The book concludes with a useful glossary of folk psychiatric syndromes. The rich case materials it presents, together with the sensible commentaries by both editors, make this book essential reading for the psychological anthropologist.

Relatively few psychological anthropologists are today prepared to deal with the medical and psychiatric complexities of mental illness; however, the imaginative work of Devereux on Mojave ethnopsychiatry, of Alexander Leighton on regional pathology, of Scheper-Hughes on rural Irish schizophrenia, and of the contributors to *The Culture-Bound Syndromes* should remind us that intensive studies of pathology may provide the key to understanding "normal" relationships between individual and cultural phenomena. This, of course, was Freud's basic assumption.

When I called for a "new synthesis in psychological anthropology... that will emphasize cognitive processes without neglecting the importance of emotion" (Bock 1980:245), I was not advocating the fusion of anthropology and psychology that Jahoda (1982:266) condemned as "neither realistic nor even desirable." Rather, I believe that we need a new generation of researchers, trained in the best traditions of both disciplines, who will critically reevaluate the work of the past, overcoming the "false dichotomies" that plague anthropology and many other fields (see Oyama 1985). In the next chapter, I shall examine some recent studies that promise such a synthesis.

Supplement, 1999

The increasing popularity of New Age thinking and writing during the 1990s has included various programs and workshops that claim to bring shamanic experience and power to anyone interested (and willing to pay). Magazines such as *Shaman's Drum* and books like Michael Harner's *The Way of the Shaman* (1990) relay anthropological studies and anecdotes to a popular audience. Interest continues in these exotic practices despite the efforts of some traditional religions to condemn them as pagan.

Several years ago I offered an undergraduate seminar on "The Selling of the Shaman." The title was taken from an article by Donald Joralemon (1990) in which he described the marketing of an urban Peruvian healer to a North American audience of spiritual "seekers." In the seminar, I tried to alert my students to the commercialization of shamanic practice and to the deceptions of many vendors without discouraging their interest in authentic spirituality. I failed because most of the students seemed determined to believe outlandish claims (say, of the late Carlos Castaneda) and to disregard the assigned readings that were intended to produce a critical attitude (e.g., William James 1961 and Richard de Mille 1980).

On the whole, psychological anthropology remains sympathetic towards the claims of native healers, while medical anthropologists often seek to incorporate elements of native practice into biomedical settings. Joralemon, who started with a highly skeptical attitude, recognized the positive effects of the Peruvian healer's actions, and concluded that, in earlier times, Eduardo's fame likely would have spread widely, bringing patients to him from considerable distances (though not on chartered flights from southern California).

Does healing take place in alternative states of consciousness? Perhaps so. The *placebo effect* is thought to be responsible for between 30 and 60 percent of apparent improvements in many illnesses, and it has been suggested that medical personnel should try to raise that rate by more systematic use of suggestion. It seems likely that being in an altered state induced by drumming, chanting, and/or psychotropic drugs can potentiate the placebo effect, whether the treatment has other physiological effects or not. (Indeed, the "therapeutic massage" now practiced by some nurses in the U.S. resembles the !Kung healing dance described at the opening of this chapter.)

The pragmatic tendency of many New Age thinkers to consider whatever seems to work for a given person as "true" for that person, what Michael F. Brown (1997) called a "laissez faire attitude towards truth," is clearly seen in Brown's book on the channeling phenomenon. In California, New Mexico, and New York he joined groups in which "channels" claimed to contact and give voice to various ancient spiritual entities, answering questions, offering advice, and teaching others how to channel. Brown traces the origins of these practices to nineteenth century spiritualism. His account is both sympathetic and critical, as he discusses the relief some people receive together with the economic base of channeling, including the disputes that arise when different people claim to channel the same valuable entity!

Most channels (not "channelers") operate in a state of *trance*. A series of valuable studies of trance and meditation phenomena have been carried out by Erika Bourguignon and her students from Ohio State University (see Bourguignon 1994). They distinguish "possession trance," in which the individual's consciousness is taken over by a spirit, from other forms, arguing that possession trance occurs only in certain types of social situations. They have also documented a wide range of meditative states that are highly valued in many societies and have related these states to cultural values.

Probably the most thorough comparative studies of alternative states have been the work of psychologist Charles Tart (1969; 1978). Among the interesting ideas that he has developed is the concept of "state specific knowledge." Starting from the observation that people returning from an alternative state to ordinary daily consciousness are usually unable to communicate what they feel they learned in the former state, Tart suggests that this is because *all knowledge is relative to a particular state*. If this is so, we may understand why what we seem to know in dreams usually evaporates on return to a waking state, while trance experiences are usually not remembered at all, and drug induced visions are difficult to communicate to others who have not shared that state. It may also explain why intoxicated persons are so hard to reason with. (See Simons 1996 on the "startle reflex" as inducing an altered state.)

Furthermore, knowledge that we possess in "ordinary conscious-ness" makes sense only to others who are also in that state. Tart argues that doing higher mathematics and perhaps any advanced science involves a special kind of consciousness that is achieved only after years of intense preparation. I also suspect that many specialized activities such as playing chess at a Master level or improvising jazz in a small combo require non-ordinary states. Grob and Dobkin de Rios (1994) have studied the use of drugs in puberty rituals, suggesting that some drug experiences aid in the transition to adulthood. (The Society for the Anthropology of Consciousness, a unit of the American Anthropological Association, sponsors symposia and publications on these topics.)

It has become increasingly difficult to talk about "mental illness" in a simple way since the division between biological and cultural approaches has become deeper (Chisholm 1992). On the one hand, medical psychiatrists make use of a disease model and search for genetic causes of symptoms and develop drug therapies for disturbed patients. The successful development of anti-psychotic agents is surely encouraging for this approach, though the negative side effects of drugs are often minimized (e.g., Prozac severely depresses sexual functioning). On the other hand, the cultural constructionists rightly point out the relativity of illness taxonomies and subsequent treatments to the social context in which they are found.

Arthur Kleinman's important book, *Rethinking Psychiatry* (1988) attempts to mediate between these extreme positions. His excellent medical credentials combine with a long history of cross-cultural work (mainly in China) to make both doctors and anthropologists pay attention. While showing that some mental disturbances are similar across different societies and are likely to have genetic and biochemical causes, he demonstrates that, even with severe illnesses such as schizophrenia, the social context affects patterns of recurrence and likelihood of remission (cf. Eaton and Weil 1959 on depression). Kleinman's ideas are best read in his own words:

> Psychological and biological vulnerability of the person combines with local social pressures to create syndromes of distress embodying neuroendocrine, autonomic, cardiovascular, gastrointestinal, and limbic system responses. Such responses constitute a spectrum of affective, anxiety, and somatic complaints. Cultural norms reciprocally interact with biological processes to pattern these body/self experiences so that different archetypes of distress are predominant in different social groups, such as neurasthenia in contemporary China, *fatigué* in France, chronic pain in North America, *nervios* in Latin America, and so on. (1988:60; see also Jenkins 1994)

In other words, "illness behavior" is the result of a complex web of physical and social forces, in which local expectations about how people should respond to pain, anxiety and other forms of distress play important parts. Edward Sapir stated long ago that anthropology "needs the psychiatrist," but it is also true that psychiatry needs to listen to what the anthropologist can contribute.

Chapter 12

Emotions and Selfhood

William Shakespeare

In anthropology and several other fields, the concept of the *self* has lately been undergoing a revival: "The self has returned!" exclaim the editors of a recent collection of essays, *Culture and Self* (Marsella, DeVos, and Hsu 1985:ix). Some writers hope that this notion will make possible a synthesis of ideas from various disciplines (Shweder and Levine 1984). In their enthusiasm for this concept, however, many have overlooked the long-time concern with the notion of the self shared by certain anthropologists (e.g., Irving Hallowell), sociologists (Erving Goffman), and social psychologists (Morris Rosenberg). Clinical and Gestalt psychologists have always found the self concept to be an essential part of their thinking about individuals.

Fifty years ago, Gardner Murphy devoted a large section of his superb treatise, *Personality* (1947:479–618) to the self. Murphy's discussion is a good place for us to begin our thinking, for he was acutely aware of the history of the concept and of its relevance to social and cultural issues. Also, Murphy grounds this often-elusive idea in a *biosocial* matrix (in what is probably the first use of this compound term), and he provides a general theory of perception that can help us to understand the "genesis of selfhood."

Murphy uses the term *self* for "the individual person as the object of his own perception" (p. 523). The sense of self develops out of vague early perceptions of one's own body and the bodies of others, especially the mother. The self is localized (often in highly idiosyncratic ways) and gradually becomes a source of emotional satisfaction: "self-love is one of the few things about which we can be reasonably sure as we compare the experiences of infancy in varying cultures" (p. 484). Integration of the self is at first quite loose. The self-image is subject to the same kinds of distortions as other perceptual objects, especially during alternative states of consciousness (dreaming, intoxication, and so on). Complete unification of the self is never achieved, though most individuals "accept the cultural definition of selfhood, try to be consistent, strive toward external identity and inner coherence" (p. 488–89).

Murphy describes how selfhood is gradually achieved by processes of identification and role playing, projection and introjection: that is, by *activities* that are "interwoven with experiencing other individuals" (p. 491). He concludes that "most human adjustments are in some degree adjustments not to an external situation alone, but to a perceptual whole of which the self is a part, a self-in-situation field" (p. 502). Since the self is largely culturally constituted, it is legitimate to ask how the sense of self may differ across cultures.

[handwritten margin note: child finds its 'self' by role playing, trying different personalities on + choosing the one that fits the best]

224

Culture and personality theorists attributed differences in typical, or basic, personality to very early patterns of interaction between children and their caretakers, but it is equally plausible to view the early genesis of selfhood as a universal human process upon which social differences are later imposed (Shweder and LeVine 1984:12–13). Consider variations in *naming* practices. In many societies, especially those with infanticide or high infant mortality, a baby is not given a name until it is several weeks old and judged likely to survive. (Most American hospitals have a similar practice, calling a newborn "Infant Jones" or "Baby Sanchez" to indicate family membership while withholding any designation of individuality.) However, the way a name is finally assigned, and the ways it may change during the child's lifetime, suggest significant differences in cultural understandings of the self.

For example, in many societies with reincarnation beliefs, a name will not be given to a child until it can be determined *which* dead ancestor's soul has animated his or her body. Plains Indian tribes generally assigned a name only when a child performed some conspicuous action, and this name might well have changed later—when, for example, a young man distinguished himself in warfare. In many Northwest Coast Indian societies, names were taken from a "fund" of names that could be used only by members of a specific kinship group; thus, one's name always indicated to others one's group membership, and high-status names were validated by a potlatch. Again, in some societies, one's personal name is secret and known to only a few close relatives; for a stranger to utter it would be a great insult. People in such groups have secular "nicknames" that may be used in public. The Yanomamo Indians of Venezuela react violently to the mention of a dead ancestor's name: anthropologists collecting genealogies have narrowly escaped harm when they accidentally did so!

In China, the Confucian tradition placed great emphasis on social harmony, which began in the home. An individual's name placed him as a member of a family. The Chinese viewed the self as "a developing part of a continuing family lineage [rather than] an individual ego, whose subjectively experienced existence continues for all eternity as is envisaged in western religion" (Marsella, DeVos, and Hsu 1985:18). In India, "when one asks for a Hindu's identity, he will give you his caste and his village as well as his name. There is a Sanskrit formula which starts with lineage, family, house and ends with one's personal name." The Indian notion of identity, then, moves from the social to the personal, in contrast to that of many Americans and Europeans, who "Identify themselves primarily and immediately by their profession or special skill" (Marsella, DeVos, and Hsu 1985:16–17). (See also the rich interpretation of Balinese naming customs in relation to the sense of self in Geertz 1973:360–411.)

These examples of naming practices should alert us to some of the ways in which the self is culturally constituted; it is dangerous, however, to reason from cultural institutions to the (assumed) experience of individuals. Such inferences are important sources of hypotheses, but, as we have learned, they must be tested with psychological data from a representative sample of individuals to avoid the circularity of the "causal assumption" (see the Interlude, above). Most anthropological writing about the self is still highly speculative, assuming a congruence between institutions and self-concepts without much evidence. At best it draws upon linguistic habits (grammar, semantics, narrative structure) to elucidate cultural notions about self.

Interest in the self frequently leads to the study of emotion. In her fine study of Ilongot notions of self and social life, the late Michelle Rosaldo (1980) used recordings of discourse, songs, and narratives to interpret native concepts of feeling and action. The Ilongot are horticulturalists who live on the island of Luzon in the Philippines. Until quite recently they were also headhunters. Rosaldo attempted to understand what killing meant to them. She learned that a complex and subtle theory of the emotions lay behind Ilongot violence. For the Ilongot, one key constituent of personality is *liget,* which can be roughly translated as "anger, energy, passion"; it contrasts with *beya,* meaning "knowledge, civility." The Ilongot say that *beya* comes to control *liget* as an individual matures. Knowledge gives form to passion, enabling a mature man to "focus" his anger in effective action. "Men went headhunting, Ilongots said, because of their emotions. Not gods, but 'heavy' feelings were what made men want to kill; in taking heads they could aspire to 'cast off' the 'anger' that 'weighed down on' and oppressed their saddened 'hearts'" (Rosaldo 1980:19).

Rosaldo's deep understanding of Ilongot culture disposes us to accept her characterization of the Ilongot self as different in fundamental ways from the "self" as it is socially constituted in Western cultures. She writes that,

> Whereas people elsewhere stress the tensions among individuals or between the private person and her or his compelling public bonds, Ilongots see continuities, casting social life as a sort of "actualization" of the emotions, and viewing difference and division as the product of affective processes that are at once invigorating and stressful. (p. 223)

But are these apparent differences fundamental? Or is Rosaldo's distinction simply a contemporary restatement of a very old notion about the "otherness" of primitive man and his "savage passions"? (See chapter 1.)

This tension, which Rosaldo mentions, between the private person and "public bonds" is essential to a way of conceiving the self that goes back, in the Western tradition, at least to the Renaissance and probably to ancient Greece and Rome, though it was made most explicit during the Enlightenment (Sennett 1976). It is a highly self-conscious formulation, likely to be espoused by persons (and classes) in positions of authority—for example, the ruler who claims to act against personal inclination for the good of his people. Those without power are more likely to view social life as flowing directly from the emotions. A reputation for sudden anger and violence, or for a sharp tongue, is valuable to the underdog. But these views of self and society are highly situational, and the underdog who is elevated to a position of authority learns all too quickly the rhetoric of power.

In comparing Rosaldo's Ilongot texts with the plays of Shakespeare, especially in passages that refer to the *heart*, I found more resemblances than differences (Bock 1984: chap. 10). For example, Rosaldo claims that "for Ilongots, *unlike ourselves* . . . the individual man's most intense 'sense of self' is won when, casting off a victim's head, he establishes himself as an 'angry' man—autonomous because constrained by none" (1980:226, emphasis added). But when Shakespeare's Richard of Gloucester is slashing his way to the crown, he summarily disposes of one opponent (Hastings) with a false accusation of treason and the command:

> Off with his head! Now by Saint Paul I swear
> I will not dine until I see the same.
> *(Richard III*, 3.4.75–76)

The Ilongot would, I believe, recognize Richard as "a man of exceptionally high heart filled with *liget,* and they would see that his social position gave him ample opportunities to discharge his great anger" (Bock 1984:149).

Rejecting earlier interpretations of headhunting, Rosaldo teaches us to focus upon the "social meanings" of violent deeds and "the ways that personhood is understood and structured in a particular sociocultural milieu" (1980:228). However, I fear that she also reinforces the ethnocentric distinction between *them* (savage, primitive, emotional, and oral) and us (civilized, individual, rational, and literate), implying not just a difference but a superiority of self-awareness and self control in "ourselves." (For another skeptical view, see Spiro 1984:334. Jean Briggs 1970 provides an extended discussion of Eskimo emotional concepts and describes their extraordinary self control.)

Recent research into supposed differences between "traditional" and "modern" societies posits *literacy* as the crucial causal factor producing such modern traits as empathy, rationality, critical thought, and scientific progress. These studies have been brilliantly critiqued by Brian Street (1984), who reveals their ideological basis and scientific inadequacy. (See also Cole and Scribner 1981.) Yet the quest to identify polar oppositions between cultures, broadly construed, rather than to learn to recognize cultural "pluralities" continues (Stocking 1992).

A critique of the polarity between *reason* and *emotion* as it has affected anthropology is found in an important article, "Emotion, Thought, and Estrangement" (1986), by Catherine Lutz. She points out the long history in the West of negative or, at best, ambivalent attitudes toward emotion. Reason is usually associated with intelligence, morality, maturity, and masculinity, whereas emotion is viewed as inherently irrational, dangerous, natural, and female. But, Lutz argues, these attitudes are all *cultural constructions*—learned distinctions that structure "innumerable aspects of experience and discourse" and that encode "an immense portion of the Western world view of the person, of social life, and of morality" (1986:289).

When we examine the varied meanings of emotion as a cultural category, we find that it has hidden ideological functions; that is, it plays a central role in maintaining power relations among peoples, classes, age groups, and genders, for

> When the emotional is defined as irrational, all of those occasions and individuals in which emotion is identified can be dismissed; and when the irrational is defined as emotional, it becomes sensible to label emotional those who would be discounted. In this society, women, people of color, children, and the lower classes have been labeled emotional to these ends. (Lutz 1986:292)

Lutz calls for a more emotional morality—one that will incorporate "feminine" concerns for nurturance and intimacy as well as the "masculine" concern with efficient problem-solving. She cautions us that we must fully understand our Western cultural construction of emotion before we can begin to "contrast these conceptions to the ethnopsychological premises upon which the emotional lives of people of other cultures are based" (p. 304). For Lutz, the beginning of wisdom still lies in Socrates' motto—Know Thyself.

It is difficult, at least in textbook prose, to write accurately about the emotions. I agree with Lutz that emotions are culturally constructed in each society and era (to wit: how many of my readers have felt "melancholy" lately?). But I also believe that there is a universal, biological base from which the cultural construction begins (Ekman 1973;

Clynes 1977; Spiro 1984) and upon which culture operates by its usual processes of selection, labeling, emphasis, and elaboration. In general, "society acts not by adding something but by molding something already there, giving it a characteristic direction" (Murphy 1948:904). Furthermore, as Franz Boas long ago pointed out, a somewhat "different equilibrium of emotion and reason" is established in each society (quoted in Stocking 1992). Furthermore, emotions are *linked* to specific events and goals by complex historical processes.

Links between emotions and goals probably give rise to distinctive senses of the self. For example, individuals who make "personal honor," "spiritual salvation," or "secular success" their ultimate concerns will experience quite different encounters with shame, sin, guilt, and triumph (Bock 1987a; Larsen 1987). Individuals who fail to achieve an integrated identity, or who adopt personal goals that are at odds with those valued by their group, will also have characteristic life experiences. But whatever one's social position may be, there is no such thing as a "culture-free self" (Kotre 1985).

Role, Self, and Identity

To what extent do people in different times and places achieve a *unified* sense of self, and how is this related to their social and historical position? In trying to answer this question, one must avoid at least two dangers. One of these is the elitist view that only by arduous training and cultivation of the "best human material" can a few individuals reach authentic selfhood. (The preferred routes in modern American society include an Ivy League education and/or Jungian analysis.) The opposite danger is the "pastoral" fantasy that, surely, the poor (or peasants, or Pacific islanders) live more authentic, unconflicted lives than do we (Empson 1974). This latter view can lead us to romanticize the "organic" society of the Middle Ages or the "integrated" cultures of exotic tribes.

I do not deny that some cultures may be more conducive to healthy and satisfying human functioning than are others (Sapir 1949:78–119), but one must be very cautious in judging such matters. Even the assumption that an integrated personality with a secure and unified self is *desirable* turns out to be culturally constructed and thus relative to a particular era. From a Marxist perspective, the separate, socially mobile, responsible individual is a product of bourgeois society. Raymond Williams writes that notions of individuality, in the modern sense, can be related to the break-up of the medieval social, economic and religious order. In the general movement against feudalism there was a new stress on man's personal existence over and above his place or function in a rigid hierarchical society. . . . Liberal thought based on 'the individual' as starting point was criticized . . . most thoroughly in Marx, who attacked the opposition of the abstract categories 'individual' and 'society' and argued that the individual is a social creation, born into relationships and DETERMINED by them. (Williams 1976:135–6)

Now if "bourgeois individualism" is part of a passing historical moment, what are the signs of its demise? Marxists would argue that the increasing *alienation* of person from person and of the self from itself is evident in capitalist society (though they too often ignore the signs of alienation in socialist states). In the arts, too, we may find evidence of the *disintegration* of the individual self. The surrealists, the cubists, and many contemporary painters, such as Francis Bacon, dissolve the individual into loosely joined parts, suggesting a multiplicity of selves or none at all. In modern drama, as Eric Bentley writes, the threat of complete disintegration is ever-present:

In the dream plays of Strindberg the individual is dissolving in mist and mysticism. Here, instead of personalities, there are memories, bits of experience, cross references, images, names, momentary encounters. In Pirandello's plays of around 1920 the nonexistence of the individual is proclaimed [and he] projects the state of soul of . . . the disoriented, the metaphysically as well as neurotically lost: men of the twentieth century. [The plays of Brecht display the paradox that] the Independent Individual of the age of individualism . . . was formed by that age and belonged utterly to that society. (Bentley 1981:123–124)

Most Americans have difficulty with the idea that the individual is a social construct, the "I" (as Nietzsche held) "a grammatical illusion." We are disturbed by the notion of many selves (as in multiple-personality schizophrenia) and dismayed by the possibility of "non-self"—unlike Hindus and Buddhists, for whom the achievement of what might be called "non-self" is a paramount spiritual goal (Bharati 1985). As noted above, middle class Americans tend to identify themselves in terms of their profession or specialized skill, their social role in the occupational structure. This is what makes being unemployed or "just a housewife" intolerable to many people, and what made the counter-cultural emphasis on "being" rather than "doing" appear so subversive of the American Way. (See Girgus 1981.)

The concept of *primary role identification* (chapter 8) seems especially useful in analyzing a society like ours, for it leads us to ask about the range of roles that can serve as a basis for identity formation in a given community at a given time. As elaborated by John H. Rohrer and Munro S. Edmonson (1964), the concept also makes the question as to which roles (if any) are "primary" for what proportion of the community an empirical one, to be answered by field research rather than speculation. It remains to be seen how useful this concept will prove in interpreting societies with different concepts of self and of individual achievement.

It is also possible that, just as many Americans engage in serial monogamy (marriage with a series of different spouses), we may be experimenting with serial identities, trying on a number of different selves without the need or desire for lifetime commitment to any of them. Robert Jay Lifton noted this trend in the late 1960s, writing of a new psychological style that he dubbed the *self-process of protean man.* (Proteus was a Greek sea god who could change his form at will.)

Lifton draws on the ideas of David Riesman and Erik Erikson, but he argues that neither the concept of other-directedness nor that of ego identity applies exactly to protean man, for he (or she) is not particularly sensitive to the social environment and has broken entirely with the notion of ego identity. Rather, the protean self-process

> is characterized by an interminable series of experiments and explorations—some shallow, some profound—each of which may be readily abandoned in favor of still new psychological quests. The pattern in many ways resembles what Erik Erikson has called "identity diffusion" or "identity confusion," and the impaired psychological functioning which those terms suggest can be very much present. But I would stress that the protean style is by no means pathological as such, and in fact may well be one of the functional patterns of our day. It extends to all areas of human experience—to political as well as sexual behavior, to the holding and promulgating of ideas, and to the general organization of lives. (Lifton 1970:319)

Lifton cites some clinical evidence for his conclusions, but he also draws upon existential philosophy and upon literature, sculpture, film, and music. The same restless experimentation occurs in the realm of ideas; in many sectors of society, he claims, it is unusual to find a person "who has gone through life holding firmly to a single ideological vision" (p. 324). Lifton suggests two major sources of the protean style: *historical dislocation,* a break in the sense of continuity that people in the past have felt with the "vital and nourishing symbols of their cultural tradition"; and *flooding of imagery* as human consciousness is overwhelmed by "the extraordinary flow of post-modern cultural influences over mass communication networks" (p. 318). Taken together, these forces sever us from traditional symbols while exposing us to "undigested cultural elements" and "endless partial alternatives in every sphere of life" (p. 318). Our inner and outer worlds become divorced, while the constant flux in emotions and beliefs produces "a profound inner sense of absurdity, which finds expression in a tone of mockery" (p. 325). Lifton felt these qualities were especially evident in "pop art" and the "camp" aesthetic. Today, Lifton might cite music videos and "Saturday Night Live" as displaying fragmentation, absurdity, and mockery. (See Bellah et al. 1985:154.)

Lifton attempts to describe the protean style in a neutral way, suggesting that the new self-process may have positive survival value, but it seems clear that he also distrusts it. Protean man may be well adapted to an era of constant, radical change, but he seems profoundly ambivalent about the new and is afflicted with attacks of nostalgia. Free of traditional superego forms of guilt, he yet suffers from "a nagging sense of unworthiness all the more troublesome for its lack of clear origin" (p. 328). In other words, despite the amount of gratification with which it supplies us, civilization still brings its discontents!

The concept of *social role* has been temporarily eclipsed by the renewed interest in the self. This may be a response to the popular notion that roles are superficial and "role playing" necessarily inauthentic. Americans are constantly urged to get in touch with their true, inner feelings, and just a few years ago a mass-circulation magazine named *Self* began publication. Dissenting voices can be heard, however, and not only from the radical Left. Michael Wallach and Lisa Wallach (1983) have criticized the American preoccupation with the self, calling for greater social responsibility in psychology. Anthropologist Maurice Godelier (1986) calls attention to the ways that societies "produce" individuals of specific types in order to reproduce their social structures. My own recent work attempts to rehabilitate the role concept by providing a formal analysis of interaction situations that focuses on expected behavioral exchanges among role categories (Bock 1986). I believe that social roles are the crucial meeting points between sociocultural and individual phenomena and that, properly conceptualized, they can help us to understand both continuity and change.

Psychology and Cultural Change

Psychological anthropology has always had difficulty dealing with cultural change, although many attempts have been made to understand the impact of change on personality and vice versa. Returning to the Manus of New Guinea twenty-five years after her initial study, Margaret Mead wrote of the rapid transformation in Manus culture that had resulted from missionary activity, contact with Japanese and American armies during World War II, and the cargo cult that followed the war. There were, she felt, some changes for the better, including relief from the terrors of the native religion and from the stresses of the old economic system, but there were also important continuities, such as the pattern of confession to rid oneself of evil (M. Mead 1966:324–325). Mead used no formal psychological tests in this second study, but her sensitive account of *generational differences* in personality is fascinating and quite convincing, and her vivid sketches of individuals are completely persuasive (see Schwartz 1975). The concept of generational differences has recently been given a useful symbolic interpretation by Katherine Newman (1986).

Many anthropological studies of change have, understandably, focused on situations of forced *acculturation* in which native peoples have been required to adapt to the demands of powerful outsiders, usually Europeans. Irving Hallowell's influential studies of Ojibwa culture and personality used Rorschach techniques to delineate the psychological effects of differing degrees of contact. He examined three communities at increasing distances from European settlements, showing that certain "regressive" alterations in personality were associated with increased contact, although women were less affected than men (Hallowell 1955:345–357).

Similar results have been reported by George Spindler and Louise Spindler, who studied the Menomini Indians for more than twenty years. They divided their population into groups that ranged from "native oriented" to "elite acculturated" and, using the Rorschach test, demonstrated differing patterns of perceptual structure at each of four levels of acculturation. The Spindlers later become dissatisfied with their description of this process in terms of passive assimilation and began to analyze acculturative levels as

> adaptive strategies that deal actively with the situation created by the confrontation between two highly divergent, in fact incongruent, psychocultural systems—the Menomini and the North American European. . . . Each of our "levels" of acculturation were represented by groups that . . . resisted or adopted, or adopted only partially, the dominant culture, or created new combinations from old and new. (Spindler 1978:179)

The view of personality as an active factor in cultural change is found in a great deal of research on *achievement motivation*. David

McClelland has long argued that measurable increases in achievement motivation (due to changing socialization practices) *precede* economic development in Third World countries (McClelland 1961). George DeVos worked with Japanese-Americans in Chicago to understand their successful post—World War II social adaptation and the ways their children were socialized for achievement (Caudill and DeVos 1956). In later studies in rural Japan, DeVos used a variety of questionnaires and projective techniques, which complemented one another in the kinds of data they elicited; he writes that he found, "for example, that TAT stories, less directly conscious, spontaneously reflected more conservative attitudes than did answers to the Problem Situation test" (DeVos 1978:231). He attributed this to a "psychological lag" between the liberal attitudes people would express to the interviewers and their unconscious feelings or actual behavior.

Among native Japanese, DeVos found that disruption of the harmonious adjustment to social roles so damages people's self-esteem that they often resort to suicide. He defined *role narcissism* as "an intense identification of one's total self with one's professional or social role, leading to the exclusion of other social meaning" (p. 250). This condition appears to be more extreme than the primary role identifications described by Rohrer and Edmonson, but it exemplifies the same kind of identity formation. DeVos believes that young Japanese are socialized and pressured to subordinate themselves to family decisions and to commit themselves to industrial or bureaucratic roles. He concludes that the "Japanese seem unduly preoccupied with standards of excellence," which they internalize and worry about constantly. This should remind us that no culture pattern is "without cost for the individuals who maintain its continuity" (p. 256).

As we have seen, psychological anthropology is concerned both with the influence of cultural change on individuals and with the ways that individual psychological processes and personalities affect change. Perhaps the most general attempt to understand the influence of human psychology on cultural change is Homer Barnett's study *Innovation* (1953). Using a modified Gestalt psychology, Barnett analyzes a series of inventions to show the perceptual and structural processes that produce new culture traits, which may then be accepted, modified, or rejected.

Anthony Wallace (1970:165–206) discusses Barnett's ideas and outlines several general models of change in a chapter entitled "The Psychology of Culture Change." But Wallace's best known contribution to the topic of cultural change is his treatment of *revitalization movements,* which he defines as "deliberate, organized attempts by some members of a society to construct a more satisfying culture by rapid acceptance of a pattern of multiple innovations" (1970:188). Wallace breaks the revitalization process into a series of overlapping but "functionally distinct" stages that he summarizes as follows:

Steady State The sociocultural system is operating normally; some change takes place, but stress and disorganization remain within tolerable limits for most people.

Period of Increased Individual Stress The system is "pushed" out of equilibrium by forces such as climatic change, disease, war, or acculturation. Cultural disorganization is accompanied by individual disillusionment; crime and illness increase.

Period of Cultural Distortion A breakdown of institutions now follows, as individuals and interest groups attempt to "restore personal equilibrium" by illegitimate and violent means, leading to further cultural disorganization.

Period of Revitalization If the people survive as a society, a series of "functions" may be enacted, usually under the guidance of a charismatic leader or prophet. These include the following: (1) formulation of a code that outlines a new society, (2) communication of the code to make converts, (3) organization of converts into disciples and followers, (4) adaptation of the movement to hostile conditions, (5) cultural transformation of the society, and (6) routinization of the movement, leading to the final stage.

New Steady State Individuals may achieve a "resynthesis of values and beliefs," while long-term changes continue under the guidance of the new value structure. (cf. Wallace 1970:191–197)

Wallace illustrated the revitalization process by citing cargo cults, the Ghost Dance, contemporary political movements, and his own detailed study of the "Handsome Lake religion," a movement that reorganized Seneca Indian society in the early nineteenth century. First formulated more than thirty years ago, Wallace's analysis now sounds rather old-fashioned, but psychological anthropologists have yet to devise a more workable general model of rapid cultural change. (See Barnouw 1985:442; Graves and Graves 1978.)

The cognitive studies that have dominated psychological anthropology since the early 1960s have tended to be *synchronic,* that is, concerned with the analysis of cognitive structures at one point in time. Recently, however, an increasing concern with change has developed. Brent Berlin and Paul Kay's proposal concerning the evolution of color terminology illustrates this new emphasis (see chapter 10). James Fernandez provides a fascinating case study of changes in the ways the Fang of West Africa have classified "people." As summarized by Gustav Jahoda, prior to 1900 the Fang included the higher primates in their category of "people," recognizing five subclasses: gorilla, chimpanzee, pygmies, themselves, and "speakers of gibberish" (other humans). From 1900 to about 1925, the nonhuman primates and the pygmies were separated from the category of "people," and two subclasses were formed on the basis of language intelligibility (Fang and related tribes versus "speakers of gibberish"). Since 1925, however,

> Pygmies have been promoted to people, though still constituting a distinct category. Language has been dropped as a criterion and . . . the classification has become 'racist'; moreover, white men have now come to be differentiated in terms of both occupational role and nationality. Thus modes of categorization may be seen to reflect profound changes in the perception of the social environment. (Jahoda 1982:249)

Other recent articles deal with variability and change in kinship terminology, ethnic categories, color terms, and biological taxonomies (e.g., Casson 1981:269–352), while some cognitive models of decision making also attempt to represent change over time (Quinn 1975). On the whole, however, psychological anthropology has yet to come to terms with the realities of cultural change and the psychological processes associated with it. Here, again, a "synthesis" between cognitive analysis and the more emotion-oriented studies of the self is called for (Levy 1984). But this may be a task for the next generation.

Supplement, 1999

The topics of self and emotion continue to be of central importance in psychological anthropology and this will likely be true into the next century. As I observed earlier, the terminology for these phenomena has become quite complex with some authors discriminating among self, person, individual, agent, personality, and many related terms, though seldom agreeing on definitions.

Since the time of William James, the term "self" has referred to one's sense of experiencing and acting on the world, also called "subjectivity" or simply "the I." When this experiencing self is made central to a discipline the result is often referred to as "phenomenology." For instance, in *Minima Ethnographica*, anthropologist Michael Jackson writes that "ethnographic understanding of others is never arrived at in a neutral or disengaged manner, but is negotiated and tested in an ambiguous and stressful field of interpersonal relationships in an unfamiliar society" (1998:5). For Jackson and others using a phenomenological approach, the goal of research is intersubjective understanding achieved through thoughtful dialogue. The ethnologist should not hide behind supposedly objective statements about "the culture," but must grapple with the constantly changing meanings that arise out of frank and open conversations and self questioning.

Arguments continue concerning the nature of the self in different societies. An early opposition between the "Western" egocentric self and the sociocentric self found elsewhere has proven much too simplistic. Some argue for a continuum between the two polar types, while others opt for a situational approach in which individualism or group orientation are relative to circumstances. Still others investigate differences in social structure that could produce variant selves in different classes, genders, or roles. (Much of this material is summarized in Csordas 1994b).

The question persists: *is the concept of a unified, bounded self an illusion*, and if so, is it a product of historical forces peculiar to Europe and America? (See Gore 1992.) Self-esteem and self-enhancement are goals that seem to have developed in the context of modernity, but perhaps this is only a matter of emphasis. The self assertion of a Kwakiutl chief cannot easily be traced to such forces (see chapter 3), though even on the Northwest Coast an influx of trade items during the nineteenth century may have increased chiefly power. On the other hand, truly self sacrificing individuals can be found at every level of a modern society. The desire to "lose oneself" in community or in a larger spiritual entity affects most people at some time in their lives, and all of us struggle with the notion that we have a "true self" different from the various masks we present to the public and, perhaps, to our closest friends (Bock 1988).

Several interesting essays on the issue of unified versus multiple selves are found in the recent book, *Two-Spirit People*, edited by Jacobs, Thomas, and Lang (1997). The term "two-spirit" is now used by some Native Americans for people in unusual sexual situations: homosexual, bisexual, hermaphrodite, transvestite, transsexual, and so forth. Terminology is important in speaking or writing of such persons, for distinctions should be made between biology and gender, identity and orientation. The interplay among these factors can be very complicated; however, in most cases, two-spirit people have a sense of multiple selves as a consequence of interactions with others who hold conflicting expectations about them.

For example, in one chapter, Wesley Thomas shows how different Navajo categories of gender and sexuality are from white American notions, while Beatrice Medicine explores the ways Native sex roles change in an urban context. Elsewhere in the book, Terry Tafoya suggests an anthropological equivalent of the Heisenberg Principle in physics. In a fascinating chapter titled "M. Dragonfly: Two-Spirit and the

Tafoya Principle of Uncertainty," we read that: "in cross-cultural research one can have context or definition but not both at the same time. The more one attempts to establish a context for a situation or process, the more one will blur a clean, simple definition for a situation or process and the more one will lose a sense of context" (1997:198). This seems true of all ethnological work, but it is especially true of studies of sex and gender where interaction between anthropologist and "informant" quickly becomes saturated with emotion as questions of self and sexual identity are raised.

An unusual discussion of these issues is found in *The Second Self* by MIT psychologist Sherry Turkle (1984). Subtitled "Computers and the Human Spirit," her book shows ways in which children and adolescents relate to computerized games and, later, to actual computers. At each stage, boys and girls seem to attribute different qualities to the computer and to struggle with philosophical problems ("Is it alive?" "Can it cheat?" "What is mind?") in ways that suggest their own selves are being shaped by these interactions. A sensitive interviewer, Turkle summarizes part of her findings:

> "It's like somebody's there." This is something I often hear about the holding power of the computer [both] from children and from adults. Many people are lonely and isolated, but when they have a computer around it can feel like somebody is always there, always ready, always responsive, but without the responsibility of having to deal with another person. The computer offers a unique mixture of being alone and yet not feeling alone. (Turkle 1984:146)

Scholars from G. H. Mead to Erving Goffman and Howard S. Becker have held that the self is formed through interaction with "significant others." Turkle's research suggests that the computer has become such an other for a new generation of Americans. The question then arises, what kind of self will result from interactions between humans and ever more clever machines?

The self has again become a subject of interdisciplinary inquiry. A new book on *Self and Identity* (Ashmore and Jussim 1997) promises to be the first in a series of biennial conference reports from Rutgers University. It includes articles by psychologists, sociologists, and anthropologists. The editors conclude with a statement of "fundamental issues" in the study of self: Is the self unified or multiple? How contextualized is the self? Can the self be studied objectively? And, is the self a moral issue? (1997:218–229). To these questions anthropology has interesting material to contribute, but no final answers. (On the "postmodern self" see Allan 1998.)

As noted earlier, much of the anthropological work on self and person has taken place in the Pacific where highly distinctive self concepts have been postulated. In his conclusions to the anthology *Person, Self and Experience*, Alan Howard summed up the problems associated with such studies. I will let him have the last word before we turn to some of the newer approaches in psychological anthropology.

> It seems to me that we have here an issue as to whether the submersion of individuals within broader, more inclusive categories of relationship represents a prior notion of individualized selves, extended outward through socialization, or whether it represents a cultural conception that does not allow for self-differentiation. . . . Viewed from this perspective, what seems to distinguish Western folk psychology is the degree to which our notions of an inner self are elaborated and made central [whereas, for] the islanders described in this volume the reverse seems to be true. They have elaborated the public, relational aspects of their selves and seem to be much less preoccupied with the inner components. (Howard 1985:414–415)

This formulation cuts through a great deal of verbiage and states the problem in a form that might make progress possible.

Chapter 13

Some Newer Approaches

Charles Darwin

I n this chapter we shall consider several movements that have developed in recent years. Some of these approaches propose new methods while others employ an unfamiliar vocabulary, writing of "evocation," "expeditions," "embodiment," or "resonance." It is difficult to predict their eventual importance as contributions to psychological anthropology, but they have all attracted talented researchers and adherents and must be noted. Although I cannot yet place them in the outline of our field, students will be directed to some of the most important sources; teachers may choose to supplement this chapter with works that they find congenial.

Evolutionary Psychological Anthropology

I assume here that the evolution of life on earth is an undeniable fact, not a hypothesis competing with "creationism" or other ideologies (Dennett 1996). That is, new species have arisen from earlier forms, bone, blood, and behavior, over millions of years. This has occurred by a natural process of selection that propels into each successive generation the genes of those individuals that have best dealt with the problems presented by their environments, enabling them to survive, reproduce, and (in higher forms) to nurture their offspring.

Since the Pleistocene, culture has played an increasing role in this process; that is, advantages in technology, social organization and cognitive abilities interact with genetic endowment to give human individuals and groups selective advantages. Evolutionary psychologists ask how the history of our species—its descent from earlier hominids and its adaptation to Ice Age environments—has shaped the human mind as well as our bodies. That is, just as evolution from forms ancestral to the modern apes has left similarities in bones and senses (e.g., large skulls and stereoscopic color vision), this history has produced continuities in behavior and cognition, including the ability of apes to learn basic sign language and to make and use simple tools (McGrew 1992).

Psychologists working in this tradition have discovered general characteristics of the human psyche that can be plausibly explained by past adaptations. But *evolutionary psychological anthropology* takes this concern a stage further, using information from archaeology, linguistics, and ethnology to give a more nuanced picture of human development through time and space. Thus where evolutionary psychologists may rely on a general notion of the conditions that Ice Age hunters faced, anthropologists are aware of environmental and cultural variability during the Pleistocene and since then.

Similarly, when it comes to testing ideas about genetic determination of human thought or behavior, they draw on data about non-European languages and societies that may moderate or even contradict premature claims about "universals" (Barkow, Cosmides, and Tooby 1992). Instead of studying the development of, say, general intelligence or language ability in our species, evolutionary psychological anthropologists are concerned with quite specific abilities, testing ideas about the genetic basis of mate selection, social ranking, ethnocentrism, and even landscape preferences against our knowledge of social and individual variation.

Jerome Barkow is a psychological anthropologist who, while sympathetic to the goals of evolutionary psychology, insists on verification of assumptions about past environments and on specification of the mechanisms that lead from genes to culture. His chapter in the *Handbook of Psychological Anthropology* furnishes an excellent introduction to this rapidly developing field. As he concludes there:

> Ultimately, what evolutionary psychology has to offer to psychological anthropology is what psychoanalysis once seemed to make available: a respected if controversial scientific theory, generating much excitement in a host of intellectual domains, claiming applicability to all human societies and perhaps to all of human behavior, at a point in history when competing paradigms are, in the opinion of many, moribund. The next decade or two will be interesting ones for psychological anthropology. (Barkow 1994:132)

Cultural Psychology

Slowly developing over the past 15 years, cultural psychology seems to me like an approach within psychological anthropology—one that puts great emphasis on the self in social context (Stigler, Shweder, and Herdt 1990). However, its proponents (Shweder 1990; Cole 1995; Miller 1994) seem determined to contrast it with traditional psychological anthropology. While agreeing that "all psychology is cultural" (see Postlude, below), they also insist that "cultural psychology is not psychological anthropology," or ethnopsychology, or cross-cultural psychology (Shweder 1991:90). They also draw on certain ideas from contemporary philosophy of mind that are too complex to discuss here.

Another important influence on cultural psychology is the work of Russian psychologist L. S. Vygotsky, who placed great importance on the *social context of learning* and on the daily *practice* of skilled persons as prior to abstract cognitive processes (Vygotsky 1978; Lave 1988). These ideas are a healthy reaction against the exclusive concern with taxonomy and hierarchy in cognitive anthropology, but so far the practitioners of cultural psychology have had difficulty communicating its principles and findings outside of their own circle. Perhaps this is due to what advocate Joan Miller recognizes as its contradictory assumptions when she writes that "cultural psychology may be understood as a set of approaches that share many but not all of their core conceptual presuppositions and that, in many cases, maintain presuppositions that are mutually incompatible" (1994:139).

In an anthology of writings by one eminent founder of this movement (Shweder 1991) we find programmatic statements (chapters 1 and 2), critical essays (chapters 7, 8, and 9) and a series of articles (chapters 3–6) on specific topics, including a critique of "Culture and Personality Theory." I will discuss only one of these chapters because it illustrates both the strengths and difficulties of his enterprise (or, as he might prefer, "expedition").

In "Menstrual Pollution, Soul Loss and the Comparative Study of Emotions," (pp. 241–265), Shweder considers (in reverse order from the title) three topics that have attracted anthropologists of all persuasions. Regarding the study of emotion, he points out that at least six different questions can be asked in any given society. The taxonomic question involves the classification of feelings, whether or not they are "lexicalized" (given verbal labels) in the native language. Next, the *ecological* question has to do with "emotion-laden situations," whether universal (e.g., threat of physical attack) or culture-specific (e.g., violations of taboos). The *semantic* question leads us to study the different *meanings* of an emotion in various societies, for example, whether expressions of "anger" are regarded as useful or dangerous, and for whom.

The *communication* question inquires into the "codes" (facial, verbal, postural, etc.) used to display emotions, with the suggestion that most of these communicative channels are either universal or are learned very early in life. The *social regulation* question leads us to study notions of emotional display and the appropriateness of different displays to specific ages, genders, and other social statuses (e.g., should male American politicians cry or should they express shame in public.) Finally, the management question involves understanding how people handle emotions that are not directly expressed, e.g., by denial, displacement, projection, or somatization (i.e., the expression of feelings through physical symptoms). Shweder concludes that "there are universals and cultural specifics with regard to each of these six aspects of emotional functioning. It is ludicrous to imagine that the emotional functioning of people in different cultures is basically the same. It is just as ludicrous to imagine that each culture"s emotion life is unique" (1991:252). These six questions seem like a useful guide to the study of emotion by ethnographers, but this general view of emotion is not unique to "cultural psychology."

Shweder next turns to the topic of "soul loss" and its relationship to the psychiatric category of depression, arguing that "When you feel depressed you feel as though your soul has left your body." In effect, he is saying that the feeling of emptiness is evidence for the reality of the "soul," an entity that he later equates with whatever "connects the person with things beyond and with others and [that] is as real to each of us as it is immaterial. Lose it and you feel dead, cut off, alone, 'dispirited"—depressed" (1991:252, 257; see also Holland 1996, for the reaction of an anthropologist who was told that she had no soul).

In what ways is this discussion of the soul characteristic of cultural psychology? It seems that Shweder is trying to make the reader recognize the phenomenal reality of concepts such as "soul," "spirit," "the gods," and "pollution" to people in societies where such entities are taken for granted. Thus in his discussion of pollution among the Oriya Brahmans of India, he describes the people's attitudes towards contact of any kind with menstruating women:

> Both men and women believe that the touch of a menstruating woman will shorten the life of the person she touches, and that anything she touches—her clothing, her bedding, her children's clothes—must be washed and purified. Consequently, a menstruating woman does not sleep in the same bed with her husband, does not cook food or leave food for returning ancestral spirits or even enter the kitchen. (1991:262; see Bock 1967)

Shweder's point is that *touch*, normally considered a sign of affection and even of healing intention, has here been transformed into a dangerous thing due to an ideology of pollution. In this society, the temple of the god, the prayer room of the house, and the human body are all endangered by unclean influences: "The temple must be cleansed if a dog, an untouchable, or a foreigner enters" (p. 263). But for the Oriya, pollution is a *spiritual*, not a material, concept, and in a community where children play at avoiding an imagined polluting touch, the "emotional impact" of this action attains a power that non-Hindus can hardly comprehend (p. 265). Cultural psychology thus asks us to recognize the "reality" of souls (and their loss), and of gods, ghosts, spiritual pollution, and unfamiliar emotional categories for those peoples whose lives embody and express them.

About The Body

European attitudes toward the human body have varied widely, from the classical Greek idealization of our physical form and emphasis on bodily pleasures to the early Christian ascetic tradition that denies the body's importance in favor of "heavenly rewards." Between these extremes we find a great variety of values placed on the body, its beauty, comfort, decoration, and display. For example, notions of modesty vary by society, class, gender, and even decade, while postures that are considered neutral in one group may be marked as seductive, threatening, or disrespectful elsewhere.

Anthropologists have always shown interest in these topics, but in the past thirty years, emphasis has shifted from description of the kinds of differences cited above to an intense study of the body as a "cultural construction." That is, recent studies (often following research initiated by French scholars such as Michel Foucault) have examined the ways in which culture is "inscribed" on the body—not just by tattooing or scarification, but through often unconscious assumptions about body structure and function, gender differences, and the relationship of physical factors to emotional and spiritual expression.

Virtually everything in social life has by now been claimed to be "culturally constructed" and/or a product of "discourse." This research tradition, most easily viewed in the journal *Cultural Anthropology*, emphasizes that the ways in which people speak and write about phenomena (from sex to history) "constitutes" or "constructs" those things.

For example, in her fascinating book, *The Woman in the Body*, anthropologist Emily Martin (1987) traces changing ideas about and actions toward female reproductive physiology in the medical and biological texts of past centuries, showing the persistence of attitudes connected with often ludicrous beliefs. In its most extreme form, the constructionist approach claims that there is only discourse in the human world and that we never directly experience reality (usually placed in quotation marks) except as it is "mediated" by oral or written "texts." Furthermore, none of these texts may be "privileged" over any others so that not only beauty but also truth is in the eye of the beholder.

While this "postmodern" point of view may seem extreme and even ridiculous when stated so baldly, its advocates have come to dominate "cultural studies" in the universities, and they argue powerfully for their ideas. Indeed, "power" is another of their concerns, and the power to control discourse turns out to be central in social and political life. For example, the current debates over racial and ethnic categories in the U. S. census and in legislation affecting immigration and economic policy or university admissions can be usefully viewed as a matter of competing discourses, with the most powerful groups imposing their view of what constitutes "minority status" worthy of separate recognition and, presumably, special treatment.

In this case, I would agree that there are no "races" or "ethnic groups" aside from the ways in which they are defined by official texts. (e.g., are immigrants from Spain who display quite varied physical types and language skills to be classed as "Hispanic," as "European," as "white" or as something else?) However, when this approach is extended to a philosophic principle implying that we can never know truth since even scientific findings are merely another kind of discourse, many anthropologists part company with this approach.

Some early studies of the *anthropology of the body* can be found in a collection edited by the late John Blacking (1977). Here we find articles on facial movement, body products, trance, and dance. While recognizing that body concepts are largely "constructed" by culture, Blacking takes a somewhat traditional view in arguing that

> It cannot be assumed that [bodily] states necessarily remain neutral until some social interpretation or value is assigned to them. Some somatic states may have intrinsic qualities that command attention, expand consciousness, and actually suggest their own interpretation. (1977:6)

Thus, for Blacking, there exists a material body that suggests and sometimes resists cultural interpretation. His own work in the comparative study of music starts from the capacities and limitations of human hands, arms, voices, and ears. Other contributors address the bodily expression of emotion through posture, gesture, and blushing, or describe the symbolic associations of body parts and oppositions (such as right versus left or upper versus lower body, associated respectively with purity versus pollution in many cultures.

A more recent approach, deriving in part from medical anthropology, uses the word *embodiment* to designate the interplay between bodily states and cultural understandings. As defined by Lambek and Strathern (1998:6) "embodiment" is now "the term for a state or a process that results from the continuous interaction of body and mind or rather their conceptualization as elements in a larger unity, the body/mind manifold." Their book examines the relationship between person and body as conceived in various African and Melanesian societies.

Embodiment and Experience (Csordas 1994c) is another recent anthology. Subtitled "The existential ground of culture and self," it treats a large number of important topics with contributions by sociologists and psychologists as well as anthropologists. According to the editor's introduction, "embodiment" refers to a real departure in studies of the body: "What we are calling for here is a more radical role for the body than that typical in the 'anthropology of the body" that has been with us since the 1970s" (1994:4). Like Shweder's six questions about emotion (above), Csordas asks us to consider *multiple bodies* such as the physical, social, consumer, and medical bodies as well as the "body politic," each of which may be conceived differently in other cultures. "Why not," he asks, "begin with the premise that the fact of our embodiment can be a valuable starting point for rethinking the nature of culture and our existential situation as cultural beings?" (1994:6). Csordas also questions the use of the "metaphor of the text" in dealing with the body, suggesting that instead of approaching the body as something to be read or interpreted for its "meaning" (semiotics) we should begin with the analysis of "lived experience" (phenomenology).

These are not easy concepts to grasp, so let us examine a specific example from the same volume. Thomas Ots has lived in China on and off for many years. When he was there during the 1980s he witnessed a movement known as the *"qigong* craze." *Qi* (often rendered in English as *chi*) is a life-giving force central to traditional Chinese medicine. *Qigong* is a kind of therapy involving breathing and very gentle bodily movements that direct *qi* to acupuncture points in the body, producing healing effects. But in the aftermath of the Cultural Revolution, new forms of *qigong* evolved. In one form, called "spontaneous-*qigong*," after practitioners have attained a state of harmony and calm, they may suddenly

> shake their hands or limbs, the head or even the whole body; they may jump up and down . . . or fall down to the ground; they may shout, scream, laugh or cry, touch or embrace others, etc. In 1984, when I first observed practitioners . . . I was surprised by this "non-Chinese" behavior. Many of the practitioners were in a state of limited control of their actions; others seemingly had entered varying states of trance, ecstasy, or emotional catharsis. (p. 122)

Ots's description recalls behavior observed during some Pentecostal church services, but such actions are most unusual in Chinese public places. At first, participants gave Ots explanations of their experience in terms of traditional Chinese medicine; however, after many months of participation in *qigong* (during which he too experienced trance), Ots learned about "an immense emotional world" that he had not previously encountered.

> With our developing intimacy, they stopped referring to [traditional] models, and eventually talked about their feelings and their sufferings, and about the manner in which they believed spontaneous-*qigong* had helped them to alleviate their individual burdens.

They progressively revealed a thick, rich and complex emotional world which had been previously hidden from me. (Ots 1994:126)

Many lessons may be drawn from Ots's description, among them the ways in which embodied experience can lead thought and feeling in new directions. But there are also important implications for anthropological research for, as Ots suggests, we are too often content with rather superficial understandings of a culture so long as "the data suit our expectations." With longer, more intimate participation in another way of life we may come to understand the "private levels of perception and discourse that can so easily evade the Western anthropologists' attention" (p. 133).

My own early field experience confirms this lesson. After I had spent two summers on an Indian reservation in Colorado and drawn some conclusions about the stolid, humorless character of men in this tribe, an airplane crash in the nearby mountains started a forest fire. I joined an Indian fire-fighting unit and it was in this crisis situation that I realized my error. Far from being "humorless," the men slowly revealed the subtlety of their joking, much of it directed at the anthropologist and other non-Indians. (For similar experiences among the Western Apache see K. Basso 1979.)

The article by Ots takes such observations even further and shows that it is possible, with tact and patience, to approach the embodied experience of others. When relieved of the depression brought about by persecution under the Cultural Revolution, the practitioners of spontaneous-*qigong* "floated around the practice ground, movements became light and rhythmic, and very often they would raise and swing their arms and start to shout and laugh" (p. 134).

Interpretation of other people's emotions is always risky, but I take Ots's materials as support for my conviction that a biologically-based, universal responsiveness underlies cultural interpretations, and that whether these experiences are called *qigong* or the Holy Spirit, startle or *susto*, hot flashes or *el calor*, panic attack or *nervios*, we are dealing with experiences that all humans are capable of. And though we left William James in chapter 1 of this book, it may be time to reconsider his theory of religious conversion and even the James-Lange theory of emotion, which hypothesized that "first we run, then we feel fear." (Other articles in Csordas 1994c are also challenging to received ideas about culture and the self; on William James, see Simon 1998 and Jackson 1998.)

Person-Centered Ethnology

In one of his enigmatic statements, the late George Devereux, anthropologist and psychoanalyst, opined that "Depth equals breadth." By this he meant that a sufficiently deep, dynamic examination of one person's psyche was equivalent to what could be learned by surveying the behavior of many individuals from the same group. Margaret Mead had made a similar claim in her studies of national character, provided, she said, that the social position of that individual be specified. There is no way to test the validity of these claims; however, a most interesting approach in contemporary psychological anthropology seems to take this idea seriously. In their intensive studies of an Inuit (Eskimo) child and a young Balinese woman, respectively, two adventurous anthropologists have shown what can be accomplished by focusing on a single individual. As yet we have no accepted name for this type of study, but for ease of reference, I have borrowed a term from Robert LeVine (1982) and labeled it "person-centered" ethnology.

Jean L. Briggs is best known in anthropology for her book, *Never in Anger* (1970). There she described and analyzed the way of life of an Eskimo family and the community in which they lived with special emphasis on the control of anger and aggression. In the Arctic, people depend on one another for everyday survival, and expressions of anger are strictly forbidden (as the anthropologist learned to her own regret). But how is this kind of control learned? At the time of writing, Briggs had only general answers to this question. (On the "socialization of affect" in other societies, see Harkness and Kilbride 1983.)

In the following decades, Briggs produced a series of fascinating and provocative papers on the "management of aggression" in the socialization of Eskimo children. Her recent book, *Inuit Morality Play* (1998), goes a step further by focussing on the behavior and experiences of one three-year-old child, whom she calls "Chubby Maata." Briggs shows how close attention to intimate verbal and non-verbal interactions between various adults and this child can reveal the ways that children learn to participate as *moral actors* in their society.

Briggs analyzes several "dramas" in which Chubby Maata was involved, attending to the sequence of events, the persons present, their relationships to the child, and especially the *tone* of the games and "interrogations" that make up an important part of an Inuit child's experience with adults. Using both dynamic psychology and her understanding of Inuit culture, Briggs is able to offer provisional interpretations of the little girl's moral development. Without sampling, counting or coding specific behaviors (methods discussed in chapter 9), she clearly describes the apparently playful interactions that teach Chubby Maata which actions are acceptable for a "baby" and which are required of an older child who has mastered Inuit concepts of decorum.

Part of this process involves learning the correct attitude towards powerful others. Briggs explicates the Inuit concept of *kappia-*, roughly, fear of injury from angry people or evil spirits. She shows that it includes *ilira-*, a feeling similar to English "respect" and even "awe" in the face of superior power; but the latter is also

> a fear of being disapproved of, criticized, scolded. . . . *Ilira-* is a social-
> izing and socialized fear, one that children have to *learn* to feel . . .
> nobody likes to feel *ilira-*; it makes one feel constrained, anxious,
> inhibited . . . [Thus, to] say that a person does not cause *ilira-* is high
> praise. Nevertheless, people who never cause *ilira-* may be considered
> a little childish, unworthy of respect [while] a person who never feels
> *ilira-* is dangerously unsocialized (p. 148; compare Lutz's (1988) dis-
> cussion of the learning of *metangu* on Ifaluk).

The goal of this teaching is to inculcate in the young an appreciation of *nallik-*, 'loving nurturance,' which is "the highest Inuit value"
(Briggs 1998:141). Thus, when Chubby Maata's mother asks her again
and again, "Are you (still) a baby?" she is pointing out both the rewards
of receiving *nallik-* and the necessity to grow out of babyish dependence
into a more autonomous (and fearful) stage of life in which she will be
expected to control her aggressive tendencies and to nurture others.

It is tempting to give an extended example of one of these games,
but I refer interested readers to Briggs's book, especially chapter 4,
"Want to Come Live with Me?" in which the child learns to value her
own family and to fear strangers. While she has developed a distinctive
style of "person-centered" ethnology, Briggs is also close to the ideals of
Edward Sapir and Margaret Mead when she writes of her interest in
"the processes through which culture may be organized and created in
the minds and bodies of those who participate in it" (p. 209). I share her
conviction that "in all cultures people create associations among ideas
and emotions in modes of thought that are not verbally articulated or
perhaps even susceptible of articulation" (p. 16; compare M. Polanyi
1964, on "tacit knowledge").

Other scholars (e.g., Edward Brunner and Victor Turner) have
written about an "anthropology of experience," and some (e.g., Paul
Radin and Vincent Crapanzano) have given us sensitive biographies of
"native" people. But it is in the works of Briggs and of Norwegian
anthropologist Unni Wikan that the inner life of another culture is best
displayed by focusing on the experiences of one person. Wikan lived
among the desperately poor families of Cairo and gave us an unforgetta-
ble portrait of a middle-aged mother in *Tomorrow, God Willing* (1996,

discussed in chapter 8) but in her other book, *Managing Turbulent Hearts* (1990), we are taken into the very soul of Suriati, an attractive young Balinese woman who experiences a tragic loss.

Wikan takes a position opposed to much writing about Bali (from Gregory Bateson to Clifford Geertz). She argues that this society which "appears so peaceful and harmonious, is actually ridden with violence in covert and indirect forms" (p. 58). Balinese fear black magic from virtually all quarters, while gossip and ridicule follow any display of inappropriate, negative emotion. Balinese women of all ages have "a moral obligation to manage their hearts, entailing that they should present the world with a 'clear, bright" face" (p. 52).

Thus, when Suriati's sweetheart dies just weeks before their wedding, she manages to laugh and appear cheerful to convince herself and others that all was well, for it is dangerous to one's spiritual and mental balance to show sadness. "Laughter is singled out as the sensible response [to loss] because expression is perceived to shape and mold feeling" (p. 123). But through her intimate relationship with Suriati, the anthropologist learns—many months later—the depth of the young woman's grief and her fear!

Wikan also questions the use of the Western dichotomy of public vs. private spaces in societies like Bali, since these concepts imply "particular connotations like warm versus cool, intimate versus restrained, and safe versus dangerous that we have no reason to expect others to share until they have been actually found to do so" (p. 59). This is a useful caution, for it can only confuse matters to assume that we can tell which social settings are elsewhere viewed as "private," or what their qualities may be. Perhaps a more neutral concept such as Erving Goffman's "backstage" (defined as those situations in which public presentations of self are prepared and often contradicted) would be a better starting point for analysis (Goffman 1959).

Balinese understandings of individual character (*sifat*) must also be taken into account if we are to comprehend local thought and behavior. "A person's character is compounded of several aspects: a part is reincarnated, a part is attributable to the environment, including parent's influence; and a part stems from one's own soul—which in turn may be reincarnated in another when one is dead" (p. 101). Like Shweder (above), Wikan would argue for the phenomenal reality of the soul and of black magic in Bali. As part of her person-centered approach, she questions "whether an anthropology of experience really needs to take second place to the description of custom, the interpretation of culture, or the investigation of material patterns." Rather, "a direct approach to the lived significance of other people's concerns should be granted as much primacy as those other approaches" (p. xxiv). It should not detract from Wikan's argument to point out its similarity to what Regna Darnell (1986) has called the "Sapirean Alternative," with its emphasis on individual experience rather than the "official culture."

Like all modes of study, the person-centered approach could be badly abused. It requires language fluency, cultural sensitivity, and long periods of contact to build the kind of trust that allows another person to reveal his or her inner life. And personal revelations must be treated with respect. Without these qualities, they could easily give a distorted view of the person and allow ethnography to become mere gossip. But would it be possible to do a person-centered analysis of a historical figure? The type of psychohistorical biography practiced by Erik Erikson and others (see chapter 7) has fallen into disfavor; however, one remarkable work combining history, psychology, and anthropology suggests that, with rare scholarship, this might be possible.

Greg Dening is an Australian historian whose study of William Bligh, the infamous captain of the sailing ship Bounty, combines understanding of the eighteenth century British navy with anthropological information about the Polynesian societies involved in the mutiny of 1789. The result is a character study of Bligh and his crew together with an account of "passion, power and theatre on the Bounty" (Dening 1992). He shows the role of Bligh's ambiguous, "bad language" in provoking the mutiny and he leads the reader to an understanding of the "calamities" of the Captain. At the same time, Dening makes us aware of how world events such as New World slavery, English colonialism, and the French Revolution affected the people and actions in the story, and how competing discourses portrayed the mutiny and its aftermath.

Into Century Twenty-One

It would be dangerous to try to predict which if any of the newer approaches will survive and flourish into the new millennium. Evolutionary thinking and genetic research will surely have many continuing effects upon psychological anthropology, but I suspect that the tension between materialist and humanistic explanations of behavior will never vanish from our field (Nuckolls 1998). Thus, evolutionary psychological anthropology is likely to remain a stimulating alternative approach, attracting those with more biological knowledge than linguistic prowess.

I think that cultural psychology is unlikely to absorb or to replace psychological anthropology. Indeed, I agree with John Ingham that, at least to date, "cultural psychology has little to say about individual motivation [and thus] lacks a compelling story about the intrapsychic, embodied foundations of will, desire, and agency" (1996:8). Contending views of the relationship of mind and culture are not likely to be reconciled, although scholars like Richard Shweder and Bradd Shore have tried to construct philosophical bridges between them. As computers master new tasks they will again be used as models of human intelligence, but the brain will not easily give up its secrets, and premature conclusions will need constant revisions.

By the time this book is published, the faddish aspects of interest in "the social construction of the body" may have passed, leaving, it is hoped, a core of better understandings about embodiment and a renewed concern with the body as a regular part of anthropological research. (My own body, for what it is worth, is willed to the osteology collection of the University of New Mexico Anthropology Department!) New fads appear regularly in all academic disciplines, but the "body," being always with us, should provide a good point of departure for ethnographic writing as well as a useful topic for comparative research (Lambek and Strathern 1998).

As for "person-centered" studies, I have pointed out the extraordinary qualifications necessary to conduct successful work using this demanding approach; the same is true of the kind of psychohistorical work represented by Greg Dening's book. Fortunately, remarkable young scholars are joining our field every day, and it is for this new generation to find ways to move forward, overcoming false dichotomies, reviving what is valuable from the past, and developing methods that will allow them to test all kinds of ideas. (For example, see Nuckolls 1996.) We should remain open to stimulation from social psychology, psychiatry, medical anthropology, cognitive studies, and personality psychology, for, as Ingham has written, "psychological anthropology is a good deal more than a branch of cultural anthropology that studies the individual; it is the place where we can begin to reimagine a holistic understanding of human beings and the human condition" (1996:ix).

I am curious to see what new understandings the millennium will bring.

Postlude

All Psychology Is Cultural

I began this book with the intentionally provocative statement "All anthropology is psychological." I then offered arguments (some of which I believe to be correct) to support that position. Now it is time to turn the tables and ask, To what extent is psychology cultural?

To begin with, the academic discipline of psychology shows the features of any cultural system: it has a complex social structure, technology, and a language that, at its worst, is virtually incomprehensible to outsiders. It also has mighty founding figures—quasi-totemic ancestors whose emblems are the rat, the pigeon, the couch, and the mandala. Within this discipline, revitalization movements have emerged and disappeared, each with its own ideology and true believers. Commitment to particular schools of psychology, from psychoanalysis to behaviorism, can be explained by the same principles that explain participation in esoteric cults or patriotic wars. Also, as Richard A. Shweder (1977) has demonstrated, "magical thinking" is as prevalent in clinical judgments of personality as it is in shamanistic performances and folk science.

Too, what I have called "psychology" in this book is actually a very limited class of theories, derived exclusively from European and American research. Other psychologies and psychotherapies exist, arising from quite different cultural roots (see Murphy and Murphy 1968). As Alan Watts wrote,

> Historically, Western psychology has directed itself to the study of the psyche or mind as a clinical entity, whereas Eastern cultures have not categorized mind and matter, soul and body, in the same way as the Western. [Western psychotherapists are] interested in changing the consciousness of peculiarly disturbed individuals. The disciplines of Buddhism and Taoism are, however, concerned with changing the consciousness of normal, socially adjusted people. (Watts 1969:16)

Failure to recognize the origins of Western psychology in our own cultural tradition, with its unconscious values, biases, and habits of thought, is the crudest kind of ethnocentrism. Even within Euro-American psychology, great provincialism exists, producing distinctive French, British, and American "schools," while the student who dips into such Russian works as A. N. Leont'ev's *Activity, Consciousness, and Personality* (1978) finds himself in a different world—one whose challenging ideas are corroborated with quotations from Marx and Lenin! Besides being biased by their own culture, most Western psychologists introduce further biases into their results by using experimental subjects exclusively from their own societies. Robert Serpell has observed that

> a science of behaviour which can account only for the behaviour of a minority of the world's population is far more appropriately designated a limited specialty than the search for explanations which account for the full range of human behaviour patterns around the world. (Serpell 1976:16)

This argument does not deny the possibility of a *transcultural psychiatry* that would transcend the biases of a particular tradition to define the parameters of healthy human functioning, but it should serve to caution us against mistaking our own culture's implicit ideals for ultimate truths. (See Kiev 1972.)

Still another argument for the social—or cultural—basis of all psychology is found in the following statement:

> In the individual's mental life someone else is invariably involved, as a model, as an object, as a helper, as an opponent; and so from the very first individual psychology [is] social psychology as well.

Most students are surprised to learn that this is a quotation from Sigmund Freud (1959:1), but the "first Freudian" clearly recognized the influence of social relations and group allegiances upon individual mental processes. Erik Erikson extended psychoanalytic thought by insisting on the relevance of history and culture to the individual's sense of identity, while Rohrer and Edmonson combined individual striving and social structure in their concept of primary role identification. And it is possible to move even further in this direction, perhaps by using the concept of self to overcome the false dichotomy between culture and personality, or by combining the perspectives of "both psychological and symbolic anthropology... in a model not yet forged" (Peacock 1984).

In chapter 10, I showed that concepts of intelligence are relative to particular cultural contexts. This is true of many other psychological ideas, including concepts of self and personality. Gardner Murphy has cautioned us that the Western concept of personality as a self-contained unity can be traced back at least to Platonic idealism. According to Murphy, many of us prefer this "encapsulated" view of the individual to a social or interactionist view for reasons that are basically moralistic:

> People can be relied on if their boundaries are definite and fixed; you know where to put them; you know they will stay put. Above all, they can be held responsible. A society made up of persons of this sort . . . can be conveniently managed from above. (Murphy 1947:10; see also Brown 1966:90–161)

The cultural basis of our psychological conceptions has been further revealed by a number of thinkers. The British psychiatrist R. D. Laing (1967) has written persuasively on the *political* basis of concepts of madness, suggesting that, for many persons, schizophrenia can be a healthy response to an insoluble dilemma. Thomas Szasz (1961) has argued that "mental illness" is a *myth* that should be replaced by more humane understanding based on an analysis of the communication process (cf. Siegler and Osmond 1974). Sociologist Philip Rieff (1966) has pointed out the moral implications of contemporary notions of therapy, especially as they relate to individual responsibility and initiative. All these writers would support Ruth Benedict's ideas about the *relativity of normality* (pp. 52–53, above). Psychological anthropology must continually sensitize itself to the ways that a society's basic values influence the behavior and cognition of its members. In this case, clarity begins at home.

We must clarify our understanding of everyday notions such as "emotion" and "self" if we wish to use them cross-culturally. We must constantly beware of hidden assumptions about uniformity, continuity, causality, and so forth, lest we import them into our research. And we have much to learn from informed criticism: Gustav Jahoda's *Psychology and Anthropology* (1982), as one example, contains a sympathetic yet critical account of our field from the perspective of modern psychology. It is an essential work for the serious student. (See also Edgerton 1974, for a discussion of the differences between psychological anthropology and cross-cultural psychology.)

Viewed over the first century of its existence, psychological anthropology exhibits two complementary tendencies: it examines in ever finer detail the cultural and interactional constraints on individuals' behavior while simultaneously considering the widest possible context for any action. Our survey of issues and approaches in psychological anthropology brings us to this question, *Why does a particular society, school of thought, or individual choose at a given point in history to attribute behavior to a particular set of causes?* To answer this question we would need a psychohistory of the behavioral sciences (see Devereux 1978:373–

375). Difficult as this sounds, it may be a necessary prolegomenon to any future synthesis.

Only the most tentative answers to our question are now available. In this book I have surveyed a series of scientific approaches that attribute behavior to every sort of cause, from early psychic trauma to the immediate interaction situation, from patterns of child training to "the selfish gene." In the cases of a few individuals (Sapir, Benedict, Bettelheim) and of several approaches (modal personality, cross-cultural correlations, interactionism), I have been able to trace the personal experiences and institutional arrangements that shaped certain points of view. I believe that we *can* understand why individuals and groups are drawn to particular theories of "human nature," and I also believe that if we repress the motives for our own studies we are certain to fail. Though the sentiment expressed resonates with psychoanalysis, it was not Freud, but George Santayana who wrote, "Those who cannot remember the past are condemned to repeat it."

Personal Epilogue, 1999

The history of our subject, from folk psychology to culture and personality and onward to psychological anthropology and, perhaps, cultural psychology, is long and complex. In this text I have really only skimmed the surface, introducing readers to the major figures and schools as well as the most productive ideas and syntheses. Philosophical and ethical issues have been slighted and many contributions abridged or neglected. But this book is not intended as the last word on the subject. For a fuller understanding, students must read some of the classics in the field as well as contemporary monographs and anthologies that will carry the research forward into the twenty-first century.

Yet an underlying theme of this book is the demonstration that, like nations, anthropologists who "fail to remember the past" are likely to "repeat it." The issues that concerned the earliest contributors to our field are still with us: psychic unity, cultural relativism, individual and society, and the influence of childhood, environment, history, biology, language, and social status on behavior—all of these call out for continued study. My hope is that by outlining the concepts and methods that have been used by the best of our predecessors we can learn from them and avoid their errors. If I have been critical of some recent work, it is because I see it falling into errors that would be preventable with more attention to the past.

It is essential to be aware of the *continuities* within any field of study. Thus, to return to a once important topic (say, incest taboos) or method (such as dream interpretation) with care and imagination can be very healthy. To conclude, then, I want to consider the four articles in a recent issue of *Ethos*, the Journal of the Society for Psychological Anthropology (September, 1998, Volume 26, Number 3). Although they do not represent all of the varied interests in our field, they do demonstrate continuity and change in a useful way.

The first article, by Brian P. Farley, takes up the issue of the nature of conformity in a sociocentric community. Many scholars distinguish between egocentric and sociocentric societies, claiming that the very nature of the "self" varies with relative emphasis on the individual or the group. The literature on this issue is large, growing, and necessarily of uneven quality. Farley's excellent article inquires into how conformity is produced in the Mexican peasant community that he studied in the middle 1990s.

Farley's research is a useful antidote to those who would romanticize the peasant village, seeing it as the opposite of the anxious, crime-ridden, and individualistic city. There are surely benefits to be had in a small community, but there are always costs as well, and Farley concludes that, "In the case of San Bartolomé the sociocentric-oriented self, conditioned and maintained through an inconstant and threatening environment, conforms as a result of realistic anxiety and harbors deep resentment toward the surrounding community" (1998:290).

The second article, by Allen Johnson, centers on the Freudian concept of repression, and asks how useful it is in the interpretation of folktales. Johnson and Douglas Price-Williams (1996) had recently published a prize-winning book on the Oedipus theme in world folklore. In this article, Johnson focuses on a single Brazilian folktale, starting from Kardiner's notion of the "projective system," and asking whether, in this tale, "hostility toward landlords" is conscious or unconscious, and to what degree. He then discusses the kinds of listeners that are implied by the concept of repression as it has developed in ego psychology, suggesting a new concept of the "whole self as a listener." It sometimes seems that each development in psychological theory soon brings us back to myth, folktales, and literature to seek confirmation of our ideas.

The next article by A. Kimball Romney and Carmella C. Moore takes up another long-standing issue in anthropology: to what extent can culture be defined as shared ways of thinking, what these authors call "cognitive structures"? Focusing on the domains of kinship terms and animal names in English, the authors use certain ethnosemantic and statistical methods to represent judgments of similarity among sets of common terms (e.g., deer, goat, sheep; or, alternatively, father, mother, son, daughter). Following D'Andrade's statement that "similarity judgments can be used to decide [how] individuals actually discriminate among terms" (1995:50), they arrive at a "theory of culture as shared cognitive representation."

I am personally skeptical about the move from this small data set (obtained from college students?) to the sweeping conclusion that "one can confidently assume that every individual shares the same structure" and the claim that their model is "universally applicable to all human beings and to all semantic domains" (1998:332); however, this is likely to be a common mode of research in the next century. (See the three articles on "consensus analysis" in de Munck and Sobo 1998:165–210.)

The final article in this issue of *Ethos* is by Ian Davies and Greville Corbett who take up the question of linguistic and physiological influences on *color terminology*. Using data from speakers of English, Russian, and Setswana (South Africa), the authors test the Berlin and Kay theory of universals described in chapter 10. They point out "patterns of data that are inconsistent with the theory," but also admit that "there is a reasonable fit to some of the theory's predictions" (Davies and Corbett 1998:356). In sum, it seems clear that, after thirty years of intensive research on color terms, this issue will be alive into the next century.

The authors of this last study, by the way, are professors of psychology and of Russian at a British university (Surrey). The background for their work is more likely to be cross-cultural psychology than psychological anthropology, and this can make studies of the same topic difficult to compare. Most likely, Berlin or Kay (at U.C. Berkeley) will respond to their findings, starting another round of research.

I do not mention these facts to discredit anyone, but to point out that certain traditions of research ("paradigms") are still associated with particular schools and universities, even within a single state. Thus, the semantic and statistical methods used by Romney and Moore are characteristic of, though not limited to, U.C. Irvine, where they both taught. Folklore studies such as Johnson's are likewise associated with U.C.L.A., where he teaches, while the concern of Farley with self and emotion is closely linked to faculty research at U.C. San Diego, where he was a doctoral student; however, some of these topics are also research foci in programs at other major universities.

Although interdisciplinary research is not as popular or as well funded as it was in the past, I believe it is essential that adjoining fields try to understand one another's jargons, concepts and goals. This is particularly true of anthropology and psychology, each of which is incomplete without the other. You need not accept my arguments that "all anthropology is psychological" or that "all psychology is cultural" to recognize the interdependence that exists between these fields, or the difficulty involved in bringing them together. The phenomenon of "cultural lag" means that scholars in one field often use obsolete and discredited material from another, but this can only lead to embarrassment and misunderstanding.

If more productive relations are to take place, it will be up to members of both fields to reach out more to one another, and not just to those few colleagues who agree with us and write positive reports on our grant applications. Dialogue begins at home, and anthropologists of different theoretical persuasions need to talk to one another as well as to psychologists and cognitive scientists. There are some signs that this is beginning to happen (e.g., Ashmore and Jussim 1997) but more can be done on both a personal and an institutional level. At the very least, to quote a celebrity victim, "Can't we all just get along?" This seems like a good query to take into the next century.

References

Most citations are to recent, inexpensive editions. When the publication date of the cited edition is more than 10 years later than that of the original publication, the earlier date is shown in parentheses.

Abel, Theodora M., Rhoda Métraux, and Samuel Roll
  1986   *Psychotherapy and culture.* Albuquerque: University of New Mexico Press.

Aberle, David F.
  1960   The influence of linguistics on early culture and personality theory. In *Essays in the science of culture,* G. E. Dole and R. L. Carneiro, (eds.), pp. 1–29. New York: Crowell.

Adorno, Theodore, et al.
  1950   *The authoritarian personality.* New York: Harper & Row.

Ainsworth, Mary D. S.
  1967   *Infancy in Uganda.* Baltimore: Johns Hopkins University Press.
  1977   Infant development and mother-infant interaction among Ganda and American families. In *Culture and infancy,* P. Leiderman et al., (eds.), pp. 119–149. New York: Academic Press.

Alexander, Richard D.
  1979   *Darwinism and human affairs.* Seattle: University of Washington Press.

Allan, Kenneth
  1998   *The meaning of culture.* Westport, CT: Praeger.

Aronson, Eliot
  1980   *The social animal.* 3d ed. New York: W. H. Freeman.

Arthur, Ransom J.
  1971   *An introduction to social psychiatry.* Baltimore: Penguin.

Ashmore, Richard D. and Lee Jussim, eds.
  1997   *Self and identity: fundamental issues.* New York: Oxford University Press.

263

Ayres, Barbara
    1967   Pregnancy magic: A study of food taboos and sex avoidances. In
                Cross-cultural approaches, C. S. Ford, (ed.), pp. 111–125. New
                Haven: HRAF Press.

Banfield, Edward
    1958   *The moral basis of a backward society.* New York: Free Press.

Barash, David P.
    1982   *Sociobiology and behavior.* 2d ed. New York: Elsevier.

Barkow, Jerome H.
    1984   The distance between genes and culture. *Journal of Anthropolog-
                ical Research* 40:367–379.

Barkow, J. H., L. Cosmides, and J. Tooby, eds.
    1992   *The Adapted Mind.* New York: Oxford University Press.

Barnett, Homer G.
    1953   *Innovation.* New York: McGraw-Hill.

Barnouw, Victor
    1958   *Culture and personality.* 4th ed. Homewood, IL: Dorsey.

Barry, H., M. K. Bacon, and I. L. Child
    1959   The relation of child training to subsistence economy. *American
                Anthropologist* 61:51–63.

Bartlett, F. C.
    1923   *Psychology and primitive culture.* New York: Macmillan.

Basso, Keith H.
    1979   *Portraits of "the whiteman."* New York: Cambridge University
                Press.

Bateson, Gregory
    1958   *Naven.* 2d ed. Palo Alto, CA: Stanford University Press.
    (1936)
    1972   *Steps to an ecology of mind.* New York: Ballantine.

Bateson, Gregory, and Margaret Mead
    1942   *Balinese character: A photographic analysis.* New York: New York
                Academy of Science.

Bateson, Mary Catherine
    1984   *With a daughter's eye: a memoir of Margaret Mead and Gregory
                Bateson.* New York: Morrow.

Beals, Ralph L.
    1978   Sonoran fantasy or coming of age? *American Anthropologist*
                80:355–362.

Befu, Harumi
    1971   *Japan: An anthropological introduction.* San Francisco: Chandler.

Bellah, Robert N., et al.
    1985   *Habits of the heart.* New York: Harper & Row.

Benedict, Ruth F.
1923   The concept of the guardian spirit in North America. *Memoirs of the American Anthropological Association* 29:1–97.

1928   Psychological types in the cultures of the Southwest. In *Proceedings of the 23d International Congress of Americanists*, New York, pp. 527–581.

1932   Configurations of culture in North America, *American Anthropologist* 34:1–27.

1934   Anthropology and the abnormal. *Journal of General Psychology* 10:59–82.

1946a   *Patterns of culture.* New York: Mentor.
(1934)

1946b   *The chrysanthemum and the sword.* Boston: Houghton Mifflin.

Bennett, John W.
1946   The interpretation of Pueblo culture: A question of values. *Southwestern Journal of Anthropology* 2:361–374.

1998   *Classic anthropology.* New Brunswick, NJ: Transaction Books.

Bentley, Eric
1981   *The Brecht commentaries.* New York: Grove Press.

Berlin, Brent, and Paul Kay
1969   *Basic color terms: Their universality and evolution.* Berkeley: University of California Press.

Berne, Eric
1964   *Games people play.* New York: Grove Press.

Berry, J. W.
1976   *Human ecology and cognitive style.* New York: Halsted.

Bettelheim, Bruno
1943   Individual and mass behavior in extreme situations. *Journal of Abnormal and Social Psychology* 38:417–452.

1962   *Symbolic wounds.* Rev. ed. New York: Collier.

1967   *The empty fortress.* New York: Free Press.

1969   *The children of the dream.* New York: Avon.

1971   *The informed heart.* New York: Avon.

1974   *A home for the heart.* New York: Knopf.

1976   *The uses of enchantment.* New York: Vintage.

1982   *Freud and man's soul.* New York: Vintage.

Bharati, Agehananda.
1985   The self in Hindu thought and action. In *Culture and self*, A. Marsela, G. DeVos and F. L. K. Hsu, (eds.), pp. 185–230. London: Tavistock.

Blacking John, ed.
1977   *The anthropology of the body.* (A.S.A. Monograph 15) New York: Academic Press.

Blumer, Herbert
   1969   *Symbolic interactionism: Perspective and method.* Englewood
             Cliffs, NJ.: Prentice-Hall.

Blurton Jones, N. G., ed.
   1972   *Ethological studies of child behavior.* Cambridge: Cambridge Uni-
             versity Press.

Boas, Franz
   1939   *The mind of primitive man.* New York: Macmillan.
   (1911)

   1966   *Race, language and culture.* New York: Macmillan.
   (1940)

Bock, Philip K.
   1964   Social structure and language structure. *Southwestern Journal of
             Anthropology* 20:393–403.

   1967   Love magic, menstrual taboos, and the facts of geography. *Ameri-
             can Anthropologist* 69:213–217.

   1968   Some generative rules for American kinship terminology. *Anthro-
             pological Linguistics* 10:1–6.

   1974   *Modern cultural anthropology.* 2d ed. New York: Knopf.

   1979   Oedipus once more. *American Anthropologist* 81:905–906.

   1980   *Continuities in psychological anthropology.* 1st ed. (of the present
             work). San Francisco: W. H. Freeman.

   1981   Review of *The Don Juan Papers* by Richard de Mille et al. *Ameri-
             can Anthropologist* 83:712–714.

   1983   The Samoan puberty blues. *Journal of Anthropological Research*
             39:336–340.

   1984   *Shakespeare and Elizabethan culture.* New York: Schocken.

   1985   Edward Sapir as psychological anthropologist. Paper presented to
             the annual meeting of the American Anthropological Association,
             Washington, D.C.

   1986   *The formal content of ethnography.* Dallas: International Museum
             of Cultures.

   1987   Success in Shakespeare. In *Literature and Anthropology,* Lub-
             bock: Texas Tech University Press.

   1988   The importance of Erving Goffman to psychological anthropology.
             Ethos 16:3–20.

   1992   Music in Mérida, Yucatán. *Latin American Music Review* 13:33–
             55.

   1993   "Neither two nor one": Dual unity in the Phoenix and Turtle. In
             The Undiscover'd Country, B. J. Sokol, (ed.), pp. 39–56. London:
             Free Association Books.

   1994   *Handbook of psychological anthropology* (edited with introduction
             and two chapters). Westport, CT: Greenwood. (Paperback edition
             available from Praeger.)

1996a   Many cultures, many musics. *Reviews in Anthropology* 25:225–232.

1996b   Review of Roy G. D'Andrade, The development of cognitive anthropology. *Journal of Anthropological Research* 52:361–2.

1996c   Psychological anthropology. In *Encyclopedia of Cultural Anthropology*, vol. 3. D. Levinson and M. Ember, (eds.), pp. 1042–45. New York: Henry Holt.

1999   Culture and personality revisited. To appear in special issue of *American Behavioral Scientist* on "Personality Traits and Culture."

Bodley, John
1982   *Victims of progress.* 2d ed. Palo Alto, CA: Mayfield.

Bornstein, Marc H.
1975   The influence of visual perception on culture. *American Anthropologist* 77:774–798.

Bourguignon, Erika
1979   *Psychological anthropology.* New York: Holt, Rinehart and Winston.

1994   Trance and mediation. In *Handbook of psychological anthropology*, P. K. Bock, (ed.) pp. 297–314. Westport, CT: Greenwood.

Bowlby, John
1973   *Attachment and loss.* 2 vols. New York: Basic Books.

Brain, James L.
1977   Sex, incest and death: Initiation rites reconsidered. *Current Anthropology* 18:191–208.

Briggs, Jean L.
1970   *Never in anger.* Cambridge, MA: Harvard University Press.

1998   *Inuit morality play: The emotional education of a three-year-old.* New Haven: Yale University Press.

Bronfenbrenner, Urie
1967   The changing American child—a speculative analysis. In *Personality and social life*, R. Endleman, (ed.), pp. 189–201. New York: Random House.

1973   *Two worlds of childhood: US and USSR.* New York: Pocket Books.

Brown, Michael F.
1997   *The channeling zone: American spirituality in an anxious age.* Cambridge: Harvard University Press.

Brown, Norman O.
1959   *Life against death.* New York: Vintage.

1966   *Love's body.* New York: Vintage.

Bukharin, Nikolai
1969   *Historical materialism.* Ann Arbor: University of Michigan Press.
(1931)

Burling, Robbins
1970   *Man's many voices: Language in its cultural context.* New York: Holt, Rinehart and Winston.

Calogeras, Roy C.
1971   Géza Róheim: Psychoanalytic anthropologist or radical Freudian? *American Imago* 28:146–157.

Cancian, Frank
1967   Stratification and risk taking. *American Sociological Review* 32:912–927.

Carson, Robert C.
1969   *Interaction concepts of personality.* Chicago: Aldine.

Carstairs, G. Morris
1957   *The twice born.* London: Hogarth Press.

Castaneda, Carlos
1968   *The teachings of Don Juan.* Berkeley: University of California Press.

1971   *A separate reality.* New York: Simon & Schuster.

1972   *Journey to Ixtlan.* New York: Simon & Schuster.

1974   *Tales of power.* New York: Simon & Schuster.

Casson, Ronald W., ed.
1981   *Language, culture, and cognition.* New York: Macmillan.

Caudill, W., and G. DeVos
1956   Achievement, culture and personality. *American Anthropologist* 58:1102–1126.

Cazenueve, Jean
1972   *Lucien Lévy-Bruhl.* New York: Harper & Row.

Chisholm, James S.
1983   *Navajo infancy.* New York: Aldine.

1992   Putting people in biology. In *New directions in psychological anthropology,* T. Schwartz, G. White and C. Lutz, (eds.), pp. 125–149. New York: Cambridge University Press.

Classen, Constance
1993   *Worlds of sense.* London and New York: Routledge.

Clynes, Manfred
1977   *Sentics.* Garden City, New York: Anchor.

Cohen, Yehudi A.
1961   *Social structure and personality: A casebook.* New York: Holt, Rinehart and Winston.

1964   *The transition from childhood to adolescence.* Chicago: Aldine.

Colby, B. N.
1966   The analysis of cultural content and the patterning of narrative concerns in text. *American Anthropologist* 68:374–388.

Cole, Michael
1995   *Cultural psychology.* Cambridge, MA: Belknap Press.

Cole, Michael, and Barbara Means
1981   *Comparative studies of how people think.* Cambridge, MA: Harvard University Press.

Cole, Michael, and Sylvia Scribner
1974   *Culture and thought: A psychological introduction.* New York: Wiley.
1981   *Psychology and literacy.* Cambridge, MA: Harvard University Press.

Coles, Robert
1970   *Erik H. Erikson: The growth of his work.* Boston: Little, Brown.
1973   *The old ones of New Mexico.* Albuquerque: University of New Mexico Press.

Conklin, Harold C.
1972   *Folk classification (a bibliography).* New Haven: Yale University Department of Anthropology.

Costa, Paul and Robert McCrae
1992   *Revised NEO personality inventory and NEO five-factor inventory.* Odessa, FL: Psychological Assessment Resources.

Costigan, G.
1965   *Sigmund Freud.* New York: Macmillan.

Coult, Allan D.
1977   *Psychedelic anthropology.* Philadelphia: Dorrance.

Crapanzano, Vincent
1980   *Tuhami, portrait of a Moroccan.* Chicago: University of Chicago Press.

Csordas, Thomas J.
1994a   *The sacred self: A cultural phenomenology of Christian healing.* Berkeley: University of California Press.
1994b   Self and person. In *Handbook of psychological anthropology,* P. K. Bock, (ed.), pp. 331–350. Westport, CT: Greenwood.

Csordas, Thomas J., ed.
1994c   *Embodiment and experience: The existential ground of culture and self.* New York: Cambridge University Press.

Cumming, Elaine, and John Cumming
1957   *Closed ranks.* Cambridge, MA: Harvard University Press.

D'Andrade, Roy G.
1984   Cultural meaning systems. In *Culture theory,* R. Shweder and R. LeVine, (eds.), pp. 88–119. Cambridge: Cambridge University Press.
1994   *The development of cognitive anthropology.* New York: Cambridge University Press.

D'Andrade, Roy G. and Claudia Strauss, eds.
> 1992   *Human motives and cultural models.* New York: Cambridge University Press.

Darnell, Regna
> 1987   Personality and culture: The fate of the Sapirian alternative. In *Malinowski, Benedict, Rivers and Others*, G. Stocking, (ed.), pp. 156–183. Madison: University of Wisconsin Press.

Dasen, P. R.
> 1972   Cross-cultural Piagetian research: A summary. *Journal of Cross-cultural Psychology* 3:23–40.

Davies, Ian and Grenville Cobett
> 1998   A Cross-cultural study of color-grouping: Tests of the perceptual-physiological account of color universals. *Ethos* 26:338–360.

Davis, Allison, and John Dollard
> 1964   *Children of Bondage.* New York: Harper & Row.
> (1940)

Dawkins, Richard
> 1978   *The selfish gene.* New York: Oxford University Press.
> 1982   *The extended phenotype.* Oxford: W. H. Freeman.

Dement, William C.
> 1974   *Some must watch while some must sleep.* San Francisco: W. H. Freeman.

De Mille, Richard, ed.
> 1980   *The Don Juan papers.* Santa Barbara, CA: Ross-Erikson.

DeMunck, Victor C. and Elisa J. Sobo, eds.
> 1998   *Using methods in the field.* Walnut Creek, CA: AltaMira Press.

Dening, Greg
> 1992   *Mr. Bligh's bad language.* New York: Cambridge University Press.

Dennett, Daniel
> 1996   *Darwin's dangerous idea.* New York: Simon & Schuster.

Devereux, George
> 1961   *Mojave ethnopsychiatry and suicide.* Bulletin no. 175. Bureau of American Ethnology, Washington, D.C.
> 1967   *From anxiety to method in the behavioral sciences.* The Hague: Mouton.
> 1969   *Reality and dream.* Garden City, NY: Anchor.
> (1951)
> 1978   The works of George Devereux. In *The making of psychological anthropology,* G. Spindler, (ed.), pp. 361–406. Berkeley: University of California Press.
> 1980   *Basic problems of ethnopsychiatry.* Chicago: University of Chicago Press.

DeVos, George
> 1978   The Japanese adapt to change. In *The making of psychological*

anthropology, G. Spindler, (ed.), pp. 219–257. Berkeley: University of California Press.

Dollard, John, et al.
1939 *Frustration and aggression.* New Haven: Yale University Press.

Dollard, John, and Neil Miller
1950 *Personality and psychotherapy.* New York: McGraw-Hill.

Dougherty, Janet W. D., ed.
1985 *Directions in cognitive anthropology.* Urbana: University of Illinois Press.

Douglas, Jack D.
1967 *The social meanings of suicide.* Princeton: Princeton University Press.

Dower, John W.
1996 *War without mercy.* New York: Pantheon.

Draper, Patricia
1973 Crowding among hunter-gatherers: The !Kung Bushmen. *Science* 182:301–303.

Draper, P., and H. Harpending
1982 Father absence and reproductive strategy. *Journal of Anthropological Research* 38:255–273.

Driver, Harold
1966 Geographical-historical *versus* psycho-functional explanations of kin avoidances. *Current Anthropology* 7:131–182.

DuBois, Cora
1961 *The people of Alor.* 2 vols. New York: Harper & Row.
(1944)

Dumont, Louis
1970 *Homo Hierarchicus.* Chicago: University of Chicago Press.

Dundes, Alan
1962 Earth-diver: Creation of the mythopoeic male. *American Anthropologist* 64:1032–1051.

1984 *Life is like a chicken coop ladder.* New York: Columbia University Press.

Eaton, J. W., and R. J. Weil
1953 The mental health of the Hutterites. *Scientific American* 189:31–37.

Edgar, Iain
1994 Dream imagery becomes social experience. In *Anthropology and Psychoanalysis,* S. Heald and A. Deluz, (eds.), pp. 99–113. London: Routledge.

Edgerton, Robert B.
1970 Method in psychological anthropology. In *Handbook of method in cultural anthropology,* R. Naroll and R. Cohen, (eds.), pp. 338–352. Garden City, NY: Natural History Press.

1971   *The individual in cultural adaptation.* Berkeley: University of California Press.

1974   Cross-cultural psychology and psychological anthropology: One paradigm or two? *Reviews in Anthropology* 1:52–65.

Eggan, Dorothy
1961   Dream analysis. In *Studying personality cross-culturally,* B. Kaplan, (ed.), pp. 551–577. New York: Harper & Row.

Ekman, Paul
1973   Cross-cultural studies of facial expression. In *Darwin and facial expression,* P. Ekman, (ed.), pp. 169–222. New York: Academic Press.

Ember, Melvin
1978   Size of color lexicon: Interaction of cultural and biological factors. *American Anthropologist* 80:364–367.

Ember, Melvin and Carol R. Ember
1997   Facts of violence. *Anthropology Newsletter* 39(7):14.

Empson, William
1974   *Some versions of pastoral.* New York: New Directions.

Endleman, Robert, ed.
1967   *Personality and social life.* New York: Random House.

Endleman, Robert
1981   *Psyche and society.* New York: Columbia University Press.

Erickson, Mark T.
1989   Incest avoidance and familial bonding. *Journal of Anthropological Research* 45:267–291.

In press   Incest avoidance: Clinical implications of the evolutionary perspective. In W. Trevathan, J. J. McKenna and E. O. Smith, eds., *Evolutionary medicine.* New York: Oxford University Press.

Erikson, Erik H.
1958   *Young man Luther.* New York: Norton.

1963   *Childhood and society.* 2d ed. New York: Norton.
(1950)

1969   *Gandhi's truth.* New York: Norton.

1975   *Life history and the historical moment.* New York: Norton.

Evans, Richard I.
1967   *Dialogue with Erik Erikson.* New York: Harper & Row.

Ewing, Katherine
1998   Crossing borders and transgressing boundaries. *Ethos* 26:262–267.

Fanon, Frantz
1965   *The wretched of the earth.* New York: Grove.

Farley, Brian P.
1998   Anxious conformity: Anxiety and the sociocentric-oriented self in a Tlaxcalan community. *Ethos* 26:271–294.

Fenichel, Otto
1945   *The psychoanalytic theory of neurosis.* New York: Norton.

Fisher, S., and R. P. Greenberg
1977   *The scientific credibility of Freud's theories and therapy.* New York: Basic Books.

Flaubert, Gustave
1957   *Madame Bovary,* trans. by Francis Steegmuller. New York: Modern Library.

Flügel, J. C.
1950   *The psychology of clothes.* London: Hogarth Press.

Fogelson, R. D., ed.
1976   *Contributions to anthropology: Selected papers of A. I. Hallowell.* Chicago: University of Chicago Press.

Foster, George M.
1965   Peasant society and the image of limited good. *American Anthropologist* 67:293–315.

Foulks, E. F.
1972   *The Arctic hysterias of the North Alaskan Eskimo.* Washington, DC: American Anthropological Association.

Fox, Robin
1962   Sibling incest. *British Journal of Sociology* 13:128–150.
1967   *Kinship and marriage.* Baltimore: Penguin.
1994   Myth as evidence of social process. In *Handbook of psychological anthropology,* P. K. Bock, (ed.), pp. 211–229. Westport, CT: Greenwood.

Fox, Robin, and Usher Fleising
1976   Human ethology. *Annual Review of Anthropology* 5:265–288.

Frake, Charles 0.
1962   The ethnographic study of cognitive systems. In *Anthropology and human behavior,* pp. 72–85. Washington, DC: Anthropological Society of Washington.
1980   *Language and cultural description.* Palo Alto: Stanford University Press.

Frank, Jerome D.
1963   *Persuasion and healing.* New York: Schocken.

Franklin, Karl J.
1963   Kewa ethnolinguistic concepts of body parts. *Southwestern Journal of Anthropology* 19:54–63.

Freedman, Daniel
1974   *Human infancy: An evolutionary perspective.* Hillsdale, NJ: L. Earlbaum Associates.

Freeman, Derek
1983   *Margaret Mead and Samoa.* Cambridge, MA: Harvard University Press.

1999 *The fateful hoaxing of Margaret Mead.* Boulder: Westview Press.

Freud, Anna
1946 *The ego and the mechanisms of defense.* London: Hogarth Press.
(1936)

Freud, Sigmund
1950 *Totem and taboo.* New York: Norton.
(1913)

1952 *On dreams.* New York: Norton.
(1901)

1959 *Group psychology and the analysis of the ego.* New York: Norton.
(1921)

1961 *Civilization and its discontents.* New York: Norton.
(1930)

Fromm, Erich
1941 *Escape from freedom.* New York: Farrar and Rinehart.

Garson, Barbara
1977 *All the livelong day.* New York: Penguin.

Geertz, Clifford
1973 *The interpretation of cultures.* New York: Basic Books.

1984 Anti anti-relativism. American Anthropologist 86:263–278.

Gellner, Ernest
1998 *Language and solitude.* New York: Cambridge University Press.

Gillespie, Andrea
1995 *Sign and signifier in Santa Fe: The history of a clothing style.*
Ph.D. dissertation, Department of Anthropology, University of
New Mexico.

Girgus, Sam, ed.
1981 *The American Self.* Albuquerque: University of New Mexico
Press.

Gladwin, Thomas, and Seymour B. Sarason
1953 *Truk: Man in paradise.* Chicago: University of Chicago Press.

Glenn, M., and R. Kunnes
1973 *Repression or revolution: Therapy in the United States today.* New
York: Harper & Row.

Godelier, Maurice
1986 *The making of great men.* Cambridge: Cambridge University
Press.

Goffman, Erving
1959 *The presentation of self in everyday life.* Garden City, NY: Anchor.

1961a *Encounters.* Indianapolis: Bobbs-Merrill.

1961b *Asylums.* Garden City, NY: Anchor.

1963 *Stigma.* Englewood Cliffs, NJ.: Prentice-Hall.

1967 *Interaction ritual.* Garden City, NY: Anchor.

1969   *Strategic interaction*. Philadelphia: University of Pennsylvania Press.

1971   *Relations in public*. New York: Basic Books.

1974   *Frame analysis*. New York: Harper & Row.

1979   *Gender advertisements*. New York: Harper & Row.

1981   *Forms of talk*. Philadelphia: University of Pennsylvania Press.

Goleman, Daniel
1995   *Emotional intelligence*. New York: Bantam Books.

Goodenough, Ward H.
1957   Cultural anthropology and linguistics. In *Report of the 7th annual roundtable on linguistics and language study*, P. L. Garvin, (ed.), pp. 167–173. Washington, DC: Georgetown University Press.

Gore, Albert, Jr.
1992   *Earth in the balance*. Boston: Houghton Mifflin.

Gorer, Geoffrey
1955   *Exploring English character*. New York: Criterion Books.

1964   *The American people*. New York: Norton.
(1948)

Gorer, Geoffrey, and John Rickman
1962   *The people of Great Russia*. New York: Norton.
(1949)

Graves, Nancy B., and Theodore D. Graves
1978   The impact of modernization on the personality of a Polynesian people. *Human Organization* 37:115–135.

Gregor, Thomas
1985   *Anxious pleasures*. Chicago: University of Chicago Press.

Grob, C. S. and M. Dobkin de Rios
1994   Hallucinogens, managed states of consciousness and adolescents: Cross-cultural perspectives. In *Handbook of psychological anthropology*, P. K. Bock, (ed.), pp. 315–330. Westport, CT: Greenwood.

Guthrie, George M., and Patricia P. Tanco
1980   Alienation. In *Handbook of cross-cultural psychology*, vol. 6, H. Triandis and J. Draguns, (eds.), pp. 9–60. Boston: Allyn and Bacon.

Hall, Edward T.
1959   *The silent language*. Garden City, NY: Doubleday.

Hallowell, A. Irving
1955   *Culture and experience*. Philadelphia: University of Pennsylvania Press.

Harkness, Sara
1992   Human development in psychological anthropology. In *New directions in psychological anthropology*, T. Schwartz, G. White and C. Lutz, (eds.), pp. 102–122. New York: Cambridge University Press.

Harner, Michael J., ed.
  1973   *Hallucinogens and shamanism*. New York: Oxford University Press.
  1980   *The way of the shaman*. New York: Harper & Row.
  1990   *The way of the shaman*. expanded ed. San Francisco: Harper and Row.

Harris, Judith
  1998   *The nurture assumption*. New York: Simon & Schuster.

Harris, Marvin
  1964   *The nature of cultural things*. New York: Random House.
  1968   *The rise of anthropological theory*. New York: Crowell.

Hay, Thomas H.
  1976   Personality and probability: The modal personality of the Tuscarora revisited. *Ethos* 4:509–524.

Heald, Suzette
  1994   Every man a hero: Oedipal themes in Gisu circumcision. In *Anthropology and psychoanalysis*, S. Heald and A. Deluz, (eds.), pp. 184–209. London: Routledge.

Heald, Suzette and Ariane Deluz, eds.
  1994   *Anthropology and psychoanalysis*. London: Routledge

Hendrix, Lewellyn
  1985   Economy and child training reexamined. *Ethos* 13:246–261.

Henry, Jules, and Melford E. Spiro
  1953   Psychological techniques: Projective tests in field work. In *Anthropology today*, A. L. Kroeber, (ed.), pp. 417–429. Chicago: University of Chicago Press.

Herdt, Gilbert H.
  1981   *Guardians of the flutes*. New York: McGraw-Hill.

Holland, Dorothy
  1997   Selves as cultured: As told by an anthropologist who lacks a soul. In *Self and identity*, Ashmore and Jussim, (eds.), pp. 160–190. New York: Oxford University Press.

Holloman, Regina E.
  1974   Ritual opening and individual transformation: Rites of passage at Esalen. *American Anthropologist* 76:265–280.

Horowitz, Helen L.
  1987   *Campus life*. New York: Knopf.

Howard, Alan
  1985   Ethnopsychology and the prospects for a cultural psychology. In *Person, self and experience*, G. M. White and J. Kirkpatrick, (eds.), pp. 401–420. Berkeley: University of California Press.

Howard, Jane
  1984   *Margaret Mead: A life*. London: Harvil Press.

Hsu, Francis L. K., ed.
    1972   *Psychological anthropology.* New ed. Cambridge, MA: Schenk-
             man.
    1973   Prejudice and its intellectual effect in American anthropology.
             American Anthropologist 75:1–19.

Hull, Clark L.
    1943   *Principles of behavior.* New York: Appleton-Century.

Hunn, Eugene
    1985   The utilitarian factor in folk classification. In *Directions in cogni-
             tive anthropology,* J. Dougherty, (ed.), pp. 117–140. Urbana: Uni-
             versity of Illinois Press.

Hymes, Dell, ed.
    1964   *Language in culture and society.* New York: Harper & Row.

Ingham, John
    1996   *Psychological anthropology reconsidered.* New York: Cambridge
             University Press.

Inkeles, Alex
    1961   National character and modern political systems. In *Psychological
             anthropology,* F. Hsu, (ed.), pp. 172–208. Homewood, IL: Dorsey.

Inkeles, Alex, et al.
    1967   Modal personality and adjustment to the Soviet sociopolitical sys-
             tem. In *Personality and social life,* R. Endleman, (ed.), pp. 210–
             221. New York: Random House.

Irons, William G.
    1979   Natural selection, adaptations, and human social behavior. In
             Evolutionary biology and human social behavior, N. A. Chagnon
             and W. G. Irons, (eds.), pp. 4–39. North Scituate, MA: Duxbury
             Press.

Jackson, Michael
    1998   *Minima ethnographica.* Chicago: University of Chicago Press.

Jackson, Michael, ed.
    1996   *Things as they are.* Bloomington: University of Indiana Press.

Jacobs, Melville
    1959   The content and style of an oral literature. Chicago: University of
             Chicago Press.

Jacobs, Sue-Ellen, Wesley Thomas, and Sabine Lang, eds.
    1996   *Two-spirit people: Native American gender identity, sexuality, and
             spirituality.* Urbana: University of Illinois Press.

Jahoda, Gustav
    1982   *Psychology and anthropology.* New York: Academic Press.

James, William
    1961   *The varieties of religious experience.* New York: Macmillan.
    (1902)

| 1981 | *Principles of psychology.* 3 vols. Cambridge, MA: Harvard Univer- |
| (1880) | sity Press. |

Jenkins, Janis H.

1994   The psychocultural study of emotion and mental disorder. In *Handbook of psychological anthropology,* P. K. Bock, (ed.), pp. 97–120. Westport, CT: Greenwood.

1998   The medical anthropology of political violence: Cultural considerations. *Medical Anthropology Quarterly* 12:122–131.

Johnson, Allen

1998   Repression: A reexamination of the concept as applied to folktales. *Ethos* 26:295–313.

Johnson, Allen and D. R. Price-Williams

1996   *Oedipus ubiquitous: The family complex.* Stanford: Stanford University Press.

Joralemon, Donald

1990   The selling of the shaman and the problem of informant legitimacy. *Journal of Anthropological Research* 46:195–118.

Kaplan, Bert

1954   A study of Rorschach responses in four cultures. *Papers of the Peabody Museum, Harvard University 42.* Cambridge, MA.

Kaplan, Bert, ed.

1961   *Studying personality cross-culturally.* New York: Harper & Row.

Kaplan, Bert, and Thomas F. A. Plaut

1956   *Personality in a communal society.* Lawrence: University of Kansas Publications, Social Science Studies.

Kardiner, Abram, with Ralph Linton

1939   *The individual and his society.* New York: Columbia University Press.

Kardiner, Abram, with Ralph Linton, Cora DuBois, and James West

1945   *The psychological frontiers of society.* New York: Columbia University Press.

Kardiner, Abram, and Lionel Ovesey

1951   *The mark of oppression.* New York: Norton.

Kardiner, Abram, and Edward Preble

1963   *They studied man.* New York: Mentor.

Katcher, Aaron, and Joan Katcher

1967   The restructuring of behavior in a messianic cult. In *Personality and social life,* R. Endleman, (ed.), pp. 500–514. New York: Random House.

Katz, Richard

1982   *Boiling energy.* Cambridge, MA: Harvard University Press.

Kaufman, I. Charles

1975   Learning what comes naturally: The role of life experience in the establishment of species typical behavior. *Ethos* 3:129–142.

Keesing, Roger M.
1985   Conventional metaphors and anthropological metaphysics. *Journal of Anthropological Research* 41:201–217.

Kegan, Robert
1982   *The evolving self.* Cambridge, MA: Harvard University Press.

Kelly, George A.
1963   *A theory of personality.* New York: Norton.

Kennedy, John G.
1966   *Peasant society and the image of limited good*: A critique. *American Anthropologist* 68:1212–1225.

Kennedy, J. G., and L. L. Langness, eds.
1981   *Dreams.* Special Issue of *Ethos* 9:249–390.

Kiev, Ari
1972   *Transcultural psychiatry.* New York: Free Press.

Kleinman, Arthur
1988   *Rethinking psychiatry.* New York: Free Press.

Kluckhohn, Clyde
1957   *Mirror for man.* New York: Premier.
1962   *Culture and behavior,* R. Kluckhohn, (ed.). New York: Free Press.

Konner, Melvin J.
1976   Maternal care, infant behavior and development among the !Kung. In *Kalahari hunter-gatherers,* R. B. Lee and I. DeVore, (eds.), pp. 218–245. Cambridge, MA: Harvard University Press.

Kotre, John
1985   *Outliving the self.* Baltimore: Johns Hopkins University Press.

Krake, Waud
1978   *Force and persuasion.* Chicago: University of Chicago Press.
1995   Dreams, ghosts, tales: Parintintin imagination. *Psychoanalytic Review* 84:273–280.

Kroeber, Alfred L.
1952   *The nature of culture.* Chicago: University of Chicago Press.

Kuhn, Thomas S.
1962   *The structure of scientific revolutions.* Chicago: University of Chicago Press.

LaBarre, Weston
1970   *The ghost dance: Origin of religion.* Prospect Heights, IL: Waveland Press, Inc. (reissued 1990).

Laing, R. D.
1967   *The politics of experience.* New York: Ballantine.

Lambek, M. and A. Strathern
1998   *Bodies and persons.* New York: Cambridge University Press.

Lang, Kurt
1964   Alienation. In *A dictionary of the social sciences,* J. Gould and W.

L. Kolb, (eds.), pp. 19–20. Glencoe, IL: Free Press.

Langer, Walter C.
1973   *The mind of Adolf Hitler.* New York: Signet.

Larsen, Tord
1987   Action, morality, and cultural translation. *Journal of Anthropological Research* 43:1–28.

Lave, Jean
1986   *Cognition in practice.* New York: Cambridge University Press.

Lear, Jonathan
1996   *Open minded: Working out the logic of the soul.* Cambridge: Harvard University Press.

Lee, Dorothy
1959   *Freedom and culture.* Prospect Heights, IL: Waveland Press, Inc. (reissued 1987).

Leighton, Alexander, et al.
1963   *Psychiatric disorder among the Yoruba.* Ithaca, NY: Cornell University Press.

Leonard, Jonathan
1998   Unleashing the genies in the sleeping mind. *Harvard Magazine* May–June 1998, pp. 58–68.

Leont'ev, A. N.
1978   *Activity, consciousness, and personality.* New York: Prentice-Hall.

LeVine, Robert A.
1974   *Culture and personality: Contemporary readings.* Chicago: Aldine.
1982   *Culture, behavior, and personality,* 2d ed. Chicago: Aldine.

Lévi-Strauss, Claude
1963   *Totemism.* Boston: Beacon Press.
1966   *The savage mind.* Chicago: University of Chicago Press.

Levy, Robert I.
1973   *Tahitians.* Chicago: University of Chicago Press.
1984   Emotion, knowing and culture. In *Culture theory,* R. Shweder and R. LeVine, (eds.), pp. 214–237. New York: Cambridge University Press.

Lewis, Oscar
1951   *Life in a Mexican Village.* Urbana: University of Illinois Press.

Lifton, Robert Jay
1961   *Thought reform and the psychology of totalism.* New York: Norton.
1970   *History and human survival.* New York: Random House.
1986   *The Nazi doctors.* New York: Basic Books.

Lindenbaum, Shirley
1979   *Kuru sorcery.* Palo Alto: Mayfield.

Lindesmith, A. R., and Anselm L. Strauss
    1950   A critique of culture-personality writings. *American Sociological Review* 15:587–600.

Linton, Adele, and Charles Wagley
    1971   *Ralph Linton*. New York: Columbia University Press.

Linton, Ralph
    1930   *The study of man*. New York: Appleton-Century-Crofts.
    1945   *The cultural background of personality*. New York: Appleton-Century-Crofts.

Lomax, Elizabeth, et al.
    1978   *Science and patterns of child care*. San Francisco: W. H. Freeman.

Lucy, John
    1997   Linguistic relativity. *Annual Review of Anthropology* 26:291–312.

Luhrmann, Tanya
    1987   *Persuasions of the witch's craft*. Cambridge: Harvard University Press.

Lurie, Alison
    1976   The dress code. *New York Review of Books,* November 25, pp. 17–20.

Lutz, Catherine
    1986   Emotion, thought, and estrangement: Emotion as a cultural category. *Cultural Anthropology* 1:287–309.
    1988   *Unnatural emotions*. Chicago: University of Chicago Press.

Lynch, Kevin
    1964   *The image of the city*. Cambridge, MA: MIT Press.

MacAndrew, C., and R. Edgerton
    1969   *Drunken comportment*. Chicago: Aldine.

MacCannell, Dean
    1976   *The tourist*. New York: Schocken.

MacCorquodale, K., and P. E. Meehl
    1948   Hypothetical constructs and intervening variables. *Psychological Review* 55:95–107.

MacGregor, Gordon
    1946   *Warriors without weapons*. Chicago: University of Chicago Press.

McClelland, David C.
    1967   *The achieving society*. New York: Free Press.
    1978   Making it to maturity. *Psychology Today* 12:42–53, 114.

McGrew, William C.
    1972   *An ethological study of children's behavior*. New York: Academic Press.
    1998   Culture in nonhuman primates? *Annual Review of Anthropology* 27:301–328.

McGrew, W. C. and L. Marchant
    1994   Primate ethology: A perspective on human and non-human hand-edness. In *Handbook of psychological anthropology*, P. K. Bock, (ed.), pp. 171–184. Westport, CT: Greenwood.

Madariaga, Salvador de
    1928   *Englishmen, Frenchmen and Spaniards*. London: Oxford University Press.

Mahler, M. S., Fred Pine, and A. Bergman
    1975   *The psychological birth of the human infant*. New York: Basic Books.

Malinowski, Bronislaw
    1955   *Magic, science and religion*. Garden City, NY: Anchor.
    1961   *Argonauts of the western Pacific*. New York: Dutton.
    (1922)

Manson, William C.
    1986   Abram Kardiner and the neo-Freudian alternative in culture and personality. In *Malinowski, Rivers, Benedict and others*, G. W. Stocking, Jr., (ed.), pp. 72–94. Madison: University of Wisconsin Press.
    1988   *The psychodynamics of culture*. New York: Greenwood.

Maquet, Jacques
    1978   Castaneda: Warrior or scholar? *American Anthropologist* 80:362–363.

Marcuse, Herbert
    1955   *Eros and civilization*. Boston: Beacon Press.

Marsella, A., G. DeVos, and F. L. K. Hsu, eds.
    1985   *Culture and self*. New York: Tavistock.

Martin, Emily
    1987   *The woman in the body*. Boston: Beacon Press.

Marx, Karl
    1904   *A contribution to the critique of political economy*. New York: International Library.
    (1859)

Mead, George Herbert
    1934   *Mind, self and society*. Chicago: University of Chicago Press.

Mead, Margaret
    1930   An ethnologist's footnote to *Totem and taboo*. *Psychoanalytic Review* 17:297–301.
    1932   An investigation of the thought of primitive children with special reference to animism. *Journal of the Royal Anthropological Institute* 62:173–190.
    1942   *And keep your powder dry*. New York: Morrow.
    1949   *Coming of age in Samoa*. New York: Mentor.
    (1928)
    1953a   *Growing up in New Guinea*. New York: Mentor.
    (1930)

1953b   *National character.* In *Anthropology today,* A. L. Kroeber, (ed.), pp. 642–667. Chicago: University of Chicago Press.

1959   *An anthropologist at work: Writings of Ruth Benedict.* Boston Houghton Mifflin.

1963   *Sex and temperament in three primitive societies.* New York:
(1935)   Apollo.

1966   *New lives for old.* New York: Morrow.
(1956)

1972   *Blackberry winter.* New York: Morrow.

1974   *Ruth Benedict.* New York: Columbia University Press.

Menget, Patrick
1982   Time of birth, time of being: The couvade. In *Between belief and transgression,* M. Izard and P. Smith, (eds.), pp. 193–209. Chicago: University of Chicago Press.

Merton, Robert K.
1957   *Social theory and social structure.* Rev. ed. Glencoe, IL: Free Press.

Métraux, Rhoda, and Margaret Mead
1954   *Themes in French culture.* Palo Alto: Stanford University Press.

Milgram, Stanley
1974   *Obedience to authority.* New York: Harper & Row.

Miller, Daniel R., and Guy E. Swanson
1966   *Inner conflict and defense.* New York: Schocken.

Miller, Neil, and John Dollard
1941   *Social learning and imitation.* New Haven: Yale University Press.

Minturn, Leigh, and William Lambert
1964   *Mothers of six cultures.* New York: Wiley.

Mitchell, Timothy
1989   *Violence and piety in Spanish folklore.* Philadelphia: University of Pennsylvania Press.

1990   *Passional culture.* Philadelphia: University of Pennsylvania Press.

1992   *Blood sport.* Philadelphia: University of Pennsylvania Press.

1993   *Flamenco deep song.* New Haven: Yale University Press.

1998   *Betrayal of the innocents: Desire, power and the Catholic Church in Spain.* Philadelphia: University of Pennsylvania Press.

Morgan, Lewis Henry
1877   *Ancient society.* Chicago: Kerr.

Munroe, Robert L.
1980   Male transvestism and the couvade. *Ethos* 8:49–59.

Munroe, Robert L., and Ruth Munroe
1975   *Cross-cultural human development.* Prospect Heights, IL: Waveland Press, Inc. (reissued with changes 1987)

Munroe, R. H., R. L. Munroe, E. Westling, and J. Rosenberg
1997   Infant experience and late-childhood dispositions: An eleven-year

follow-up among the Logoli of Kenya. *Ethos* 25:359–372.

Murdock, George P.
    1949   *Social structure*. New York: Macmillan.
    1957   World ethnographic sample. *American Anthropologist* 59:664–687.

Murphy, Gardner
    1947   *Personality: A biosocial approach to origins and structure*. New York: Harper & Brothers.

Murphy, Gardner, and Lois B. Murphy, eds.
    1968   *Asian psychology*. New York: Basic Books.

Murphy, Robert
    1971   *The dialectics of social life*. New York: Basic Books.

Murray, Frank B., ed.
    1972   *Critical features of Piaget's theory of the development of thought*. New York: MSS Information Corporation.

Nachman, Steven R.
    1986   Discomfiting laughter: *Schadenfreud* among Melanesians. *Journal of Anthropological Research* 42:53–68.

Naroll, Raoul, and Ronald Cohen, eds.
    1970   *A handbook of method in cultural anthropology*. Garden City, NY: Natural History Press.

Needham, Rodney
    1965   Review of *Lucien Lévy-Bruhl,* by Jean Cazenueve. *American Anthropologist* 67:1291–1292.

Neisser, Ulrich
    1976   *Cognition and reality*. San Francisco: W. H. Freeman.

Newman, Katherine S.
    1986   Symbolic dialects and generations of women. *American Ethnologist* 13:230–252.

Newman, Philip
    1964   "Wild man" behavior in a New Guinea Highlands community. *American Anthropologist* 66:1–19.

Nuckolls, Charles W.
    1996   *The cultural dialectics of knowledge and desire*. Madison: University of Wisconsin Press.
    1998   *Culture: A problem that cannot be solved*. Madison: University of Wisconsin Press.

Orlansky, Harold
    1949   Infant care and personality. *Psychological Bulletin* 46:1–48.

Orwell, George
    1954   *A collection of essays*. Garden City, NY: Anchor.

Ots, Thomas
    1993   The silenced body. In *Embodiment and experience*, T. J. Csordas,

(ed.), pp. 116–138. New York: Cambridge University Press.

Ottenberg, Simon
   1994   Initiations. In *Handbook of psychological anthropology*, P. K. Bock, (ed.), pp. 351–377. Westport, CT: Greenwood.

Oyama, Susan
   1985   *The ontogeny of information.* Cambridge: Cambridge University Press.
   1994   Rethinking development. In *Handbook of psychological anthropology*, P. K. Bock, (ed.), pp. 185–196. Westport, CT: Greenwood.

Paul, Robert A.
   1976   Did the primal crime take place? *Ethos* 4:311–352.
   1989   Psychoanalytic anthropology. *Annual Review of Anthropology* 18:177–202.
   1995   Act and intention in Sherpa culture and society. In *Other intentions*, L. Rosen, (ed.), pp. 15–46. Santa Fe: School of American Research Press.

Peacock, James
   1984   Symbolic and psychological anthropology. *Ethos* 12:37–53.

Pettit, Philip
   1975   *The concept of structuralism.* Berkeley: University of California Press.

Phillips, Herbert P.
   1965   *Thai peasant personality.* Berkeley: University of California Press.

Piaget, Jean
   1971   *Genetic epistemology.* New York: Norton.
   1973   *The child and reality.* New York: Grossman.

Piers, Gerhart, and Milton Singer
   1953   *Shame and guilt.* Springfield, IL: Charles C. Thomas.

Piker, Steven
   1966   The image of limited good: Comments on an exercise in description and interpretation. *American Anthropologist* 68:1201–1211.

Pitt-Rivers, Julian A.
   1960–1961 "Interpersonal relations in peasant society": A comment. *Human Organization* 19:180–183.

Polanyi, Michael
   1964   *Personal knowledge.* New York: Harper & Row.

Price-Williams, D. R.
   1975   *Explorations in cross-cultural psychology.* San Francisco: Chandler & Sharp.

Price-Williams, D. R., W. Gordon, and M. Ramirez
   1969   Skill and conservation. *Developmental Psychology* 1:769.

Prince, Raymond, ed.
   1982   *Shamanism and endorphins.* Special issue of *Ethos* 10:299–423.

Quinn, Naomi
  1975   Decision models of social structure. *American Ethnologist* 2:19–
            46.
  1992   The motivational force of self-understanding: Evidence from
            wives' inner conflicts. In *Human motives and cultural models*, R.
            D'Andrade and C. Strauss, (eds.), pp. 90–126. New York: Cam-
            bridge University Press.

Radin, Paul
  1957   *Primitive man as philosopher.* 2d rev. ed. New York: Dover.
  (1927)

Redfield, Robert
  1953   *The primitive world and its transformations.* Ithaca, NY: Cornell
            University Press.
  1955   *The little community.* Chicago: University of Chicago Press.

Rickers-Ovsiankina, M. A.
  1977   *Rorschach psychology.* 2d ed. Huntington, NY: Krieger.

Rieff, Philip
  1961   *Freud: The mind of the moralist.* Garden City, NY: Anchor.
  1966   *The triumph of the therapeutic.* New York: Harper & Row.

Riesman, David
  1954   *Individualism reconsidered.* Garden City, NY: Anchor.

Riesman, David, with Nathan Glazer and Reuel Denney
  1961   *The lonely crowd.* New Haven: Yale University Press.
  (1950)

Rogoff, B. and G. Morelli
  1994   Cross-cultural perspectives on children's development. In *Hand-
            book of psychological anthropology*, P. K. Bock, (ed.), pp. 231–242.
            Westport, CT: Greenwood.

Róheim, Géza
  1943   *The origin and function of culture.* Nervous and Mental Disease
            Monographs No. 69. New York.
  1974   *The riddle of the sphinx.* New York: Harper & Row.
  (1934)

Rohrer, John H., and Munro S. Edmonson, eds.
  1964   *The eighth generation grows up.* New York: Harper Torchbooks.

Romney, A. Kimball and Carmella Moore
  1998   Toward a theory of culture as shared cognitive structures. *Ethos*
            26:314–337.

Rosaldo, Michelle Z.
  1980   *Knowledge and passion: Ilongot notions of self and social life.*
            Cambridge: Cambridge University Press.

Rosch, Eleanor, et al.
  1975   *Basic objects in natural categories.* Berkeley: Language Behavior
            Research Laboratory.

Rosen, Lawrence, ed.
    1995   *Other intentions*. Santa Fe: School of American Research Press.

Rosenbaum, Ron
    1998   *Explaining Hitler.* New York: Random House.

Sahlins, Marshall D.
    1976   *The use and abuse of biology.* Ann Arbor: University of Michigan Press.

Sapir, Edward
    1921   *Language.* New York: Harcourt, Brace.

    1949   *Culture, language and personality.* Berkeley: University of California Press.

    1994   *The psychology of culture: A course of lectures*. Reconstructed and edited by Judith T. Irvine. Berlin: Mouton de Gruyter.

Saucier, J. F.
    1972   Correlates of the long postpartum taboo: A cross-cultural study. *Current Anthropology* 13:238–249.

Schachtel, Ernest G.
    1959   *Metamorphosis*. New York: Basic Books.

Schachter, Stanley, and Jerome Singer
    1962   Cognitive, social, and physiological determinants of emotional states. *Psychological Review* 69:379–399.

Schefflen, Albert E.
    1974   *How behavior means*. Garden City, NY: Anchor.

Scheper-Hughes, Nancy
    1979   *Saints, scholars and schizophrenics*. Berkeley: University of California Press.

    1985   Culture, scarcity, and maternal thinking. *Ethos* 13:291–317.

    1992   *Death without weeping*. Berkeley: University of California Press.

Schlegel, Alice
    1994   Comparisons in psychological anthropology. In *Handbook of psychological anthropology,* P. K. Bock, (ed.), pp. 19–39. Westport, CT: Greenwood.

Schwartz, Theodore
    1975   Relations among generations in time-limited cultures. *Ethos* 3:309–322.

Schwartz, T., G. M. White and C. A. Lutz, eds.
    1992   *New directions in psychological anthropology.* New York: Cambridge University Press.

Scott, James C.
    1976   *The moral economy of the peasant.* New Haven: Yale University Press.

    1985   *Weapons of the weak*. New Haven: Yale University Press.

Seeger, Anthony
1987   *Why Suyá sing*. New York: Cambridge University Press.

Segall, Marshall H., D. T. Campbell, and M. J. Herskovits
1966   *The influence of culture on visual perception*. Indianapolis: Bobbs-Merrill.

Sennett, Richard
1976   *The fall of Public man*. New York: Knopf.

Sennett, Richard, and Jonathan Cobb
1973   *The hidden injuries of class*. New York: Vintage.

Serpell, Robert
1976   *Culture's influence on behavior*. London: Methuen.

Seymour, Susan
1983   Household structure and status and expression of affect in India. *Ethos* 11:263–277.

Shirley, R. W., and A. Kimball Romney
1962   Love magic and socialization anxiety. *American Anthropologist* 64:1028–1031.

Shore, Bradd
1982   *Sala'ilua: A Samoan mystery*. New York: Columbia University Press.
1996   *Culture in Mind*. New York: Oxford University Press.
1997   Keeping the conversation going: An interview with Jerome Bruner. *Ethos* 25:7–62.

Shweder, Richard A.
1977   Likeness and likelihood in everyday thought: Magical thinking in judgments about personality. *Current Anthropology* 18:637–658.
1979–80 Rethinking culture and personality theory. *Ethos* 7:255–311; 8:60–94. (Reprinted in Shweder 1991.)
1984   Anthropology's romantic rebellion against the enlightenment. In *Culture theory: Essays on mind, self, and emotion*, R. A. Shweder and R. A. Levine, (eds.). New York: Cambridge University Press.
1991   *Thinking through cultures: Expeditions in cultural psychology*. Cambridge: Harvard University Press.

Shweder, R., and R. LeVine
1984   *Culture theory*. Cambridge: Cambridge University Press.

Siegler, Miriam, and Humphrey Osmond
1974   *Models of madness, models of medicine*. New York: Harper & Row.

Simmel, Georg
1950   *The sociology of Georg Simmel*. New York: Free Press.

Simon, Linda
1998   *Genuine reality: A life of William James*. New York: Harcourt Brace.

Simons, Ronald C.
　　1996　　*BOO! Culture, experience and the startle reflex*. New York: Oxford
　　　　　　University Press.

Singer, Milton
　　1961　　A survey of culture and personality theory and research. In *Study-*
　　　　　　ing personality cross-culturally, B. Kaplan, (ed.), pp. 9–90. New
　　　　　　York: Harper & Row.

Sisk, John P.
　　1970　　*Person and institution*. Notre Dame, IN: Fides Books.

Slater, Philip L.
　　1970　　*The pursuit of loneliness*. Boston: Beacon Press.

Smith, E. E., and D. L. Medin
　　1981　　*Categories and concepts*. Cambridge, MA: Harvard University
　　　　　　Press.

Spain, David H.
　　1972　　On the use of projective tests for research in psychological anthro-
　　　　　　pology. In *Psychological Anthropology*, new ed., F. Hsu, (ed.),
　　　　　　pp. 67–308. Cambridge, MA: Schenkman.

Spindler, George D., ed.
　　1978　　*The making of psychological anthropology*. Berkeley: University of
　　　　　　California Press.

Spiro, Melford E.
　　1951　　Culture and personality: The natural history of a false dichotomy.
　　　　　　Psychiatry 14:19–46.

　　1958　　*Children of the kibbutz*. Cambridge, MA: Harvard University
　　　　　　Press.

　　1965　　Religious systems as culturally constituted defense mechanisms.
　　　　　　In *Context and meaning in cultural anthropology*, M. E. Spiro,
　　　　　　(ed.), pp. 100–113. New York: Free Press.

　　1976　　A. Irving Hallowell (an obituary). *American Anthropologist*
　　　　　　89:608–611.

　　1984　　Some reflections on cultural determinism and relativism with spe-
　　　　　　cial reference to emotion and reason. In *Culture theory*, R.
　　　　　　Shweder and R. LeVine, (eds.), pp. 323–346. Cambridge: Cam-
　　　　　　bridge University Press.

　　1997　　*Gender ideology and psychological reality*. New Haven: Yale Uni-
　　　　　　versity Press.

Spiro, Melford E., and Roy G. D'Andrade
　　1958　　A cross-cultural study of some supernatural beliefs. *American*
　　　　　　Anthropologist 60:456–466.

Spradley, James P., ed.
　　1972　　*Culture and cognition: Rules, maps and plans*. San Francisco:
　　　　　　Chandler.

Srole, Leo R., et al.
   1961   *Mental health in the metropolis: The Midtown Manhattan study,*
            vol. 1. New York: McGraw-Hill.

Starr, Kenneth W.
   1997   *The Starr report.* Edited with an introduction by Phil Kuntz. New
            York: Pocket Books.

Stein, Howard F.
   1985   Alcoholism as a metaphor in American culture. *Ethos* 13:195–235.

   1986   *Developmental time, cultural space: Studies in psychogeography.*
            Norman: University of Oklahoma Press.

   1994   *The dream of culture.* New York: Psyche Press.

   1998   Death imagery and the experience of organizational downsizing,
            or, is your name on Schindler's list? *Administration and Society*
            29:222–247.

Stephens, William N.
   1962   *The Oedipus complex.* Glencoe, IL: Free Press.

Stocking, George W.
   1992   Polarity and plurality: Franz Boas as psychological anthropolo-
            gist. In *New directions in psychological anthropology,* T. Schwartz,
            G. White and C. Lutz, (eds.), pp. 311–323. New York: Cambridge
            University Press.

Stocking, George W. Jr., ed.
   1986   *Malinowski, Rivers, Benedict and others. Essays on culture and
            personality.* (History of Anthropology, Vol. IV) Madison: Univer-
            sity of Wisconsin Press.

Stoetzel, Jean
   1955   *Without the chrysanthemum and the sword.* New York: Columbia
            University Press.

Street, Brian V.
   1984   *Literacy in theory and practice.* Cambridge: Cambridge University
            Press.

Sugerman, A. Arthur, and Ralph E. Tarter, eds.
   1978   *Expanding dimensions of consciousness.* New York: Springer.

Sutton, Nina
   1999   *Bruno Bettelheim: A life and a legacy.* Translated by David Sharp.
            New York: Basic Books.

Szasz, Thomas S.
   1961   *The myth of mental illness.* New York: Dell.

Tafoya, Terry
   1996   M. Dragonfly: Two-spirit and the Tafoya principle of uncertainty.
            In *Two spirit people,* S. E. Jacobs, W. Thomas and S. Lang, (eds.),
            pp. 192–202. Urbana: University of Illinois Press.

Tart, Charles
   1978   Altered states of consciousness: Putting the pieces together. In

Expanding dimensions of consciousness, A. A. Sugerman and R.
E. Tarter, (eds.), pp. 58–78. New York: Springer.

Tart, Charles. ed.
1969   *Altered states of consciousness.* New York: Wiley.
1975   *States of consciousness.* New York: Dutton.

Tedlock, Barbara
1993   *The evidence from dreams.* In *Handbook of psychological anthropology,* P. K. Bock, (ed.), pp. 279–295. Westport, CT: Greenwood.

Tedlock, Barbara, ed.
1987   *Dreaming: Anthropological and psychological interpretations.*
New York: Cambridge University Press.

Tobin, Joseph J.
1986   (Counter) transference and failure in intercultural therapy. *Ethos*
14:120–143.

Tocqueville, Alexis de
1954   *Democracy in America.* 2 vols. New York: Vintage.
(1830)

Tolman, Edward Chace
1958   Cognitive maps in rats and men. In *Behavior and psychological man, selected essays E. C. Tolman,* pp. 241–264. Berkeley: University of California Press.

Triandis, Harry, et al.
1971   Cross-cultural psychology. In *Biennial review of anthropology,* B. J. Siegel, (ed.), pp. 1–84. Palo Alto: Stanford University Press.

Turkle, Sherry
1984   *The second self: Computers and the human spirit.* New York: Touchstone.

Turner, Roy, ed.
1974   *Ethnomethodology.* Baltimore: Penguin.

Tyler, Stephen A., ed.
1969   *Cognitive anthropology.* New York: Holt, Rinehart and Winston.

Tylor, Edward B.
1889   On a method of investigating the development of institutions applied to laws of marriage and descent. *Journal of the Royal Anthropological Institute* 18:245–269.

1858   *Primitive culture.* 2 vols. New York: Harper & Row.
(1871)

Vargas Llosa, Mario
1986   *The perpetual orgy: Flaubert and* Madame Bovary. Trans. by Helen Lane. New York: Farrar Straus Giroux.

Vygotsky, L. S.
1978   *Mind in society.* Cambridge: Harvard University Press.

Wagner, Roy
1975   *The invention of culture.* Englewood Cliffs, NJ.: Prentice–Hall.

Wallace, Anthony F. C.
1952   The modal personality structure of the Tuscarora Indians as revealed by the Rorschach test. *Bureau of American Ethnology Bulletin* 150. Washington, DC: Smithsonian Institution.
1958   Dreams and the wishes of the soul. *American Anthropologist* 60:234–248.
1965   Driving to work. In *Context and meaning in cultural anthropology*, M. E. Spiro, (ed.), pp. 277–292. New York: Free Press.
1966a   Review of *The revolution in anthropology* by I. C. Jarvie. *American Anthropologist* 68:1254–1255.
1966b   *Religion: An anthropological view*. New York: Random House.
1970   *Culture and personality*. 2d ed. New York: Random House.
(1961)

Wallace, Edwin R. IV
1983   *Freud and anthropology*. New York: International Universities Press.

Wallach, Michael, and Lisa Wallach
1983   *Psychology's sanction for selfishness*. New York: W. H. Freeman.

Watts, Alan W.
1969   *Psychotherapy East and West*. New York: Ballantine.

Werner, Oswald, and Mark Schoepfle
1987   *Systematic ethnography*. 2 vols. Beverly Hills: Sage Publications.

Westermeyer, J.
1989   *Psychiatric care of migrants: A clinical guide*. Washington, DC: American Psychiatric Press.

White, Leslie A.
1949   *The science of culture*. New York: Grove Press.

Whiting, Beatrice, ed.
1963   *Six cultures: Studies of child-rearing*. New York: Wiley.

Whiting, Beatrice, and John W. M. Whiting
1974   *Children of six cultures*. Cambridge, MA: Harvard University Press.

Whiting, John W. M.
1941   *Becoming a Kwoma*. New Haven: Yale University Press.
1964   Effects of climate on certain cultural practices. In *Explorations in cultural anthropology*, W. H. Goodenough, (ed.), pp. 511–544. New York: McGraw-Hill.

Whiting, John W. M., et al.
1966   *Field guide for a study of socialization*. New York: Wiley. (First published in B. Whiting 1963.)

Whiting, John W. M., and Irvin L. Child
1953   *Child training and personality: A cross-cultural study*. New Haven: Yale University Press.

Whiting, John W. M., Richard Kluckhohn, and Albert Anthony
  1958   The function of male initiation ceremonies at puberty. In *Readings in social psychology*, 3d ed., E. Maccoby, T. Newcomb, and E. Hartley, (eds.), pp. 359–370. New York: Holt.

Whyte, Lancelot Law
  1960   *The unconscious before Freud.* New York: Basic Books.

Whyte, William H.
  1956   *The organization man.* New York: Simon and Schuster.

Wikan, Unni
  1990   *Managing turbulent hearts.* Chicago: University of Chicago Press.
  1996   *Tomorrow, God willing.* Chicago: University of Chicago Press.

Williams, Patricia J.
  1997   Dearly beloved. *The Nation*, 267 (19):10. December 7, 1998.

Williams, Raymond
  1976   *Keywords.* New York: Oxford University Press.

Wills, Garry
  1971   *Nixon agonistes.* New York: Signet.

Wilson, Edward O.
  1975   *Sociobiology: The new synthesis.* Cambridge, MA: Belknap Press.
  1998   *Consilience: The unity of knowledge.* New York: Knopf.

Witkin, H. A.
  1967   A cognitive style approach to cross-cultural research. *International Journal of Psychology* 2:233–250.

Wolf, Arthur P.
  1970   Childhood association and sexual attraction: A further test of the Westermarck hypothesis. *American Anthropologist* 73:503–515.
  1993   Westermarck redivivus. *Annual Review of Anthropology* 22: 157–175.

Wolman, Benjamin B., ed.
  1973   *Handbook of general psychology.* Englewood Cliffs, NJ.: Prentice-Hall.

Woodworth, Robert S.
  1948   *Contemporary schools of psychology.* Rev. ed. New York: Ronald Press.

Worthman, Carol M.
  1992   Cupid and psyche. In *New directions in psychological anthropology.* T. Schwartz, G. White and C. Lutz, (eds.), pp. 150–178. New York: Cambridge University Press.

Wrong, Dennis H.
  1961   The oversocialized conception of man in modern sociology. *American Sociological Review* 26:183–193.

Wundt, Wilhelm
  1916   *Elements of folk psychology.* New York: Macmillan.

Wylie, Philip
  1946   *Generation of vipers.* New York: Rinehart.
Young, Frank W.
  1965   *Initiation ceremonies.* Indianapolis: Bobbs-Merrill.

Index